Judas the Galilean

Judas the Galilean

The flesh and blood Jesus

Daniel T. Unterbrink

iUniverse, Inc.
New York Lincoln Shanghai

Judas the Galilean
The flesh and blood Jesus

All Rights Reserved © 2004 by Daniel T. Unterbrink

No part of this book may be reproduced or transmitted in any form or by any means, graphic, electronic, or mechanical, including photocopying, recording, taping, or by any information storage retrieval system, without the written permission of the publisher.

iUniverse, Inc.

For information address:
iUniverse, Inc.
2021 Pine Lake Road, Suite 100
Lincoln, NE 68512
www.iuniverse.com

ISBN: 0-595-32197-6

Printed in the United States of America

CONTENTS

TERMINOLOGY AND ORGANIZATION		ix
CHAPTER ONE	A CHALLENGE	1
CHAPTER TWO	THE BIRTH OF JESUS	10
CHAPTER THREE	THE BIRTH OF JUDAS THE GALILEAN	19
CHAPTER FOUR	THE BIRTH OF JUDAS THE GALILEAN—PART 2	29
CHAPTER FIVE	WHAT REALLY HAPPENED	42
CHAPTER SIX	THE PLAYERS	52
CHAPTER SEVEN	THE DEAD SEA SCROLLS	82
CHAPTER EIGHT	THE LIFE OF JESUS—A LOGICAL APPROACH	98
CHAPTER NINE	THE FOURTH PHILOSOPHY	124
CHAPTER TEN	GOSPEL TRUTH OR GREAT DECEPTION?	164
CHAPTER ELEVEN	RAMIFICATIONS	188
CHAPTER TWELVE	CONCLUSION	197
APPENDIX 1	SIMILARITIES—JUDAS THE GALILEAN AND JESUS JUDAS THE GALILEAN AND JUDAS	201
APPENDIX 2	TIME LINE	211

APPENDIX 3	FAMILY TREE OF JESUS 215
APPENDIX 4	THE GOSPELS, ACTS AND JOSEPHUS 219
APPENDIX 5	NAME GAMES 229
APPENDIX 6	PAUL—I DO NOT LIE 233
APPENDIX 7	PILATE'S REIGN 261

BIBLIOGRAPHY 267

NOTES 269

TIMELINES

The Births of Jesus and Judas the Galilean 18

The Deaths of Jesus and Judas the Galilean 50

The Players 77

The Problem of Paul 79; 258

The Four Philosophies 95

The Fourth Philosophy—The Kingdom of Heaven 157

The Fourth Philosophy—The Imminent Return of Jesus 159

The Fourth Philosophy—Disintegration 162

Dating the New Testament 186

TERMINOLOGY AND ORGANIZATION

Christianity as we know it today has not changed much over the past two thousand years, at least in its core beliefs. Names and events contained within the New Testament pages are familiar to most people throughout the world. This familiarity and vast history tends to bias our objectivity; we dare not question the long-established truths. Even the names of the main characters come down to us as holy or profane. For example, Jesus was holy from his mother's womb, and everything associated with that name is considered good. On the other hand, Judas (a popular name in first century AD Judea) now represents the traitor, the one who sold his soul for thirty pieces of silver. To this day, the name Judas has such a negative connotation that the mere utterance of "Judas" refers us back to those dark deeds.

The strong bias that has been instilled in us will make it difficult but not impossible to follow my hypothesis concerning Judas the Galilean. I submit that Jesus and Judas the Galilean were two names describing the same person. To avoid confusion, I use Judas the Galilean when studying the history of Josephus and Jesus when referring to the Gospels. When both sources converge, I designate this individual as Judas/Jesus.

A similar track is followed concerning the movement which grew from his teachings. Josephus referred to Judas' beliefs as the Fourth Philosophy while the New Testament used such terms as Christian and the Way. (The other three philosophies in first century Judea were represented by the Sadducees, Pharisees and the Essenes). Early Jewish followers of Jesus were known as members of the Way of Righteousness or Way for short. According to Tacitus and Suetonius, these Jewish disciples were derisively known as followers of "Chrestus" or as Christians, at least in Rome, circa 50 AD. The term Christian was also adopted by Paul's Gentile disciples and has been used historically as a designation for the whole movement. For our purposes, this one supposedly seamless Christian movement will be split into two groups: Jewish Christians and Gentile Christians. The Fourth Philosophy, the Way and Jewish

Christianity were different names for the same movement while Paul's Gentile Christianity formed a distinct and separate movement.

Other well-known Biblical figures may also confuse. Peter is known as both Peter and Cephas in the New Testament. In addition, I believe this Cephas should also be identified with Sadduc, the co-teacher with Judas the Galilean. Thus, Peter is used in studying the Gospels, Cephas when quoting the writings of Paul and Sadduc from the pages of Josephus. Another possible confusion concerns the brother pair of James and John. The Gospels claim James and John are the sons of Zebedee while Paul leads us to believe that James and John are the brothers of Jesus. I agree with Paul's version and this will be further explained in Chapters Six and Eight. In addition, the Apostle Paul is designated as both Paul and Saul in the New Testament. Saul is generally used when the Apostle interacted with Jews. Josephus also mentioned a Saul in his description of the events leading up to the war with Rome. To be consistent with these sources, I will use both Saul and Paul, dependent on his circumstances and his involvement with Jews or Gentiles.

Other terms such as Zealots and Sicarii (dagger men or assassins), usually used synonymously with the Fourth Philosophy, will be explained fully in Chapter Nine. These particular designations were not applicable to the earliest days of the Fourth Philosophy's history. So for consistency throughout the book, I will use Fourth Philosophy instead of the more common reference, Zealot.

All quotations from Josephus and the Bible are noted in the text so that readers may easily check them for accuracy. I have also used somewhat lengthy passages and have reproduced them in their entirety for those who do not possess a copy of Josephus. (Most people own a Bible). This may aid the reader in determining whether or not I am taking any passages out of context. (See the Bibliography for the translators of Josephus. The New International Version (NIV) has been used for most Bible quotes).

In regards to Josephus' terminology; he often refers to the Fourth Philosophy disciples as innovators and bandits. Innovation concerns their interpretation of the Scriptures and practices of the Law. For example, Jesus' "the Sabbath was made for man, not man for the Sabbath," was not mainstream but rather an interpretation of the Sabbath's true purpose. Also, members of the Fourth Philosophy practiced "pure communism." Josephus' mention of bandits may refer to their insistence on equality. Thus, Robin Hood may have been working the by-ways of Judea long before he entered Sherwood Forest. All this must be kept in mind when reading Josephus. As a well-to-do man, his sympathies went out to others like himself, and these were the very people most threatened by the Fourth Philosophy.

The only other item which may confuse is the dating of Jesus' crucifixion. The traditional dating places Jesus' death during the governorship of Pontius Pilate (26-37 AD), as defined by the current version of Josephus. However, in Chapter Nine and Appendix 7, I will present an alternative, where Jesus' crucifixion may have been much earlier, around 19 AD. This is based upon an analysis of Josephus where Pilate actually became procurator in 18 AD. I believe the earliest date is most probable but the hypothesis of Judas the Galilean being Jesus is not dependent on the early date. Therefore, if Jesus were crucified under Pilate, I would argue for the 19 AD date as this makes more sense based upon the writings of Josephus and Tacitus.

The organization of this book is fully dependent on most peoples' understanding of Christianity. So while I delve into the life of Judas the Galilean, I must deal with Jesus as well. Thus, the first five chapters build a sturdy bridge between Judas and Jesus, their beliefs and practices dovetailing nicely into one another. The remaining chapters assume the two are one, and the coincidences between Jewish Christianity and the Fourth Philosophy become so numerous that the reader will wonder why this has never been adequately explained before.

If my hypothesis is correct, then the whole Christian movement began a generation earlier than previously believed. To help sort out these dating inconsistencies, I have included several timelines throughout the book which compare and contrast the New Testament version of events to my interpretations of Josephus' history. For example, a timeline of Paul's career has been included in the two sections covering the Apostle to the Gentiles (Chapter Six and Appendix 6).

As an aid to the reader, I have included seven appendices which summarize data or may expand upon a subject within the main text. For example, Appendix 1 lists all the similarities between Judas the Galilean and Jesus of Nazareth. Since these are scattered throughout the text, this appendix will be quite handy. Appendix 7 details the career of Pontius Pilate as presented by Josephus. This is important as it places the date of the crucifixion at 19 AD, a full decade before the traditional dating. In Appendix 6, I have fully explained Paul's relationship to the Fourth Philosophy. Since a full history of Paul is beyond the scope of this book, his mention in the text is minimal. However, this appendix gives the reader a much more detailed account of the later Gentile Church (40-66 AD) and a clearer lens to view the current Christian world.

The use of Greek within the text is minimal since my arguments are not based upon linguistics. However, in Appendix 5, the Greek will be used to help explain some names used in the Gospels and Acts, such as Iscariot. Other than that, any additional study of the Greek text will be left to those with the ability to distinguish between linguistic styles.

CHAPTER ONE

A CHALLENGE

Why write another book about Jesus? After all, can there be anything new which might interest the religious devotee? I think there is. Although I have not uncovered a cache of previously unexplored documents, a la the Dead Sea Scrolls, I have discovered a convincing connection between Jesus of Nazareth and another historical character hidden within the pages of Josephus, namely, Judas the Galilean. From common history books found in any public library, I have pieced together my unique hypothesis. The only thing I ask is for the reader to withhold judgment until the entire argument is made, for this hypothesis runs against two thousand years of official Christian history, from the first century Gospel story to the present. Thus, the reader is left with a monumental challenge—to maintain an open mind.

New or different thinking does not arise from a vacuum. My vision of Christianity has evolved considerably throughout the years. I was raised Catholic and attended church regularly with my parents and siblings until high school. Somewhere along the way, the whole line of Jesus and God was jettisoned, as my dear mother would say, in favor of pagan living. So in high school and college, my interests focused upon living, not the living God. But this debauched lifestyle led to remorse and finally repentance, leading to conversion. At the age of twenty-one, I became immersed in religion, joining a fundamentalist Christian church. With that, I denounced my sinful ways, my upbringing and my parents. This radical departure from the real world was foolish, but it seemed like the right thing to do at the time.

The slogan "What would Jesus do?" haunted me, as it became evident that the church's interpretation of "Jesus' words" might be different from my own. Breaking away from the fundamentalist mindset was a daunting task. Unless you have belonged to such a group, you cannot imagine the control the church leaders can exert. Every word and each unthoughtful deed was monitored for religious correctness. It was this unrelenting control of every aspect of my life which drove me to the door, risking the very soul I thought had been saved.

Once through the door, the guilt vanished, and I stood alone but happy. After successfully escaping the stranglehold of the church and brotherhood, my life became better but somehow unfulfilled. I still had a burning desire to know more about Jesus, even though I had rejected this particular fundamentalist branch. These were the searching years, where I read conventional and unorthodox renderings of Jesus and his church. I had personally lived the traditional complacent and the fanatical literal interpretations of Christianity; now I intended to discover if the word truth could be applied to any or to all of it. History books and Barclay's Commentaries helped shape my evolving perspective of Christianity, softening the remaining hard edges from my beliefs and language.

Next, I moved on to the book, <u>Revolution in Judaea</u>, by Hyam Maccoby. This book is must reading for anyone interested in Christian origins. Driven by his Jewish background, Maccoby attempts to reclaim Jesus as a national hero. To Maccoby, Jesus was a devout and practicing Pharisee, his teachings similar to other Pharisees of his era. In addition, the long-held belief that Paul lived as a Pharisee was absolutely false, according to Maccoby—with this flying in the face of Paul's own admission of his Pharisaic background (Phil. 3:5; Acts 23:6). Maccoby does a credible job in overturning the traditional beliefs of Paul as Pharisee and Jesus as anti-Pharisee. This interpretation of New Testament history captured my attention for nearly a decade, for the picture of Jesus as a Jewish leader and not an anti-Jewish mystic appealed to my common sense and seemed more in line with history and probabilities.

But not all questions were answered by Maccoby's view of Jesus. For instance, why was a practicing Pharisee crucified by the Roman authorities? In fact, the majority of Pharisees were content to live by Rome's rules as long as Rome did not interfere with their religious practices. The founder of Rabbinical Judaism was a Pharisee named Johanan Ben Zakkai. He escaped the siege of Jerusalem by being smuggled out to the Roman camp. He later received Roman permission to gather together a synod at Jamnia which eventually replaced the Sanhedrin.(1) So the very survival of Judaism depended upon accommodation with Rome. This, however, hardly describes Jesus. So if Jesus were a Pharisee as claimed by Maccoby, then he must have been a different type of Pharisee. To find an answer to the Pharisee question, I had to search beyond Maccoby.

The next stop on this enlightenment tour brought me to a book entitled <u>James, the Brother of Jesus</u>, by Robert Eisenman. Eisenman, too, portrays Jesus as a popular Jewish figure, but antagonistic to the Pharisees, more in line with Essene teachings. Like Maccoby, he removes Paul from the Pharisaic ranks and lumps him in with the Herodians, those tax collectors and harlots of the day. In fact, Eisenman goes so far as to equate Paul with the "Liar" of the Dead Sea Scrolls. The hero of his book is James, the brother of Jesus. Without doubt, Eisenman proves that James was an observant Jew, even a Jewish leader. By reading between the lines of Paul's letters and the Book of Acts, this conclusion is soundly based. Opposed to the traditional view of Jesus as having lived the role of grand reformer of Judaism, Eisenman claims that Jesus was just like James—fully observant of the Jewish Law. Thus, to Eisenman, the thought that James relapsed into Judaism is absurd; James simply followed the example and teachings of his older brother, Jesus. I believe Eisenman is correct in much of his analysis, but his study concentrates on James, not Jesus.

Upon reflection, I have moved beyond both Maccoby and Eisenman and have fused their beliefs with the history of Josephus as well as a few passages from Tacitus and Suetonius, forming my own unique view of Christian origins. I believe that the only way to find the flesh and blood Jesus is through a thorough study of the source documents of the times. Maccoby relies heavily on later Jewish writers and Eisenman quotes early church sources ad nauseam. This may help in building a general picture of the life of Jesus, but the specifics are missing. These specifics are supplied primarily by Josephus and supported by Tacitus and Suetonius.

Unlike these two scholars, my education is not in religion but in accounting. This shortcoming, I am sure, will be attacked by the religious establishment. I admit to being an amateur historian but my sense is that truth can be found by anyone who searches. And as an auditor, I know what looks right and what smells fishy. In addition, an amateur is not beholding to any church or institution for financial compensation. I can say whatever I want about religion and not be fired. The point to my story is this: religious truth is not the sole possession of the academics or the religious establishment. Each of us can and should seek out truth to the best of our abilities. After all, the root of the word amateur means love, and this love of religion may yield some startling finds.

So, let us begin our challenge. What is known about our subject—Jesus? Outside the New Testament, there are only two contemporaneous mentions of him, one by the Roman historian, Tacitus and the other by the Jewish historian, Josephus. Both short passages are quoted below:

But all the endeavors of men, all the emperor's largesse and the propitiation of the gods, did not suffice to allay the scandal or banish the belief that the fire had been ordered. And so, to get rid of this rumor, Nero set up as the culprits and punished with the utmost refinement of cruelty a class hated for their abominations, who are commonly called Christians. Christus, from whom their name is derived, was executed at the hands of the procurator Pontius Pilate in the reign of Tiberius. Checked for the moment, this pernicious superstition again broke out, not only in Judea, the source of the evil, but even in Rome.... The Neronian persecution of 64, Tacitus, Annales, xv. 44.

Now, there was about this time, Jesus, a wise man, if it be lawful to call him a man, for he was a doer of wonderful works,—a teacher of such men as receive the truth with pleasure. He drew over to him both many of the Jews and many of the Gentiles. He was Christ; and when Pilate, at the suggestion of the principal men amongst us, had condemned him to the cross, those that loved him at the first did not forsake him, for he appeared to them alive again the third day, as the divine prophets had foretold these and ten thousand other wonderful things concerning him; and the tribe of Christians, so named from him, are not extinct at this day. Josephus, Antiquities of the Jews 18.63,64.

The passage by Tacitus discusses the Neronian persecution, where Nero used the Christian community as a scapegoat for the great fire of Rome. Nero was fond of architecture and his ultimate goal was the rebuilding of Rome in his own image. The great fire afforded him the opportunity to rebuild, but the suspicions of the general public made for bad press. But even Tacitus does not wholly endorse the theory that Nero torched the city. The fire, "whether accidentally or treacherously contrived by the emperor, is uncertain, as authors have given both accounts...." (Annals xv.38) Interestingly enough, another passage from Tacitus could indict either Nero or the Christians.

And no one dared to stop the mischief, because of incessant menaces from a number of persons who forbade the extinguishing of the flames, because again others openly hurled brands, and kept shouting that there was one who gave them authority, either seeking to plunder more freely, or obeying orders. Tacitus, Annals, xv.38.

The one who gave authority was either Nero or Christ. For Nero to place blame upon the Christians, there must have been a history of agitation against Rome. This history was exploited by Nero, who was not gentle with his persecutions; Christians were torn apart by animals and set ablaze to illuminate the night. Tacitus added a homey touch by saying that the populace even felt sorry for these hated Christians, for they knew all too well the cruelty of Nero.

Tacitus lived from 60-120 AD, his adult life one to two generations after the great fire. Note his description of the Christians as being "hated for their abominations" and Christianity as a "pernicious superstition." Clearly, the term Christian had a negative connotation to Tacitus and to Roman society as well, at least in the year 115 AD when this was written. However, it is quite likely that Tacitus confused the now defunct Jewish Christian movement with the Gentile "Christian" movement of the early second century.

In describing an event in 19 AD, Tacitus referred to Judaism as a superstition, and to its followers as "infected."(2) Suetonius, who also wrote his history of the Twelve Caesars in the time period of Tacitus, clears up this whole confusion.

"Because the Jews at Rome caused continuous disturbances at the instigation of Chrestus [Christ], he [Claudius in 52 AD] expelled them from the city."(3) Before 70 AD, the association of Christ was with the Jewish communities which thrived in the major urban areas of the Roman Empire. So when Tacitus and Suetonius mention Christians relating to the 64 AD fire in Rome, they were referring to the Jewish population who followed the teachings of Christ.

In 64 AD, the year of the great fire, Rome had a potential Jewish rebellion on its hands which resulted in the Jewish War and the destruction of Jerusalem and the Temple (70 AD). The fanatical disciples of Jesus persecuted by Nero were undoubtedly Jewish members of the Jesus movement, referred to as Nazirites or followers of the Way (Way of Righteousness). According to the New Testament, the term Christian was applied to Paul's Gentile disciples. (Acts 11:26) However, it is clear from Tacitus and Suetonius that the term Christian was derisively attached to the most fanatical of the Jewish religion. The confusion of terms masks the political ramifications, as the Jewish followers of Jesus were highly nationalistic, ready to foment rebellion against Rome. The Gentile Christians of Paul were taught to obey the government (Romans 13:1-7). Therefore, we can be assured that Paul's converts were not part of the persecution. This first myth may have been great public relations for the later church, but it did not fit in with the reality of the times. Books and movies have shown Pauline Christians (Gentiles) kneeling in prayer, waiting for hungry lions to devour them for the enjoyment of thousands in the Colosseum. First of all, the Roman Colosseum was not built until 69 AD, five years after the persecution, which actually occurred in the Circus Maximus, a prominent square in Rome. But more importantly, those dying were doing so for God, His Law and for their resurrected Jewish Messiah, not for a Gentile pagan man-god. This is key to understanding why the Gentile movement was so willing to divorce themselves from anything Jewish, and why even Jesus was made to oppose the Jews (Gospel of John). To live in Roman society, these Gentile Christians could not associate themselves with the hated Jews or they themselves would be hunted down and executed.

Tacitus mentioned the person of Jesus through the term "Christus" or Christ. This "Christus" was executed by Pontius Pilate in the reign of Tiberius.

Tiberius was Roman Emperor from 14-37 AD. Per Tacitus, Pilate may have been governor from 18-37.(4) Thus, the death of Jesus must have occurred between 18 and 37 AD. However, the orthodox interpretation of Josephus dates Pilate from 26-37 AD in <u>Antiquities</u> and leaves us hanging in the <u>Jewish War</u>, where the three Governors between Coponius 6-9 AD and Pilate were not even mentioned. So, it is possible than an important discrepancy exists between the dating of Pilate and the ultimate crucifixion of Jesus. In fact, I believe Jesus was crucified in 19 AD. This is determined by analyzing Josephus. (See Appendix 7). As the traditional dating of the crucifixion is approximately 30 AD, an earlier date for Pilate would throw all long-held beliefs out the window.

So where did Tacitus arrive at the Pilate era for Jesus' death? After all, he was writing in the year 115 AD, nearly ninety years after the event. The only three sources for this time period would have been Josephus, the Gospels and interviews with current Christians. Josephus was born in 35 AD and experienced first-hand the horrors of war, as he commanded the Jewish forces in Galilee in 66 AD. He later "went over" to the Roman side, where he wrote the <u>Jewish War</u> (75 AD) and <u>Antiquities</u> (93 AD). Josephus mentioned Jesus' death once, in the above passage. As we will see, this passage was probably a late third century insertion. But as argued in Appendix 7, the spurious Jesus passage may have replaced another event recorded by Josephus. Regardless, from the analysis, the dating of the material before and after the "Jesus" passage described the years 18-19 AD. It is very possible that Tacitus used the "original" Josephus material when he placed Pilate as a procurator at the time of Christ's crucifixion.

The second of Tacitus' sources was the synoptic Gospels, written between 70 and 90 AD according to many scholars and around 105 AD by my analysis. (See Appendix 4 for further data regarding these dates). These Gospels were heavily dependent on Josephus' history, which was nearly non-existent for this particular time period (7-37 AD). The mention of Pilate in the Gospel stories should not be discounted because of their second century composition. The passion play of Jesus being tried by Pilate was most likely a Jewish Christian tradition which could not be ejected by second century Gentile Christians. (These well-known Jewish traditions were simply absorbed into the Gospels, while the original documents were either destroyed or hidden away for posterity.) So, as to direct interviews, any early second century Christian would have held the Gospel line. Either from Josephus or from the Gospel accounts, Tacitus repeated the players in the drama: Christ and Pilate. The only question is this: was Pilate procurator in 18 AD or in 26 AD? Using only Tacitus, a solution can never be made. However, by combining Tacitus and Josephus, the threads of truth can be woven together to form a coherent argument for the earlier date (18 AD).

Now the above passage from Josephus is much different in tone. Although he agreed with Tacitus concerning the execution of Jesus during the reign of Pilate, nothing else is the same for his Roman readers. In fact, by this passage, Josephus appeared to be a believing Christian. Note that he called Jesus a "wise man", "a doer of wonderful works" and "the Christ." He even confessed to the resurrection. This is amazing considering Josephus only mentioned Jesus one other time in passing, the passage concerning the death of James, the brother of Jesus (Ant. 20.200). This hardly seems consistent with a true believer, considering the Jesus Movement was very powerful until at least 62 AD, the year James was murdered. It appears to me (and to many historians) that the passage about Jesus was a clip-and-paste deal. Some later Christian inserted this passage and possibly deleted something else of interest. (See Chapter Nine and Appendix 7). This becomes obvious with even a casual reading of Josephus. Josephus condemned the miracle workers as deceivers (Ant. 20.97,98) and he accorded the Star prophecy to Vespasian (Roman Emperor 69-79 AD), not Jesus.(5) (The Star prophecy stated that a world ruler would arise from Palestine.) A true Christian would have opted for Jesus over Caesar, every time.

The interesting part of the story concerns the place where the spurious Jesus passage was inserted into Josephus. In Appendix 7, I examined the surrounding text of Josephus and found it all referred to 18-19 AD. If this is the case, then all traditional calculations for dates of the early church must be thoroughly examined. I am not questioning whether Jesus was crucified. I believe he was. But I do question the date of the crucifixion and the background of the one known as Jesus Christ.

In reality, the only piece of information concerning Christ in Josephus is a mention in passing when describing James. So how could the most influential teacher in Jewish society go totally unnoticed by the great Jewish historian? This would be like writing an anthology about baseball in the 1920s and not mentioning Babe Ruth. But maybe the baseball historian called Ruth the Sultan of Swat, the Bambino or some other nickname. Could Josephus have mentioned Jesus using a different identity? I believe he did.

Sherlock Holmes based the solution to a crime upon a dog not barking when the dog notoriously barked at all strangers. The absence of the bark gave the detective a valuable lead. Likewise, the absence of material from Josephus should give us pause. Jesus was the most influential teacher in first century Palestine, and his followers were spread throughout the Roman Empire (note the Neronian persecution in Rome). How could Josephus completely ignore this figure except for a reference to his death (and even this is a later insertion)?

In addition, another figure of this time known as Judas the Galilean was written about in detail and even credited with founding a new philosophy. But in this case, Judas' death was <u>not</u> mentioned by Josephus. Why was the life of Jesus ignored as well as the death of Judas—unless they were one in the same?

Beyond the meager information in Tacitus and Josephus, we must head to the New Testament for more clues concerning the earthly life of Jesus. The earliest New Testament writings are from the pen of Paul the Apostle, around the years 40-50AD. Paul was not a contemporary of Jesus, having never met him in person, and in his writings mentioning nothing of his earthly life; not his birth, his upbringing or his teachings. (The only mention of historical content supposedly from Paul is found in 1 Tim. 6:13, where the writer speaks of Pontius Pilate. Even a Christian apologist such as William Barclay notes that this is not from Paul but from a later source.(6)) To Paul, the whole message of Christ Jesus centered upon the resurrection and the grace of God. And this gospel was given to Paul through revelations and visions of the <u>Risen</u> Christ. If it were not for the mention of James, the brother of the Lord, we might surmise that Jesus was not a real person, but a myth.(7) This school of thought (mythicist theory of Christianity) was in vogue in the late 19th and early 20th Centuries. Its arguments (championed by J.M. Robertson, whose views are detailed in his book, <u>Pagan Christs</u>)(8) drew upon the scant historical information concerning Jesus combined with data from anthropology and comparative religion. They reasoned that the telescoping of Jesus' ministry into a few scenes, culminating in the capture, trial and crucifixion made it appear to be more theater than real historical events. Jesus, if he ever existed, had been transformed into a mythical character. Thus, Jesus became a savior God, like Mithra or Osiris. However convincing their arguments (and they do make a lot of sense), they do not recognize the brother of the Lord. Therefore, James is really our <u>only</u> link to the historical Jesus. However, this one link is enough to all but guarantee the existence of a real flesh and blood Jesus.

Knowing that Jesus was a real person, not just a character in a play, we have a head start on many historians. We will not question his existence but only when he lived. Did Jesus preach during the governorship of Pilate as has been asserted from the earliest Gospel (26-37 AD by traditional reckonings) or is that claim a sleight-of-hand aimed at misdirecting us from an earlier time? Did Jesus and John the Baptist preach at the same time or was John more a contemporary of Paul? Does the crucifixion of Jesus during the later dating of Pilate make historical sense or is there a more probable date of death? These questions will be answered in our focus upon Judas the Galilean. This study will be conducted using the works of Josephus, the only historian who chronicled the events, having had some first-hand knowledge of the people and the movements which existed in first century Palestine. While Josephus did not write about Jesus, he did mention Judas the Galilean and his followers in great detail. And it is in the details where we will find Jesus.

As for Judas the Galilean, we will attempt to sort out one Judas from another. Was Judas Iscariot a real person or was his character a stand-in for Judas the Galilean? In the same way, was Barabbas flesh and blood or a literary devise used to convict the Jews concerning Jesus' crucifixion—and thus absolving the Romans? Does the name Barabbas have significance or is it just a coincidence that this means "son of the father"? Could it perhaps be that Judas the Galilean was Jesus who was Judas Iscariot who was Barabbas? These questions will be answered as we study Josephus.

But many will protest: Why should we question anything about Jesus when we have the infallible Gospels at our disposal? Surely, they argue, the Word of God is sufficient in proving the life and death of Jesus; and this Word would certainly guarantee more than just one link to the historical Jesus. We will examine the birth narratives to determine the worthiness of two thousand years of trust. If the birth narratives are faulty, then how can we trust Gospel information concerning the teachings, the actions and the death of Jesus? In fact, these birth narratives will provide a clue which will be helpful in identifying the real Jesus.

CHAPTER TWO

THE BIRTH OF JESUS

For our challenge to go forward, we must, at a minimum, attempt a partial dismantling of the New Testament. This is necessary because many people will not entertain new ideas if they believe the old ideas are correct or rather, God-given perfection. So we must, at least, make a chink in the armor. Beginning in the fourth century, the various Gospels and letters of Paul were coalesced into a larger book known as the New Testament. Since then, this New Testament has been viewed as infallible, first by the Catholic Church who authorized it and then by all Protestant denominations, including the fundamentalist branch. (Before the Nicene Council in 325 AD, different geographical areas used their own individual Bibles, some more Gnostic, some long since forgotten.) A powerful bias has been ingrained into our understanding of Jesus and his movement. So you see, this dismantling is not intended to throw dirt upon Jesus, but rather is necessary to move Jesus from myth to reality, ultimately tying Jesus to Judas the Galilean. For now, we will simply examine the birth narratives.

The birth of Jesus has been celebrated by Christians the world over for centuries, and few question the historical data supporting the event. But is the romanticized Gospel version historical fact or wishful thinking? First, the earliest Christian documents are completely silent concerning the birth of Jesus. Although Paul emphasized Jesus' death, burial and resurrection, he never mentioned his birth or life. Maybe Paul felt that these were unimportant compared to the death, or more likely was simply unaware of the details. The earliest Gospel, attributed to Mark, was penned around the year 105 AD, more than fifty years after Paul's last letter. (See Appendix 4 concerning the 105 AD date). Again, the birth of Jesus was omitted. While Paul may have deemed the birth as unworthy of comment, the same cannot be said for a document detailing the life of Jesus. If a history of the birth or first part of Jesus' life had been available, then it would have been reported. I believe such details were not known, or rather, not yet invented. Incredibly, it may have taken another generation to compose the only two versions of the birth, those of Matthew and Luke. The silence of Paul and the Gospel of Mark may speak volumes concerning the historical accuracy of Matthew and Luke, but the silence by itself is <u>not</u> conclusive.

Before we tackle the details in the two birth narratives, the purpose behind the efforts should be ascertained. As already noted, the Gospel of Mark was written a few years after the publication of Josephus' <u>Antiquities of the Jews</u>, around the year 105 AD. This earliest Gospel was meant to separate Jesus from the Jews, in a time when hatred of the Jews was pandemic throughout the Roman Empire. In writing <u>The Histories</u> around 115 AD, Tacitus stated that Israel was the "vilest of nations."(1) An intense loathing for the Jewish people and their religion was current in thought and action. Suetonius wrote this concerning the reign of Domitian (81-96 AD).

Domitian's agents collected the tax on Jews [imposed by Vespasian after the 70 AD destruction of the Temple] with a peculiar lack of mercy; and took proceedings not only against those who kept their Jewish origins a secret in order to avoid the tax, but against those who lived as Jews without professing Judaism. As a boy, I remember once attending a crowded Court where the imperial agent had a ninety-year old man inspected to establish whether or not he had been circumcised. (2)

From the above historical references, it is perfectly clear why early second century <u>Gentile</u> Christianity desired a break from its Jewish roots. That is why Jesus was made to look like an anti-Jewish religious leader instead of a liberating Jewish hero.

Once the break with Judaism was complete, Matthew and Luke added their birth narratives for the purpose of attracting those elements of the population clinging to the old gods and to those who worshipped the memory of Augustus. Jesus was crafted in a way to supercede these old and new gods. Certainly Jesus was greater than Heracles, born of a human mother but fathered by Zeus. And the divine birth of Jesus spoke to emperor worship as well. Suetonius wrote this passage of Augustus in 119 AD, approximately the time when the birth narratives were first envisioned.

A public portent warned the Roman people some months before Augustus' birth that Nature was making ready to provide them with a king....Augustus' mother, Atia...once attended a solemn midnight service at the Temple of Apollo....Suddenly a serpent glided up, entered her, and then glided away again. On awakening, she purified herself, as if after intimacy with her husband..., and the birth of Augustus nine months later suggested a divine paternity....Publius Nigidius Figulus, the astrologer, hearing at what hour the child had been delivered, cried out: "The ruler of the world is now born." Everyone believes this story. (3)

Note the similarities between the birth of Augustus and that of Jesus. Both Mary and Atia were religious women, chosen by God from all women to deliver a king. Both births were attributed to the workings of God and not men—divine paternity. And after the birth, both Augustus and Jesus were prophesied to be rulers.(See Luke 2:21-33) Possibly the most important point of this passage is that the people believed the story about Augustus. To compete with emperor worship, Jesus had to be born of God too. Now that the purpose of the birth narratives has been exposed, a further analysis of the details is necessary to feed the gnawing doubts concerning the Bible's infallibility.

Matthew and Luke both include the genealogy of Jesus in their birth narratives (Matt. 1:1-17 and Luke 3:21-38). In Matthew, three sets of fourteen generations are mentioned, from Abraham to David, from David to the Babylonian exile and from the exile to the birth of Jesus. This genealogy traces the family of Joseph, the supposed father of Jesus. Note that most Jews, with the exception of the Levites who were priests, had long since forgotten their genealogies, not even remembering their particular tribe. The detail of Matthew's list is amazing, if true. Not only does Matthew list the tribe as Judah, but he knows every generation as well. When one considers the four hundred plus years in Egypt, the Assyrian exile and the Babylonian exile, it is nearly impossible to believe the level of detail. But just because everyone else would be unable to trace such a genealogy, this does not, in itself, prove an error.

However, one must also consider modern archeology which even questions the flight from Egypt. There are serious questions about the authenticity of the early Bible stories of Moses and the Exodus. The archeology does not wholly support the Moses story and the conquests of Joshua as presented in the Old Testament. This does not mean that Moses and Joshua were fictional characters, devoid of any past. They could have been local legends, and the adoption of these early Jewish heroes may have been a way to legitimize a later king (Josiah) and an established priesthood. (This line of reasoning may explain why only the Levites could trace their original tribe. If the other tribes were only creations of convenience then no one could possibly remember them.) Moses and Joshua may have been actual people, but the writers of the Old Testament made them founders of this land (Israel) and its law.(4) So it is likely that the Bible Moses was myth built upon the framework of an individual known to the Jews in their distant past. If this Moses was a mythical character, then the genealogy of Jesus was also created in the mind of man, not God. But again, this is conjecture, not proven fact.

The genealogy of Luke also traces the ancestors of Joseph through 75 generations, through David, Judah, Abraham, Shem, Noah, Seth, Adam and God. All the important Old Testament characters are present. Note that this genealogy of Joseph is not to be reconciled to the one presented in Matthew. Maybe one list traced Joseph's father and the other, his mother. However, this solution only doubles the problem mentioned above. Now, two separate families could trace their history while all other Jews were clueless. And the list in Luke goes all the way back to Noah and Adam. This is truly amazing. Forget all the research into man's origins by paleoanthropologists. Obviously, the remains of Cro-Magnon, Neanderthal and other early hominids are misdiagnosed, as Adam is only a few thousand years old. And if Adam is much older, then the genealogy is even more unbelievable.

To further muddy the genealogy waters, the story of Noah is but a copy of an earlier recorded flood story, that of the Sumerian King, Gilgamesh.(5) In the Epic of Gilgamesh, the gods determined to extinguish mankind, but Ea warned the human hero of the impending calamity and commanded him to build a boat, giving the precise measurements. When the man finished the boat, he took his family and the "seed of all living creatures" into the belly. Then the rains came and covered the earth. When they stopped, the boat set down upon a mountain. The man set loose a dove and a swallow but they returned, finding no resting place. Finally, a raven was let loose, and it did not return. At that, the man made a sacrifice to the gods. This is incredibly close to the Noah story and precedes it by many, many centuries. So if Noah did not exist, or rather was a substitute for Gilgamesh, then this genealogy of Noah and Shem is a forgery. Needless to say, this part of the birth narratives is suspect at best, a complete falsification at worst.

The Gospel of Luke provides information about the birth of John the Baptist which is missing from Matthew's account. John's parents were named Zechariah and Elizabeth. Elizabeth was barren and both were well along in years, beyond child-bearing. However, an angel appeared to Zechariah and told him that Elizabeth was with child. This story is quaint but not an original. Remember the struggle of Abraham and Sarah concerning children. In Genesis 17:15-19, God promised Abraham that Sarah would give him a son even though Abraham was one hundred years old and Sarah, ninety. Yes, this biblical miracle was reproduced in Luke 1:5-25. One must question the veracity of the New Testament story. After all, an unbelievable miracle loses its magic if overused.

Next, Mary visited her relative Elizabeth in order to celebrate the upcoming miraculous births of John and Jesus. Note that these relatives had the same names as Moses' and Aaron's sister, Miriam, and her sister-in-law Elisheba (Aaron's wife). And like Miriam and Elisheba, the New Testament Elizabeth played second fiddle to Mary, the Greek variant of Miriam. Also, Mary's song (Luke 1:46-55) was patterned after Hannah's prayer in 1 Samuel 2:1-10. Again, there is nothing new under the sun.

In Matthew 1:18-25 and Luke 1:26-38, Mary was found to be with child through the Holy Spirit. A passage from Isaiah 7:14 was quoted as support for this miracle, "The virgin will be with child and will give birth to a son, and they will call him Immanuel." The term "virgin" has two different meanings depending on whether one uses the Hebrew Bible or the Greek version, the Septuagint. The Greek version of virgin denotes our concept of virgin (not having had sexual relations) while the Hebrew means young woman. Now, it seems to me that many young women have babies but not many virgins. So, not only is the passage taken out of context in support of the "Virgin Birth" but the Hebrew meaning is disregarded in favor of the Greek form which supports the new concept. The Jewish community in Jerusalem, the center of the early Jewish Church (Way), would never have placed the Greek version above the Hebrew one. Obviously, this "virgin birth" story came from the Gentile world where Greek would have been favored. In addition, in the history of modern Mankind, such a birth has not been recorded.

The writers of the Gospels merely placed Jesus on a level with other heroes in ancient antiquity like Apollonius and Heracles. Heracles had a human mother and Zeus for a father. If we hold the story of Heracles to be pure fantasy, why should we believe the story of Jesus? The two stories are identical: a human mother and god for a father.

The visit of the Magi or Wise Men has been a mainstay of Christmas plays and is somewhat mysterious in nature. Matthew 2:1-18 describes "wise men" or Magi from the east travelling to Jerusalem to worship the king of the Jews. They met with Herod who wanted them to reveal the infant's whereabouts to him, so that the future king might be silenced forever. The Magi might represent the Queen of Sheba, who led the fabulously rich party to Jerusalem to admire and give gifts to King Solomon (1 Kings 10:1-10). The gift of gold and adoration are present in both stories.

The desire to kill all the infants two years old or younger is missing from Herod's portrayal by Josephus. In fact, the only children murdered by Herod were his own (Alexander and Aristobulus in 7 BC), born to his Maccabean princess wife, Miriam. The motive for this murder of his own flesh and blood is similar to the Gospel story. Herod was jealous of his boys because the crowds preferred them to him, and Herod did not wish to share his crown. (War 1.535-549) And interestingly enough, Miriam (Mary) was eventually slain by Herod for allegedly sleeping with his own uncle, Joseph, who was immediately executed. (Ant. 15.65-87) Note again the overlap between stories. Miriam and Mary are both accused of infidelity, and the names Miriam and Joseph themselves lead us to great suspicion concerning the truth of the Gospels. Also, the age of Joseph the uncle reminds us of the stories of a young Mary and an older wiser Joseph at the Inn. In addition, the slaughter of innocents recalls Herod's family deeds and also mimics the life story of the greatest of Jews, Moses. In Exodus 1:15-22, Pharaoh commanded that all Jewish male children were to be killed, just as Herod supposedly ordered the same in Matthew 2:16.

The Gospel writers cannot help themselves; whenever a miracle is performed by an Old Testament hero (or Pagan Redeemer), Jesus must perform the same. Just as God called the Jews out of Egypt, Matthew declared that Jesus also was called out of Egypt. (Matthew 1:14,15) Other examples of this "creative process" include: walking on water and the floating axe of Elisha (2 Kings 6:1-7), the raising from the dead of Lazarus and the boy revived by Elisha (2 Kings 4:8-37), the fasting in the desert for forty days and the forty days spent by Moses with God in receiving the Ten Commandments (Ex 19-23) and the making of wine from water, consistent with the abilities of Dionysis.

In Matthew 2:19-23, Jesus was brought back to the town of Nazareth because Joseph feared returning to Judea. In Luke 2:1-4, Mary and Joseph lived in Nazareth and were forced to leave for Bethlehem. These two accounts are reversed. However, to be fair, it is possible that Joseph and Mary had previously lived in Nazareth, thus reconciling Matthew to Luke. As for Nazareth, this town was never mentioned in the Old Testament or in the writings of Josephus. Many historians believe that Nazareth is a corruption of Nazirite, a belief system whose most famous sons were Samson (Judges 13:7) and James, the brother of Jesus (6). I am not questioning the area of Galilee, but only the specific site, Nazareth.

All the above problems, inconsistencies and apparent plagarisms are minor compared to this following fact. Matthew claimed that Jesus was born approximately two years before the death of Herod, thus dating the birth at 6 BC. Luke, on the other hand, dated the birth to the census of Cyrenius, under the Roman Governor Coponius, around the year 6 or 7 AD. There is an 11-12 year difference between accounts. Thus, if the Word of God is perfect or infallible, then the standards must be very lax.

If we take Luke's account of the dating, we have many problems. Jesus was born in 6 AD and according to Luke 3:23, his ministry began at the age of thirty. This brings the year to 36 AD. Most Biblical scholars claim that the ministry lasted three years. Therefore, Jesus was put to death in the year 39 AD. Unfortunately, this is two years after the removal of Pontius Pilate and several years after the conversion of Paul. This will not do. I believe Luke used a passage in Josephus whose subject corresponded to Matthew's account. The reason for the switch is simple. Luke had to get Jesus from Nazareth to Bethlehem, and the census was the ideal vehicle. Unfortunately, just as Winston Smith discovered, the hero of Orwell's book <u>1984</u>, the rewriting of history often leaves tell-tale signs of truth. So if we disregard Luke's dating of the birth, we arrive at the crucifixion under Pilate in the year 27 AD (6 BC plus 30 years plus a 3 year ministry). This is probably closer to the truth than the traditional dating of 28-33 AD. And this also corresponds to the beginning of Pilate's term where the death of Jesus is recorded by Josephus. However, we will soon see that even this earlier date is not early enough. (See Chapter Nine and Appendix 7).

As you can see, there are many problems with the Biblical birth narratives. Although not mentioned in the Gospels, the day of Jesus' birth has been traditionally assigned to December 25, our Christmas Day. This day was a Roman holiday and was also attached to the pagan god Mithra. Mithra [like Jesus] was born in a cave and the newborn adored by shepherds who offered firstfruits. At the time of Jerome, Pagan worshippers celebrated the festival of the birth of the sun on Christmas Day at this very cave.(7) So not only are the pages of the New Testament filled with borrowings from Josephus, the Old Testament and pagan sources, but so too the traditions which most Christians adhere to.

So do we throw the baby out with the bathwater? Is the entire story of Jesus a lie or purposeful exaggeration? After all, if the birth narratives are patently false, then what else is to be believed? As for the Gospels, not much should be blindly believed. In this respect the Mythicists hold the trump cards. The writings of J.M. Robertson one hundred years ago explain the method of the Gospel writers. He believed the Jesus movement began much earlier than is traditionally accepted and that the person of Jesus was no more real than Heracles or the Greek Gods. The birth narratives and the death passion play were ways to express ideas about a forgotten past using a fictional character. In this, the Mythicists were correct, for the Jesus of the Gospels was not real. He was an individual crafted to meet the needs of a Gentile community, complete with all the pagan imagery (lamb of God). Unfortunately for the Mythicists, Jesus left behind James and at least one other brother, known through Paul's letters to the Galatians and Corinthians. Unlike the Mythicists, I recognize this difficulty.

Even though the Gospel presentation of Jesus is at the least, a partial fabrication, I hope to prove that much of the story is based upon a real person, a rabbi of extraordinary abilities, not the Son of God but a man, made of real flesh and blood. This man, Judas the Galilean, was detailed in the history of Josephus in 5 BC and 6 AD, the very years when Jesus was supposedly born, according to Matthew and Luke. This striking coincidence does not prove that the two men, Judas and Jesus, were one in the same, but it does whet the appetite for further investigation. (For similarities between Jesus and Judas the Galilean concerning the birth scenarios, see Appendix 1—numbers 1, 11, 20, 29 and 30).

THE BIRTHS OF JESUS AND JUDAS THE GALILEAN

New Testament

Jesus born (Matt.) (1)	Herod the Great dies (3)	Joseph goes to Galilee due to Archelaus (4)								12 year old at the Temple (6)	Jesus born (Luke) (1,6)
6	5	4	3	2	1	1	2	3	4	5	6	7
BC						**AD**						
Judas and Matthias Golden Eagle (2)	Herod the Great dies (3)	Archelaus rules(4) Barabbas release(5)	Judas King in Galilee (4)							Judas the Galilean leads tax revolt census of Cyrenius (2,6)	

JOSEPHUS

1. The New Testament is inconsistent in pinpointing the birth of Jesus. The difference in dates is eleven to twelve years.

2. The main mentions of Judas the Galilean are in 5 BC and 6-7 AD or the same interval as the birth narratives in the Gospels.

3. Herod the Great dies in 4 BC in Matthew and in Josephus.

4. During the reign of Archelaus, the Gospel of Matthew has Joseph moving to Galilee because he fears Archelaus. Josephus has Judas moving to Sepphoris in Galilee in order to escape the reaches of Archelaus. Here, Judas is crowned King.

5. Josephus records the Barabbas incident in 4 BC, when Archelaus released Judas from prison. The Gospel Barabbas incident occurred during the trial of Jesus, anywhere from 28-39 AD, depending on which birth date is used in calculating Jesus' age of 33.

6. The Gospel of Luke has Jesus being born at the time of the census of Cyrenius. The Gospel of Matthew has the boy Jesus at the Temple about this time. Josephus records that Judas the Galilean started his nationwide campaign against the census tax and Rome during the census of Cyrenius.

CHAPTER THREE

THE BIRTH OF JUDAS THE GALILEAN

The actual birth of Judas the Galilean escaped the pen of Josephus, but the birth of his movement was written about with great conviction. In fact, of all the troublemakers crisscrossing Judea about this time era, 6 BC to 70 AD, Josephus spent more time and effort recounting the highlights of Judas' career than anyone else. To Judas, Josephus attributed the downfall of Israel. But this particular viewpoint depended entirely upon one's place in society. To the Romans, Judas and his followers were bandits and murderers, causing uprisings and political turmoil wherever their ideas were free to flourish. However, to the poor and downtrodden, Judas' call for freedom and self-determination was a sign of God's working hand. Opposing Roman taxation, Judas set himself apart from other religious personalities; Judas picked his fight with the Roman empire, a brave but ultimately foolish act.

To understand this man, we must examine the writings of Josephus. In this chapter and the next, I have reproduced passages from the <u>Antiquities</u> and have bracketed { } any additional data from the <u>War</u>. All other points of interest have been italicized and will be discussed later. The first passage examined in this chapter occurred before the death of Herod the Great (5 BC) while the second came right after his death.

1. ...he [Herod] resented a sedition which some of the *lower sort of men* excited against him, the occasion of which was as follows: There was one Judas, the son of Saripheus {*Sepphoris*}, and Matthias, the son of Margalothus {Margalus}, two of the most eloquent men among the Jews, and the most *celebrated interpreters of the Jewish laws, and men well beloved by the people* {held in great esteem all over the nation}, because of their education of their youth; for all those that were *studious of virtue* frequented their lectures every day {a kind of an army of such as were growing up to be men}. These men, when they found that the king's distemper was

incurable, excited the young men that they would pull down all those works which the king had erected contrary to the law of their fathers, and thereby obtain the *reward* which the law will confer on them for such actions of piety; for that it was truly on account of Herod's rashness in making such things as the law had forbidden, that his other misfortunes, and this distemper also, which was so unusual among mankind, and with which he was now afflicted, came upon him: for Herod had caused such things to be made, which were contrary to the law, of which he was accused by Judas and Matthias; for the king had erected over the great gate of the temple a large golden eagle, of great value, and had dedicated it to the temple. *Now, the law forbids those that propose to live according to it, to erect images, or representations of any living creature.* So these *wise men* persuaded [their students] to pull down the golden eagle: alleging, that although they should incur any danger which might bring them to their deaths, the virtue of the action now proposed to them would appear much more advantageous to them than the pleasures of life; since they would die for the preservation and observation of the law of their fathers; since they would also *acquire an everlasting fame and commendation*; since they would be both commended by the present generation, and leave an example of life that would never be forgotten to posterity; since that common calamity of dying cannot be avoided by our living so as to escape any such dangers; that therefore it is a right thing for those who are in love with a virtuous conduct, to wait for that fatal hour by such a behaviour as may carry them out of the world with praise and honor; and that this will alleviate death to such a degree, thus to come at it by the *performance of brave actions*, which bring us into danger of it; and at the same time to leave that reputation behind them to their children, and to all their relations, whether they be men or women, which will be of great advantage to them afterward {it was a glorious thing to die for the laws of their country; because that the soul was immortal, and that an *eternal enjoyment of happiness did await such as died on that account*}.

And with such discourses as this did these men excite the young men to this action; and a report being come to them that the king was dead, this was an addition to the *wise men's* persuasions, so, in the very middle of the day they got upon the place, they pulled down the eagle, and cut it into pieces with axes, while a great number of people were in the temple. And now the king's captain, upon hearing what the undertaking was, and supposing it a thing of higher nature than it proved to be, came up thither, having a great band of soldiers with him, such as was sufficient to put a stop to the multitude of those who pulled down what was dedicated to God: so he fell upon them unexpectedly, and as they were upon this bold attempt, in a foolish presumption rather than a cautious circumspection, as *is usual with the multitude*, and while they were in disorder, and incautious of what was for their advantage,—so he caught no fewer than forty of the young men, who had the courage to stay behind when the rest ran away, together with the authors of this bold attempt, who thought it an ignominious thing to retire upon his approach, and led them to the king. And when they were come to the king, and he had asked them if they had been so bold as to pull down what he had dedicated to God, "Yes," said they, "what was contrived we contrived, and what has been performed we performed it; and that with such a virtuous courage as become men; for we have given our assistance to those things which were dedicated to the majesty of God, and we have provided for what we have learned by hearing the law: and it ought not to be wondered at, if we esteem those laws which Moses had suggested to him, and were taught him by God, and which he wrote and left behind him, more worthy of observation than thy commands. Accordingly, *we will undergo death, and all sorts of punishments which thou canst inflict upon us, with pleasure, since we are conscious to ourselves that we shall die, not for any unrighteous actions, but for our love to religion.*" {and when he [Herod] asked them by whose command they had done it, they replied at the command of the law of their country; and when he further asked them how they could be so joyful when they were to be put to death, they replied, because *they should enjoy greater happiness after they were dead.*} And thus they all said, and their courage was equal to their profession, and equal to that with which they readily set about this undertaking. And when the king had ordered them to be bound, he sent them to Jericho, and called together the principal men among the Jews; and when they were come, he made them assemble in the theatre, and because he himself could not stand, he lay upon a couch, and enumerated the many labours he had long endured on their account, and his building of the temple, and what a vast charge that was to him; while the Asamoneans, during the hundred and twenty-five years of their government, had not been able to perform any so great a work for the honour of God as that was: that he had also adorned it with very valuable donations; on which account he hoped that he had left himself a memorial, and procured himself a reputation after his death. He then cried out, that these men had not abstained from affronting him, even in his lifetime, but that, in the very daytime, and in sight of the multitude, they had abused him to that degree, as to fall upon what he had dedicated, and in that way of abuse, had pulled it down to the ground. They pretended indeed, that they did it to affront him; but if any one consider the thing truly, they will find that they were guilty of sacrilege against God therein.

But the people, on account of Herod's barbarous temper, and for fear he should be so cruel as to inflict punishment on them, said what was done, was done without approbation, and that it seemed to them that the actors might well be punished for what they had done. But as for Herod, he dealt more mildly with others [of the assembly]; but he deprived Matthias of the high priesthood, as in part on occasion of this action, and made Joazar, who was Matthias's wife's brother, high priest in his stead. Now it happened, that during the time of the high priesthood of this Matthias, there was another person made high priest for a single day, that very day which the Jews observe as a fast. The occasion was this:—This Matthias the high priest, on the night before the day when the fast was to be celebrated, *seemed in a dream, to have conversation with his wife;* and because he could not officiate himself on that account, Joseph, the son of Ellemus, his kinsman, assisted him in that sacred office. But Herod deprived this Matthias of the high priesthood, *and burnt the other Matthias, who had raised the sedition, with his companions, alive.* And that very night there was an eclipse of the moon. {[Herod] ordered those that had let themselves down, together with the rabbins, to be burnt alive....} Ant. 17.149-167 and War 1.648-653

2. There was also *Judas, the son of that Ezekias {Hezekiah} who had been head of the robbers;* which Ezekias was a very strong man, and had with great difficulty been caught by Herod. This Judas having gotten together a multitude of men of a profligate character about *Sepphoris in Galilee,* and made an assault upon the palace [there] and seized upon all the weapons that were laid up in it, and with them armed every one of those that were with him, and carried away what money was left there; and he became terrible to all men, by tearing and rending those that came near him; and all this in order to raise himself, and out of an ambitious desire of the royal dignity; and he hoped to obtain that as the reward, not of his virtuous skill in war, but of his extravagance in doing injuries. {Judas attacked those who were so earnest to gain the dominion.} Ant. 17.271-2 and War 2.56.

These two passages are together quite lengthy and are reproduced so that we can systematically discover the facts concerning Judas and his possible link to Jesus. In Antiquities, Josephus began his narrative of a sedition (a popular uprising) against an old and ailing Herod by depicting the rebels as "some of the lower sort of men." This was not unusual for Josephus to describe rebels as of the lower sorts, or as bandits or even as murderers. A few sentences later these same "lower sorts" were described as young men "studious of virtue". Perhaps the derogatory "lower sorts" applied to one's social standings. After all, Josephus was writing for the Emperor and had close ties to the ruling elites in Israel during his early years. Needless to say, these rebels were not wealthy but young impressionable men studying at the feet of two widely respected teachers, eloquent and well beloved by the people.

The two teachers, "most celebrated interpreters of the Jewish laws," were named Judas and Matthias. These names suggest a relationship with the Maccabean movement, a tradition of struggle against foreign rule. The Maccabean fight against Greek rule (approximately 170-140 BC) was led by a

Mattathias and his five sons, the most famous being Judas Maccabee. This Judas is remembered to this day by the Jewish Festival of Lights or Hanukkah, commemorating the rededication of the Temple by Judas after the defilement by Antiochus Epiphanes. Could the names be mere coincidences or were the "two teachers" purposely named after these earlier heroes? From an analysis of names in Appendix 5, the use of Maccabean names was no coincidence.

The event in question occurred in 5 BC, right before the death of King Herod. (Herod died in 4 BC). The dating of this sedition correlates precisely to the birth date of Jesus, according to Matthew (see Chapter Two). Note also the close relationship between Jesus as a twelve year old in the temple (Luke 2:41-52) and the circumstances concerning Judas and Matthias' lectures on the law: both were located at the temple in Jerusalem and both centered upon young men thirsting for righteousness.

The origin of the sedition was attributed to Judas and Matthias, who incited their students to destroy a golden eagle which had been dedicated to the temple by Herod. Judas and Matthias accused Herod of breaking the law by erecting "images or representations of any living being." Thus, the young men were persuaded by the "wise men" to pull down the eagle, and so they did. (Also note that the only passage attributed to Jesus by Josephus—Chapter One—used the same term, wise man, in describing Jesus.) To the untrained eye, this type of act appears purely religious on the surface, but political undertones were clearly present. Pulling down the eagle was tantamount to pulling down Herod himself. Once again, this passage correlates to the birth narrative in Matthew, where Herod was searching for a usurper to the crown. And in both accounts, many innocents died from his wrath: the children under two years old in the Gospel account and forty young students in this rebellion.

This first passage detailed ad nauseam the supposed rewards for the students in the rebellion. These rewards remind us of the Muslim terrorists in the 9/11/01 attack and the even more recent Palestinian attacks on the state of Israel. Josephus wrote in the War, "it was a glorious thing to die for the laws of their country; because that the soul was immortal, and that an eternal enjoyment of happiness did await such as died on that account." and again, "…when he [Herod] further asked them how they could be so joyful when they were to be put to death, they replied, because they should enjoy greater happiness after they were dead."

The following can be deduced from the above. First, the followers of Judas and Matthias were dedicated to the point of putting the cause (love of the law) above their own lives. This "army of such as were growing up to be men" was a dangerous group, just waiting to explode into action. An army of martyrs is a difficult group to fight as the United States and Israel are realizing in the war on terrorism. This was the reason why Herod killed so many and chased those who escaped. The Temple Cleansing gave Herod political cover, making it a perfect time to defuse this dangerous bomb. This dedication of belief over life corresponds with the Fourth Philosophy as described by Josephus in <u>Antiquities</u>. (This will be examined later, in Chapter Four). Such an attitude also fits precisely with what we know of the early Jewish Christians, who were persecuted under Nero as recorded by Tacitus. These Christians "were clad in the hides of beasts and torn to death by dogs; others were crucified, others set on fire to serve to illuminate the night when daylight failed."(1) In fact, it is my belief that the martyrdom of Judas' students fits perfectly with the martyrdom of Jewish Christians before 70 AD. (After 70 AD, the Jewish Christians were minor players as their Messiah did not materialize during the Jewish War. The post war Christians were primarily Gentiles who did their best to distance themselves from their Jewish forerunners in the faith (See Chapter Six)).

Secondly, the belief in the afterlife was part of Pharisaic doctrine. This agreed to the Fourth Philosophy of Judas the Galilean (Chapter Four) and to Christian faith. In fact, such a belief in the afterlife was necessary in order to control the masses. Why would you give your life for a cause if there were no rewards? The afterlife and martyrdom go hand-in-hand.

Thirdly, the place and cause of the rebellion was similar to an event which occurred right before the one mention of Jesus in <u>Antiquities</u>. Here, Pontius Pilate sent his soldiers to Jerusalem (19 AD—see Appendix 7) with Caesar's effigies upon their banners. This was against the law, similar to the Golden Eagle affair in which Herod also defamed the Temple (5 BC). Those that opposed Pilate had the same disregard for their own lives. They bared their necks and told Pilate that they would rather die than transgress their law. On this occasion, Pilate blinked and had the banners removed. His next action was to raid the temple treasury to build an aqueduct. Here the anger was such that Pilate ordered an attack, where a great number of Jews were slain while others ran away wounded. This may very well mirror the Gospel portrayal of Jesus cleansing the temple, where the thieves were the Romans and their hirelings, the Herodians. Not long after, Jesus was arrested and crucified. Could this have been Judas re-enacting an episode of his own life, the cleansing of the temple? In fact, it would have been Judas' second temple cleansing. This corresponds with the Gospel of John which places the temple cleansing at the beginning of Jesus' ministry while the Synoptics had it at the end. Like Judas, the Jesus of the Gospels cleansed the temple at the beginning and end of his career.

If Judas/Jesus were crucified during the Pilate era, then the above scenario makes sense. However, the odds against Judas surviving until the traditional dating of Pilate (27 AD) seem overwhelmingly long. It is much more likely that

Judas was crucified shortly after his entry into Jerusalem, some time after the tax rebellion of 6-7 AD. Judas the Galilean was a clever man. He knew the power of Rome and was not easily fooled. The only things which could have drawn him to Jerusalem were the acts of Pilate. However, per Appendix 7, the dating of Pilate should be 18-37 AD. It is my contention that Judas the Galilean died at the hands of Pilate in 19 AD. This is the smoking gun! This earlier date corresponds with the time of Judas the Galilean and flies in the face of the mythical Jesus of the Gospels. The Gospel Jesus would have been twelve years old by Luke's account and twenty-three by Matthew's birth narrative.

The next coincidence involved the sending of the rebels to Jericho, where Herod could interrogate the prisoners. A similar occurrence was recorded in Luke 23:6-12, where Pilate sent Jesus to Herod for questioning. This only occurred in Luke's account. I believe Luke was simply using the data from Josephus and incorporating it into the story of Jesus.

Later in the account, one of the priests dreamed that he had "conversation" with his wife, making him unfit to perform his priestly duties. Matthew 27:19 parodied that thought, "While Pilate was sitting on the judge's seat, his wife sent him this message: 'Don't have anything to do with that innocent man, for I have suffered a great deal today in a dream because of him.'" Again, the passage in Josephus was used to develop the story of Jesus.

How did the story end? According to the War, those involved in the rebellion and the rabbis were put to death, burnt alive. So there goes the basis of this book, that Judas was Jesus. This is the reason why historians and scholars have overlooked Judas and this whole era concerning the life of Jesus. But further analysis is needed. In Antiquities, only Matthias was put to death, with no mention of Judas being killed. This is further enhanced by a later sedition where the Jews were revolting because of the death of Matthias (Ant. 17.206-218). The rebels were in the temple, lamenting the loss of Matthias and Judas; Matthias to death, Judas to flight or to imprisonment.

If Matthias were immediately put to death, then why would Herod delay the execution of Judas? Perhaps the execution of Matthias was part one of a strategy by Herod, where the innovators would be temporarily stopped. The imprisonment of the other teacher, Judas, could be seen as an insurance policy to keep the mob at bay. Soon after the Temple Cleansing, Herod died and his son Archelaus assumed control. In a way to appease the seditious mob, Archelaus released prisoners captured during the reign of his father.(Ant. 17.204) This was at the same time when the crowd lamented the loss of Matthias and Judas. Perhaps the crowd insisted on the release of Judas, crying out, "Barabbas," son of the Father. It is possible that Judas was well known for his prayers to God just as Jesus was in the Lord's Prayer in Matt. 6:9: "Our

Father in heaven, hallowed be thy name...." Or this name Barabbas might have signalled a familial tie of Judas to Matthias. It is possible that Matthias was the father and Judas the son, built on the pattern of Mattathias and Judas Maccabee.

Note that the second passage from Josephus described another Judas (the same Judas?), the son of Hezekiah. Now Hezekiah could represent two distinct possibilities. First, in 2 Chronicles 29-31, Hezekiah purified the temple, just as Judas and Matthias had done. Or the second possibility was given by Josephus: that this Hezekiah was a bandit or robber, the code language for freedom fighter. Either way, this Judas may be connected with the Judas from the first passage.

Next, Judas was said to have come from Sepphoris in Galilee. This Sepphoris is only a few miles from Nazareth, although the very existence of Nazareth is questionable at this time as it escaped mention in the Old Testament and the writings of Josephus. In the War, Judas the rabbi was the son of Sepphoris. Note that the place name has replaced the father's name. This also happened with Jesus. Jesus the Nazirite became Jesus of Nazareth. Thus, I think it is probable that the Judas of the second passage is the same as Judas, the rabbi of passage one.

This composite Judas travelled back and forth from Jerusalem to Galilee in the same way as Jesus. On the run from the authorities, Judas could never put down permanent roots. In Matthew 12:1-4, Jesus and his disciples were eating grain from the fields on the Sabbath. They were accused of working on the Sabbath by the Pharisees. However, Jesus defended his party by comparing their situation to that of David, who ate consecrated bread in his flight from Saul. Likewise, Jesus and his disciples were in flight from the authorities. Their constant movement was of necessity, but it should also remind us of the robbers and innovators represented by Judas.

How did the temple defeat affect Judas? He lost his best friend or father, Matthias, and at least forty of his disciples. The events may have radicalized Judas even more. Much has recently been made of the transformation of Osama Bin Laden. His radicalization was a product of Western influence or an unhealthy backlash against Western values. In the same way, Judas had decided to mix weapons with preaching. However, Judas' use of weapons was strictly defensive. He knew that his small army was no match for Rome. Any attack on Rome would have to be accomplished through the hand of God. Only God could defeat such a great power as Rome.

At Sepphoris, he seized all the weapons at the palace and "carried away what money was left there." Thus, he was a robber. But from his point of view, the weapons were a necessity and the money could be no better spent. Our own myths have produced a character named Robin Hood, the outlaw who stole from the rich and gave to the poor. Note the attitude about wealth in the New Testament. "Blessed are the poor," said Jesus. James, the brother of Jesus, wrote:

Now listen, you rich people, weep and wail because of the misery that is coming upon you. Your wealth has rotted, and moths have eaten your clothes. Your gold and silver are corroded. Their corrosion will testify against you and eat your flesh like fire. You have hoarded wealth in the last days. Look! The wages you failed to pay the workmen who mowed your fields are crying out against you. The cries of the harvesters have reached the ears of the Lord Almighty. You have lived on earth in luxury and self-indulgence. You have fattened yourselves in the day of slaughter. You have condemned and murdered innocent men, who were not opposing you. (James 5:1-6)

You will never find a writer more opposed to the misuse of wealth than James, and he was the blood brother of Jesus.

Josephus also stated that after Judas raided the armory and carried away the money, he "became terrible to all men." By this, Josephus meant that Judas and his followers tried to persuade others to "adopt" his philosophy. Josephus wrote about Judas Maccabee in the same way:

...where Judas met him [Lysias] with ten thousand men; and when he saw the great number of his ememies [60,000], <u>he prayed to God that he would assist him</u>, and joined battle with the first of the enemy that appeared, and beat them, and slew about five thousand of them, and thereby <u>became terrible</u> to the rest of them. Nay, indeed, Lysias observing the great spirit of the Jews, how they were <u>prepared to die rather than lose their liberty</u>, and being afraid of their desperate way of fighting [Lysias returned to Antioch].... When, therefore, the generals of Antiochus's armies had been beaten so often, Judas assembled the people together, and told them, that after these many victories which God had given them, they ought to go up to Jerusalem, and purify the temple, and offer the appointed sacrifices. (<u>Ant</u>. 12.314-316)

In fact, this episode of Judas Maccabee defeating the foreign invaders must have inspired Judas to do the same things. Note that they were prepared to die rather than lose their liberty. This was a central teaching of Judas the Galilean, as will be presented in Chapter Four. And realize that after the victory, Judas Maccabee went to Jerusalem to purify the temple which had been polluted by Antiochus Epiphanes. After arming his followers and defeating other claimants to the throne, it is very possible that Judas/Jesus was crowned king or Messiah about this time. Josephus said this concerning the time in question, after the death of Herod the Great:

And now Judea was full of robberies; and, as the several companies of the seditious lighted upon anyone to head them, he was created a king immediately, in order to do mischief to the public. (Ant. 17.285)

It is possible that Judas/Jesus was crowned king of a small area in Galilee but had to fight others who also had similar designs. Thus, the Messiahship of Judas/Jesus may have lasted from 4 BC to 19 AD or shortly after the arrival of Pilate. This long-lasting Messiahship may have been necessary to build his movement, for we know that Judas the Galilean became a national figure in 6 AD at the census. This longer kingship makes much more sense than the Gospel version, where an unknown Jesus took the nation by storm. After all, we must realize that the ruling authorities (Herodians and Romans) were constantly harassing or killing the seditious. Thus, the movement's growth would be a slow but progressive march from Galilee to Jerusalem, after the model of Judas Maccabee.

There is one passage in Josephus which definitely ties the Judas of 4 BC to Judas the Galilean of 6 AD (Chapter Four).

Menahem, the son [probably grandson] of Judas, that was called the Galilean...took some of the men with him, and retired to Masada, where he broke open King Herod's armory and gave arms not only to his own people, but other robbers also. These he made use of for a guard, and returned in the state of a king to Jerusalem. (War 2.433,434)

Interestingly, a son or grandson of Judas the Galilean (6 AD) did the exact deeds as Judas of Sepphoris (4 BC). He broke into an armory, armed his followers, was made king and then marched upon Jerusalem. Surely, he was acting on the memory of his father or grandfather, Judas the Galilean.

Thus, the radical rabbi, teaching adherence to the law in the Temple, became a freedom fighter, not just with words but now also with swords, (although his use of weapons was limited per the analysis in Chapter Nine). Against the power of Rome, such an undertaking would be foolish in our eyes and certainly from the viewpoint of our only historian of this time period, Josephus. Judas patterned his war against Rome and their Herodian puppets after Judas Maccabee, and like contemporary freedom fighters/terrorists, he believed his way was the way of God. And with God, all things are possible.

CHAPTER FOUR

THE BIRTH OF JUDAS THE GALILEAN PART 2

Just as Luke recorded a second birth of Jesus, at the time of the census of Cyrenius, so too was Judas reborn, his movement also traced from this census. This may seem like a harmless coincidence, but the number of coincidences goes beyond mere chance. It is true that Luke used the census to transport Joseph and Mary from Galilee to Jerusalem, but where did this idea originate? From an examination of the Gospel of Luke and the book of Acts, it appears as if Luke was quite adept at using and often twisting the details of Josephus in the telling of his own story. For example, in Acts 5:36,37, Luke wrote, "Some time ago Theudas appeared, claiming to be somebody, and about four hundred men rallied to him. He was killed, all his followers were dispersed, and it all came to nothing. After him, Judas the Galilean appeared in the days of the census and led a band of people in revolt. He too was killed and all his followers scattered." Luke badly mangled the history of Josephus as noted below.

Now it came to pass, that while Fadus was procurator of Judea, that a certain magician, whose name was Theudas, persuaded a great part of the people to take their effects with them, and follow him to the river Jordan; for he told them he was a prophet, and that he would, by his own command, divide the river, and afford them an easy passage over it; and many were deluded by his words. However, Fadus did not permit them to make any advantage of his wild attempt, but sent a troop of horsemen out against them; who falling upon them unexpectedly, slew many of them, and took many of them alive. They also took Theudas alive, and cut off his head, and carried it to Jerusalem. This was what befell the Jews in the time of Cuspius Fadus's government. Then came Tiberius Alexander as successor to Fadus;…and besides this, the sons of Judas of Galilee were now slain; I mean of that Judas who caused the people to revolt, when Cyrenius came to take an account of the estates of the Jews, as we have shown in a foregoing book. The names of those sons were James and Simon, whom Alexander commanded to be crucified. <u>Ant</u>. 20.97-102

Josephus claimed Theudas was killed by Fadus, governor from 44-46 AD. The sons of Judas of Galilee were crucified by Tiberius Alexander in the years following, somewhere between 46-48 AD. And we already know the census of Cyrenius occurred in 6 AD. Now, let's see how Luke twisted these pieces of history. His speaker in Acts 5 was Gamaliel, and this speech occurred some short time after Pentecost, approximately, 27-33 AD (depending on the traditional dating of Jesus' death). It is uncanny how Gamaliel could foresee the future and claim it to be the past. First, he said that Theudas died some time ago, and then he stated that Judas, not the sons of Judas, died after Theudas. In addition, Luke's reference to Judas the Galilean (put into words by Gamaliel) claimed that Judas was killed and his followers scattered. Gamaliel then said in Acts 5:38:

Leave these men alone [Apostles]! Let them go! For if their purpose or activity is of human origin, it will fail. But if it is from God, you will not be able to stop these men; you will only find yourselves fighting against God.

But as you will soon see, Josephus stated that the movement of Judas the Galilean grew and strengthened from 6-70 AD. (It only ended in 70 AD, the year the temple was destroyed by Rome, because so many of its members were slaughtered in the war.) The movement of Judas may have been temporarily scattered at his death, but it grew tremendously afterwards. And coincidentally, the movement of Jesus grew as well after his death. As this example illustrates, Luke used names and even events, but he distorted them to meet his unhistorical time frames and story lines. So it follows that even the speech put into the mouth of Gamaliel was pure fantasy. Luke simply invented the speech to make a good story. And what a story it was! Even today, Christian scholars try to find a Theudas in Josephus' writings before the census. These pathetic efforts are as laughable as the history of Luke.

Thus, Luke liked to copy names and events from Josephus without real concern for accuracy. After all, his audience had no concept of Jewish history. The same can be said for most people throughout the world today. We're lucky if most U.S. citizens have a grasp of our own history. The odds against us knowing the writings of Josephus are astronomically high. This is true of the masses, but what about the religious scholars. These individuals can be placed in two categories. The first are well-meaning souls who accept the party line from their particular organizations. These people would never think of questioning the accuracy of the Bible, and therefore will never see contradictions or incredible coincidences. The second type of scholar sees and even publicly recognizes errors but somehow spiritualizes the problems away, a type of historical gymnastics. But our goal should be to identify errors or coincidences and explain the possible ramifications. As we study this next passage from Josephus, let your mind go beyond the confines of standard orthodoxy, because this time period concerning Jesus (6-7 AD) has never been adequately explored before. All I ask is that you <u>attempt</u> to give a fair hearing to my interpretation of Judas the Galilean being none other than Jesus of Nazareth.

The following lengthy passage from Josephus' <u>Antiquities</u> describes the movement of Judas the Galilean, termed the Fourth Philosophy. Text within parentheses {} comes from the <u>War</u>. Important points will be italicized.

Now Cyrenius, a Roman senator, and one who had gone through other magistracies, and had passed through them till he had been consul, and one who, on other accounts, was of great dignity, came at this time into Syria, with a few others, being sent by Caesar to be a judge of that nation, and to take account of their substance: Coponius also, a man of the equestrian order, was sent together with him, to have the supreme power over the Jews. Moreover, Cyrenius came himself into Judea, which was now added to the province of Syria, to take an account of their substance, and to dispose of Archelaus's money; but the Jews, although at the beginning they took the report of a taxation heinously, yet did they leave off any further opposition to it, by the persuasion of Joazar, who was the son of Boethus, and high priest. So they, being over-persuaded by Joazar's words, gave an account of their estates, without any dispute about it; yet there was one Judas, a Gaulonite, of a city whose name was Gamala {This man was a rabbi with a sect of his own and was quite unlike the others.}, who taking with him Sadduc, a Pharisee, became zealous to draw them to a revolt, who said that this taxation was no better than an introduction to slavery, and exhorted the nation to assert their liberty {*saying that they would be cowards if they submitted to paying taxes to the Romans, and after serving God alone accepted human masters*}; as if they could procure them happiness and security for what they possessed, and an assured enjoyment of a still greater good, which was that of the honor and glory they would thereby acquire for magnanimity. They also said that God would not otherwise be assisting to them, then upon their joining with one another in such counsels as might be successful, and for their own advantage; and this especially, if they would set about great exploits, and not grow weary in executing the same; so men received what they said with pleasure, and this bold attempt proceeded to a great height. All sorts of misfortunes also sprang from these men, and the *nation was infected with this doctrine to an incredible degree*; one violent war came upon us after another, and we lost out friends, who used to alleviate our pain; *there were also very great robberies and murders of our principal men. This was done in pretense indeed for the public welfare, but in reality for the hopes of gain to themselves*; whence arose seditions, and from them murders of men, which sometimes fell on those of their own people, (by the madness of these men towards one another, while their desire was that none of the adverse party might be left,) and sometimes on their enemies; a famine also coming upon us, reduced us to the last degree of despair, as did also the taking and demolishing of cities; nay, the sedition at last increased so high, that the very temple of God was burnt down by their enemy's fire. Such were the consequences of this, that the customs of our fathers were altered, and such a change was made, as added a mighty weight toward bringing all to destruction, which these men occasioned by thus conspiring together; for Judas and Sadduc, who excited a fourth philosophic sect among us, and had a great many followers therein, filled our civil government with tumults at present, and laid the foundation of our future miseries, by this system of philosophy, which we were before unacquainted withal; concerning which I shall discourse a little, and this the rather, because the infection which spread thence among the younger sort, who were zealous for it, brought the public to destruction. [Josepus then goes on to describe the Pharisees, Sadducees and Essenes before returning to the fourth philosophy.]...But the fourth sect of Jewish philosophy, Judas the Galilean was the author. *These men agree in all other things with the Pharisaic notions; but they have a inviolable attachment to liberty; and they say that God is to be their only Ruler and Lord. They also do not value dying any kinds of death, nor indeed do they heed the deaths of their relations and friends, nor can any such fear make them call any man Lord*; and since this immovable resolution of theirs is well known to a great many, I shall speak no further about that matter; nor am I afraid that anything I have said of them should be disbelieved, but rather fear, that what I have said is beneath the resolution they show when they undergo pain; and it was in Gessius Florus's time that the nation began to grow mad with this distemper, who was our procurator, and who occasioned the Jews to go wild with it by the abuse of his authority, and to make them revolt from the Romans; and these are the sects of Jewish philosophy. <u>Ant</u>. 18.1-10;23-25. <u>War</u> 2.117,118.

The disparate parts of a movement coalesce when there is an outside influence, attempting to shape the future of their collective lives. The outside influence was the Roman Empire, the movement being the Fourth Philosophy of Judas the Galilean. The central issues in the above passage concerned the willingness of Jews to pay taxes and to surrender their liberty to Rome. Now, the average U.S. citizen openly complains about paying taxes to the IRS. We go through all types of manipulations of income in order to minimize our tax burden, yet most grudgingly pay. And this payment is to our own democratically elected government. Consider how onerous the tax burden would be if we had to support an occupying power.

In our own history, patriots rallied the people behind the slogan, "No taxation without representation." Even though the colonies were part of the British Empire, these subjects wanted a say in regards to taxation policy. Eventually, the taxation revolt led to the War of Independence. The tax issue was devisive, pitting brother against brother, yet enough souls were brave enough to fight the great power of that day—England. Just imagine how intense the colonists would have felt if their tax monies were given to Germany or Russia, lands not heavily represented in North America at that time.

In Israel, a new era was dawning. The year was 6 AD, the same year that Luke assigned the birth of Jesus. Rome sent Cyrenius to begin a tax assessment along with a governor, Coponius. Coponius was to have "supreme power over the Jews." So the tax was more than just money; it was the submission of national sovereignty. The high priest, Joazar, from the line appointed by Herod, strongly supported the taxation, thereby endorsing the occupation as well. This is not unusual. Throughout history, those in power have usually worked together against the have-nots.

However, Judas the Galilean convinced the people to revolt, arguing that paying taxes to Rome was no different than accepting slavery. In the War, Judas was called a rabbi, a teacher of his own peculiar sect. In Chapter Three, we examined the life of a Judas, a rabbi who incited the people to cleanse the temple and who escaped to Galilee to arm his followers for a future fight. From this beginning sprang forth the Fourth Philosophy, the desire for national independence from usurpers of power, such as Herod and later, the Romans. Note also that Judas had a co-teacher with him called Sadduc. This Sadduc undoubtedly replaced the slain Matthias. The Fourth Philosophy was consciously imitating the Maccabean movement. (This co-teacher arrangement was first started with Mattathias and Judas Maccabee, and when Mattathias died, the reigns of leadership fell upon Judas and his brother, Simon.)

The Dead Sea Scrolls spoke of a Root of Planting, a Righteous Teacher and a Wicked Priest. Matthias must have been a very popular teacher as the people mourned his death in the Temple (Ant. 17.264). It would be such a martyr who would be the culmination of the "Root of Planting" or the beginning of a movement. It is my contention that Judas was the Righteous Teacher, upholding the law and defending the nationalistic fervor of the masses. To support this, James argued that the "Rich" had killed the righteous man, referring to Jesus. (James 5:6) In addition, the Cairo Damascus Document (1.9-11) revealed a twenty year period of "groping for the Way" from the time of the Root of Planting to the rise of the Righteous Teacher.(1) Twenty years passed from the first risings against Herod the Great (25 BC) to the death of Matthias and the rise of Judas. Joazar best represented the Wicked Priest, supporting the invaders against God and His Law. There was such a stark contrast between Judas and Joazar; from taxation to independence. And upon these differences, a movement was fomenting, a war looming in the not so distant future. (See Chapter Seven for full explanations of the Root of Planting, Righteous Teacher and Wicked Priest.)

At this time, we should also examine the views of Jesus concerning taxes to Rome. Luke 23:1,2 states, "Then the whole assembly rose and led him off to Pilate. And they began to accuse him saying, 'We have found this man subverting our nation. He opposes payment of taxes to Caesar and claims to be Messiah, a king.'" Note that the main charge against Jesus concerned the refusal to pay taxes to Rome, thus not accepting the rule of Rome. The claim of Messiah or king is understandable in this context. And of course, this charge was true, however hard it is for the Gospel writers to accept. The Gospels even reported that the refusal to pay taxes was a false charge. However, the Romans believed the charge to be true, and Jesus paid dearly with his life. Crucifixions were reserved for political prisoners, a most horrible way to die.

The passage in Luke 20:21-25 demonstrates Jesus' position on taxes.

So the spies questioned him: "Teacher, we know that you do not show partiality but teach the way of God in accordance with the truth. Is it right for us to pay taxes to Caesar or not?" He saw through their duplicity and said to them. "Show me a denarius. Whose portrait and inscription are on it?" "Caesar's," they replied. He said to them, "Then give to Caesar what is Caesar's, and to God what is God's."

Jesus' answer is not as straightforward as first imagined. We have been taught that this passage proves that Jesus did not oppose Roman taxation, consistent with the position held by Paul, who in Romans 13:6,7 stated:

This is why you pay taxes, for the authorities are God's servants, who give their full time to governing. Give everyone what you owe him: If you owe taxes, pay taxes; if revenue, then revenue; if respect then respect; if honor then honor.

Paul's position on Roman taxation was the same as Joazar, the high priest I have pegged as the Wicked Priest. But Paul's siding with the authorities should not be surprising. Paul had a long history with the household of Herod, and his complicitous dealings with Herodians and Romans is one reason the Jewish Christians excommunicated him (Galatians) (also see Appendix 6).

If we jettison the later views of Paul and study the passage in question without prejudice, then we can arrive at a consistent interpretation in light of the times. The passage notes that the enemies of Jesus were trying to trap him into making statements against the Roman occupation. Jesus saw through their designs and gave them a very sophisticated answer to their question. If he answered 'yes', then the masses would be angered, since the taxation was not popular with the common man. If he answered 'no', then the authorities would have ample evidence to arrest and convict him of sedition. Jesus answered the question of paying taxes to Caesar as follows. He said that Caesar should take his money, thus appearing to support the taxation. He then followed that assertion by saying that what is God's should be given to God. What did he mean by this?

The land of Israel was promised to Abraham in the book of Genesis. This is what Jesus meant in his reply: You Romans and Herodian supporters (tax collectors), take your money and leave our country. In fact, this reply would have infuriated the authorities. So his reply went farther than just answering the question of taxation; it also spoke to the occupation. The Romans would have to leave. Unfortunately for Jesus, the Romans had other ideas.

So identifying Jesus with Judas the Galilean on the tax question is not a difficult task. Both taught against this bondage to Rome. It is not surprising that the Roman coinage itself would be replaced by a Jewish coin during the Jewish War (66-70 AD). These coins of rebellion have been located in the Qumran area where the Dead Sea Scrolls were discovered.

As mentioned earlier, Judas worked with an individual named Sadduc by Josephus. This Sadduc was a Pharisee and I link him with Cephas, or Peter of the Gospels. Remember that Judas had once worked with Matthias. This fellow teacher was martyred by Herod, shortly before Herod's death in 4 BC. In all probability, Matthias and Judas had a dual ministry going on. They had an influence in Jerusalem and one in Galilee. This modus operandi is also evident with the ministry of Jesus as presented in the Gospels. Jesus spent much of his time outside of Jerusalem, but the real play for power coincided with his entry into Jerusalem. Cephas was the right hand man of Jesus, the one who escaped after the arrest of Jesus. This escape or denial by Cephas might have been deemed necessary considering Judas' arrest in the Golden Eagle Temple Cleansing a generation earlier. In fact, the leaders of the movement were probably careful to maintain distance from one another in case an arrest was made. Someone in a leadership role had to carry on the mission. Surely, Judas realized that it was unlikely for a Roman procurator to release prisoners as did Archelaus in 4 BC.

But it goes even further. When Jesus was crucified, a new leader emerged to complement Cephas, so that the ministry did not rely upon one person. That new leader was James, the brother of the Lord. In reading the New Testament, one must ask the question: who's in charge? In some places, it appears that

Cephas is the main man, in others, James. Luke's story of the two men on the road to Emmaus may answer that question. (Luke 24:13-35) One man was named Cleopas (really Cephas) and the other man was unnamed. According to Luke, these were the first two to see Jesus arisen from the grave. This agrees with Paul's account:

…that he was buried, that he was raised on the third day according to the Scriptures, and that he appeared to Cephas, (and then to the Twelve. After that, he appeared to more than five hundred of the brothers at the same time, most of whom are still living, though some have fallen asleep.) Then he appeared to James, then to all the apostles…. (1 Cor. 15:4-7)

The part of the passage in parentheses is a later addition. Note that the use of Twelve apostles is unlike any other mention of apostles by Paul where a definite number is used. Also, according to the Gospels, there were only Eleven left at this time. So, in reality, the first two to meet Jesus after the resurrection were Cephas and James.

Cephas knew that the revolution must continue. His sojourn on the road to Emmaus with James was more a planning strategy than anything else. The resurrection was necessary to continue the movement, and the election of James would once again place a representative in Jerusalem and one in Galilee and beyond. Note that in the book of Acts and in Paul's letters, James is always in Jerusalem and Cephas in the field, preaching the revolution to the Jews. This pattern fits perfectly: Judas with Matthias and Sadduc with Judas.

After speaking of Sadduc, Josephus then stated that the nation was exhorted to "assert their liberty" from taxation (and Rome), that "they were cowards if they would endure to pay a tax to the Romans, and would, after God, submit to mortal men as their lords." The followers were assured a greater glory in the afterlife, similar to the promises made in the Golden Eagle affair with Herod (Chapter Three). So again, there is a tie back to the earlier movement led by Judas and Matthias.

After this, Josephus tells how the nation suffered because of these men, how the wealthy were killed and how the burning of the temple was due to their "infection" of the younger men, who were zealous for this teaching. So Josephus claimed the Fourth Philosophy of Judas was exceedingly prosperous; that they endured for sixty-five years until the slaughter by the Romans in the Jewish war. Earlier in this chapter, a passage from Acts 5 was mentioned, where Gamaliel supposedly said: "For if their purpose or activity is of human origin, it will fail. But if it is from God, you will not be able to stop these men; you will only find yourselves fighting against God." This was uttered after he claimed that the movement of Judas the Galilean had already failed miserably. Gamaliel (Luke's invention) could not have meant the Fourth Philosophy, because it became stronger and stronger and "the nation was infected with this doctrine to an incredible degree." (Ant. 18.6)

In fact, we can tie the movement of Jesus quite closely with that of Judas. Of the Twelve apostles listed, Simon was called a Zealot, Judas Iscariot was really Judas the Sicarios (dagger man or assassin), and the Sons of Thunder imply power in battle. Also, in Acts 21:20, the followers of James who numbered in the thousands, were denoted as "zealous for the law." These followers, "zealous for the law", were no different in belief than those disciples reported by Josephus in the Judas, Matthias sedition in 5 BC. So again, the movements of Judas and Jesus perfectly coincide.

In Ant. 18.11-22, Josephus followed his first mention of Judas and the Fourth Philosophy with descriptions of the other three Jewish philosophies: the Pharisees, the Sadducees and the Essenes. It is important to understand these philosophies because the Fourth Philosophy relied heavily upon the Pharisees and Essenes. In fact, since the Fourth Philosophy was a liberation movement, men from the other three could join. This may be why John the Essene was mentioned as a war leader even though the Essenes were generally described as peace loving. (War 2.567)

The Pharisees were consistently denigrated in the Gospels, where they were depicted as hypocrites and fodder for the fires of hell. However, there are several passages which portray a different type of Pharisee. In Luke 13:31, some Pharisees warned Jesus that Herod wanted to kill him, thus showing their allegiances. Also, in Luke 10:25-37, the expert in the law (Pharisee) was in agreement with Jesus concerning the two greatest commandments. So there might have been two sets of Pharisees, one siding with Jesus and the people, the other siding with the rulers and establishment.

Per Josephus, Pharisees believed in the immortality of the soul and that rewards and punishments awaited the dead depending upon the virtue of their lives. The evil doers would exist in an everlasting prison while the virtuous would live again in glory. This doctrine was very attractive to the downtrodden who had very little hope in the present life. They also believed in the freedom of men to act good or bad, so that men had a responsibility to work towards their own betterment. They also respected their elders.

Sadducees believed that the souls died with the bodies, not an attractive doctrine for the masses. They were few in number and when forced to serve as administrators, they often attached themselves to the Pharisees for protection from the masses. Sadducees aligned themselves with the ruling elites such as the Herodians and Romans, and certainly were not prospective members of the Fourth Philosophy.

The Essenes believed the same doctrines as the Pharisees concerning the immortality of the soul. They also followed a strict life of righteousness, not claiming property for their own but insisting that all things be shared in common (pure communism). Most lived a chaste lifestyle, despising riches and earthly pleasures, (though one sect of Essenes did condone marriage and child rearing). The initiation into the group lasted three years, time to determine if the initiate was worthy. And in death, they would endure any type of torture rather than blaspheme their God.

Josephus wrote that the Fourth Philosophy agreed in all things with the Pharisees, "but they have an inviolable attachment to liberty; and they say that God is to be their only Ruler and Lord."(Ant. 18.23) Like the Pharisees, Judas and Sadduc taught about the resurrection from the dead and the rewards in the afterlife based upon one's virtuous or vicious life. (This belief was also shared with the Essenes). Note that Sadduc is described by Josephus as a Pharisee. It is my contention that Sadduc was picked by Judas as a co-leader because of his Pharisaic ties. This may have also been the background of Matthias, Judas' former co-leader.

Not only is there a close tie with the Pharisees, but many similarities with the Essenes are evident. As noted above, Essenes believed in the resurrection and valued righteousness, in concert with the Fourth Philosophy. In addition, both the Essenes and the followers of Judas would undergo all types of torture rather than blaspheme God. Josephus wrote this about the Essenes:

Their spirit was tested to the utmost by the war with the Romans, who racked and twisted, burnt and broke them, subjecting them to every torture yet invented in order to make them blaspheme the Lawgiver or eat some forbidden food, but could not make them do either, or ever once fawn on their tormenters or shed a tear. Smiling in their agony and gently mocking those who tortured them, they resigned their souls in the joyous certainty that they would receive them back. (War 2.152,153)

Josephus said the Fourth Philosophy "do not value dying any kinds of death, nor indeed do they heed the deaths of their relations and friends, nor can any such fear make them call any man Lord;...that what I have said is beneath the resolution they show when they undergo pain."(Ant. 18.23,24) Thus, the Essenes and followers of Judas appear fairly indistinguishable from one another. It must be noted that the early Jewish Christians also underwent horrible tortures at the hands of Roman power. In Chapter One, the Neronian persecution, as recorded by Tacitus, detailed the spectacle of burning

Christians which amused the Roman crowds, or at least Nero. So in this respect, Essenes, Jewish Christians and followers of Judas the Galilean all suffered in the same way.

Like the Essenes, the followers of Judas rejected wealth and shared all things. Josephus confirmed this when he wrote:

...there were also very great robberies and murders of our principal men. This was done in pretence indeed for the public welfare, but in reality for the hopes of gain for themselves. (Ant. 18:7)

This Robin Hood approach to the wealthy was not acceptable behavior with the Romans or for wealthy Jews. Josephus even claimed that this redistribution of wealth often found its way into the pockets of the robbers. (Note that Judas Iscariot was portrayed as a thief in the Gospel of John—John 12:4-6). This aside, the popularity of the Fourth Philosophy emanated from the pledge of equality, where distinctions based upon wealth and power would be abolished. Thus, the Herodian partnership with Rome was a main target. This also is tracked exactly by the teachings of Jesus and James and is perfectly summed up in Acts 2:44: "All the believers were together and had everything in common. Selling their possessions and goods, they gave to anyone as he had need." Again, the Essenes, Fourth Philosophy and early Jewish Christians all practiced pure communism, the sharing of all possessions.

From the above, we can note the similarities between the Fourth Philosophy and the Pharisees as represented by Sadduc, a Pharisee. In addition, followers of Judas had many things in common with the Essenes. I believe that while Sadduc linked the liberation movement to the Pharisees, Judas provided the same type of link with the Essenes. (Note that there was one major difference between Judas and the Essenes: marriage. The followers of Judas married as did the brothers of Jesus, while the majority of Essenes abstained from marriage and temptation. (Ant. 18.21) However, Josephus described a second order of Essenes which differed only in marriage and the begetting of children.(War 2.160-161) This second order was more in agreement with Judas and earliest Jewish Christianity.) As a nationalistic liberation movement, the Fourth Philosophy reached out to other groups and likewise adopted other groups' practices and philosophies. So Judas took the best from the Pharisees and the Essenes and fused them together with nationalistic fervor.

Since Judas' Fourth Philosophy flourished for such a long time (4 BC-73 AD), it would be simplistic on our part to assume that it was a philosophy which did not evolve over the years. Consider the current day position of the Republican Party concerning the progressive income tax; most deride it as

Socialistic and a hindrance to the economy's growth. But the current system was implemented under the Republican presidency of Teddy Roosevelt during the Progressive Era. He, like many in his time, believed that such a tax system was the only fair way to raise federal revenues. So from Teddy Roosevelt to Ronald Reagan, the Republican viewpoint of progressive taxation flip-flopped. The Fourth Philosophy may have also been transformed due to outside influences. Josephus described the religious fervor of Judas' followers as well as their similarities to the Pharisees and Essenes. Thus, Judas the Galilean could be accurately classified as a righteous teacher, loved by the masses. But Josephus claimed he was also associated with assassins or the Sicarii. How can this be?

Josephus plainly blamed Judas and Sadduc for the troubles which befell Israel during the Jewish War, around 70 AD. It is very possible that Judas' Fourth Philosophy began as a nationalistic religious movement, emphasizing righteousness and the power of God in removing the Romans. (See Chapter Nine for a full explanation). Thus, Jesus appeared almost foolhardy in his approach to Rome; two swords against the Romans in the Garden of Gethsemane. Obviously, he believed God would perform a great miracle. This failure may have convinced others that a more prudent approach to Rome should be attempted; some may have taken the law into their own hands, using assassination as an opposition tactic. So it is very possible that circumstances turned the more religious movement into a terrorist one, although both had the same goal, the removal of Roman influence from Israel.

It is my contention that the Fourth Philosophy was another name for Jewish Christianity. Judas the Galilean was none other than Jesus of Nazareth. Note that the story of Christianity in its earliest years was marked by struggles against Rome and Herodian sycophants. Jesus was crucified for claiming to be king and opposing the payment of taxes to Rome. And it was Judas who was associated with this stance on foreign taxation in the writings of Josephus. In fact, it is the writings of Josephus which show the signs of a switch. If Jesus of Nazareth were such a marvelous teacher, a king, a Messiah, then why was he not mentioned (the only mention was obviously a late addition)? It seems that Josephus spent all his time chronicling the life and deeds of Judas the Galilean, stating that it was this Judas, not Jesus, who developed a new philosophy. With the "coincidence" of the birth stories through their deaths, Judas and Jesus appear inseparable. And if they were the same, then the problem of Josephus' omission of Jesus from his history is solved. In fact, Josephus was obsessed with Jesus and his followers but referred to them using <u>first century Jewish</u> terms.

Appendix 1 has a detailed listing of all similarities between Judas and Jesus and all similarities tying the Judas of Chapter Three to the Judas of Chapter Four. These listings will make any further analysis into first century Christianity much easier. In the next chapter, the data concerning Judas the Galilean has been placed into one easily understood narrative. In this way, we will be able to fully concentrate our efforts on the similarities between Judas and Jesus.

CHAPTER FIVE

WHAT REALLY HAPPENED

Throughout Chapters Three and Four, I have endeavored to unravel the mystery of Jesus of Nazareth by examining the life of Judas the Galilean. Certainly, some may be confused while others have a hazy understanding of all that has gone before. Therefore, I deem it necessary to chronologically recount the life of Judas the Galilean and his movement, the Fourth Philosophy. This is done to tie together any loose ends which may be troubling the reader. This history will focus primarily upon the writings of Josephus. How closely this corresponds to the story of Jesus as revealed in the Gospels is left up to your good judgment.

THE STORY OF JUDAS THE GALILEAN

In the year 5 BC, two learned teachers of the law gazed out upon their students, an army of young men thirsting for righteousness. Every day this throng of Israel's future sat and listened to the wizened Matthias and his younger partner Judas preach the Kingdom of Heaven. The relationship between the two wise men can be argued as well as their ages, but the pattern of the Maccabees suggests that Matthias was the older father figure (or literal father) and Judas the son. How they came to the Temple, to this point in the history of Israel can be deduced from what preceded them.

Herod the Great may have been a good ruler in that he built fine cities and restored the Temple itself, but his introduction of pagan ways (athletic events, the theater and images within the Temple) alienated a portion of the populace. Surely, to these religious fanatics, the reign of Herod was inconsistent with the Scriptures and the Reign of God. In 25 BC, a group of ten men planned to assassinate Herod, using short knives hidden within their garments. The plot was exposed, and the ten were put to death. But the struggle against Herod and pagan influences had just begun. A movement was forming that was based upon the distant exploits of Mattathias and his son Judas Maccabee (170 BC). In this new Jewish sect, a leader named Matthias taught about the true meaning of God's promises, freedom from pagan influences and the equality of all Jews. Whether or not Matthias began in Jerusalem or among the cities of Galilee, we will never know. But his teachings did bring him to Jerusalem by 5 BC, along with his son, Judas.

To Matthias and Judas, the Temple was dedicated to the unseen God, the God of Abraham, Isaac and Jacob. But Herod had purposely adorned the Temple with a Golden Eagle, an image of beauty to Herod and his followers but a slap in the face to those who strictly interpreted the Scriptures. After all, did not God command His followers to abstain from idols (Deut. 5:8,9), and did He not punish the children of Israel who fashioned a calf from gold while Moses received the Ten Commandments (Ex. 32). To Matthias, the Golden Eagle was no different than the calf authorized by Aaron. God would certainly reward those who destroyed such idols.

The young impressionable students were whipped into a frenzy by the seditious teachers. They were convinced that God expected them to rise up against Herod and his graven image. Such a show of devotion would be richly rewarded not only in this life but in the life to come. In this life each would be remembered as a martyr, bringing fame upon the household. In the life to come, God would honor them with eternal happiness. So, like the martyrs of today, these followers of Matthias and Judas were all too willing to attack the power structure, that being Herod the Great.

In broad daylight, the students brought down the Golden Eagle, crashing it to the ground. But in their enthusiasm, the students were oblivious to Herod's guards, who quickly brought an end to the uprising and imprisoned those caught at the Temple. Included among the prisoners were the authors of the sedition, Matthias and Judas.

A trial of sorts was arranged, but the sentence was known already. The prisoners were bound and sent to Jericho awaiting Herod's final decision. Herod was bitter about the whole affair. After all, had he not provided the Jews with a beautiful Temple and the Golden Eagle as well. This act against the Golden Eagle was no different than an attack upon himself. So there was no doubt in the matter; the prisoners were guilty and deserved death. In a related matter, the high priest with the same name, Matthias, was also punished as a result of this sedition. Reminiscent of Pilate relinquishing power to the mob due to his wife's dream, this Matthias had once before stepped down from his office for a day because of a dream where he had sexual relations with his wife. But now he was being permanently replaced by Joazar, who was his wife's brother.

The sentence of death was the expected outcome. Herod had Matthias and his followers burnt alive. Josephus stated in the <u>War</u> that both rabbis were killed, but in <u>Antiquities</u> mentioned only Matthias. What most likely occurred was the execution of the movement's leader, Matthias, and a number of his followers. Those remaining, including Judas, were imprisoned in order to dangle their fate in the face of the seditious. In short, Judas was an insurance policy against any other rebellious acts against Herod. A second powerful motive in imprisoning Judas involved Herod's desire for true mourning at his own death. Josephus stated that Herod planned to kill a number of people at the time of his death so that there would be mourning throughout Israel. Judas and his followers may have been part of this plan. Either way, it was just a matter of time until Judas would meet the same doom as Matthias.

Judas and his fellow prisoners were spared an eventual death for only one reason: Herod the Great had died (4 BC), and his insane orders of murder were not obeyed. In terms of stability, the death of this tyrannical yet able administrator rocked the country. But it also presented a great opportunity for those who had been persecuted and oppressed for so many years. Herod's death coincided with the Passover feast, a time when pilgrims flocked to Jerusalem to celebrate Israel's deliverance from Egypt. This left Herod's son, Archelaus, with a dilemma: how could he gain firm control of the government without offending the masses?

The crowds sensed that Archelaus was not dealing from strength and that he might be swayed by their desires. They asked if he would ease their annual taxes and remove all taxes related to sales and purchases. These were very serious requests, for a king must have revenues to rule effectively. Even so, Archelaus assented to their will, pretending to agree with these requests. And a segment of the people, those who mourned the death of Matthias, asked one other favor: release those who had been imprisoned by Herod. And once again, Archelaus agreed. Judas was now a free man.

Archelaus soon realized that any concession to the followers of Matthias and Judas was fruitless, for these fanatics could never be won over by friendly intentions. In this, he was correct, for this new movement had no intention of meekly following the Herodian dynasty. In fact, they wished to upset this structure in order to fully implement their theocracy. Predictably, tensions arose and the military slaughter began. Judas escaped with a group of disciples and headed to Galilee, to the city of Sepphoris.

Judas had witnessed the execution of Matthias and many of their students and had just fled from a massacre in Jerusalem. His thoughts must have been upon the security of the small group he now led. In a bold move, he attacked the armory with its large cache of weapons. His followers were now well armed and could defend themselves from all except the army of Archelaus. His reliance upon these weapons of man diminished as he witnessed the awesome power he was up against. Consistent with guerrilla warfare, Judas and his bandit followers blended into the countryside as the Roman army marched upon Sepphoris and burnt it to the ground, enslaving all its inhabitants. Surely, this sight hardened Judas against Rome and the Herodian sycophants.

But safety depended upon guile and resourcefulness. The message of fealty to God and refusing to be a slave to human masters (Rome) was transmitted to eager hearers throughout Galilee on a small-scale basis. Judas did not draw too much attention to himself by setting up base in any city. Instead, he moved throughout the countryside, always prepared for a quick getaway.

As his popularity grew in Galilee, Judas asked his disciples this question: Who do people think I am? A teacher, a prophet, the Messiah were the answers. Unlike our heavenly vision of the Messiah, the Jews held that the King or Anointed One was the Messiah. In fact, in this particular era, many warlords and popular teachers were crowned King by their own disciples. In this way, Judas was no different. His disciples led the way to Mount Tabor where they anointed Judas King and Messiah. This probably occurred some short time after his release from prison, between 4-2 BC. Thus, the Messiahship of Judas in Galilee lasted anywhere from eight to ten years, depending on the date of his anointment. During this time, Judas widened his appeal among the downtrodden in Galilee, always being careful not to directly engage the authorities.

But an event stirred the pot, where all Jews were affected. The census of Cyrenius (6-7 AD) was meant as a way for Rome to separate Judea from its wealth. The Roman Governor Coponius was appointed to lend the power of Rome to this taxing situation. At first, the population was outraged. But this opposition soon melted away as the High Priest, Joazar, convinced the people that such a tax was for their own good. In this he may have been correct as the Romans were adept at building and improving the means of transportation throughout the Empire. But to Judas the Galilean, this taxation was nothing other than support for another king, another power. Judas preached that only God was their master, and that the foreigners were merely slave masters. Thus, his opposition to this taxation was direct and to the point. Whom do you support, God or Rome?

The census was the launching pad for Judas' nationwide campaign. His Kingship in Galilee had been solid, and his reputation was beyond reproach, but not since his brush with death in the Golden Eagle Temple Cleansing (5 BC) had Judas returned to Jerusalem. The time must have seemed right for action. Judas' popularity soared, and the call against Rome was a strong rallying cry. God would deliver the Jews from the hands of the invader just as He had done in the days of Judas Maccabee.

At this fateful time in history, Judas the Galilean was a middle-aged man, somewhere in his early forties. His ministry had begun at the side of an older mentor, Matthias. It is quite likely that he was only thirty at that time and the passage of twelve years would have logically placed Judas at forty-two in 7 AD. Like his co teacher Matthias, Judas also worked with a lieutenant. He was named Sadduc according to Josephus and was probably younger than Judas by as many as ten years. Although age and wisdom went hand in hand in Jewish culture, the second-in-command could be a younger more vigorous man. Moses chose Joshua, a much younger man, to lead the nation of Israel into the Promised Land.

This question of age is very important as one other figure must also be counted in the equation. James the Just, or the brother of the Lord, would have been forty-one years old in 7 AD, the younger brother of Judas by a year. (Tradition says that James was ninety-six years old at his death in 62 AD). And the age of Judas is necessary to compute the ages of his sons and grandsons. If Judas and Mary were married at twenty and had sons every third year for twelve years, then the ages of Judas' sons in 7 AD would have been twenty-two, nineteen, sixteen and thirteen. Two of these sons were crucified under Tiberius Alexander in 47 AD. The range of ages would have been fifty-three to sixty-two. The two grandsons mentioned by Josephus were both associated with Masada. Menahem was killed in Jerusalem in 66 AD while Eleazar led the Sicarii at Masada in 73 AD. He committed suicide with nine hundred and sixty others instead of surrendering to the Roman army. Both would have been around fifty years old at their deaths.

Josephus does not record anything else about Judas directly. But much more can be deduced from other materials about his grandson, Menahem. This Menahem overtook the king's armory at Masada in the same way that Judas had captured the armory at Sepphoris, some seventy years earlier. After the capture of Masada, Menahem marched as king to Jerusalem, where he assumed control for a short while before being murdered. This action of Menahem closely followed the pattern set by Judas. After Judas captured Sepphoris, his disciples proclaimed him King or Messiah. This title he kept, but his influence was centered primarily in Galilee. It was the nationwide census and the arrival of the Roman Governor which drove Judas to Jerusalem.

The exact date of Judas' triumphal entry into Jerusalem may be forever a mystery. His nationwide ministry began with the census in 6 AD, but his actions at that point are not so certain. He may have rallied the troops and headed straight to Jerusalem. However, this does not appear to be the modus operandi of that "clever rabbi". He most likely built a large opposition to the census tax by traveling from city to city. This would have taken many years to accomplish. In addition, he may have gone beyond the bounds of Israel, even to Rome itself. The history of Josephus is curiously missing data between 7-37

AD, as if someone had purposely expunged his information. But the Roman historian, Tacitus, may help in identifying the date of Judas' death. Between 16-18 AD, in the reign of Tiberius, he wrote: "The provinces too of Syria and Judaea, exhausted by their burdens, implored a reduction of tribute."(1) It appears likely that Judas' movement was having an impact on the nation's attitude towards taxation. Whether or not Judas was still alive at this point may be answered by what was happening in Rome in 19 AD.

There was a debate too about expelling the Egyptian and Jewish worship, and a resolution of the Senate was passed that four thousand of the freedman class who were infected with those superstitions and were of military age should be transported to the island of Sardinia, to quell the brigandage of the place, a cheap sacrifice should they die from the pestilential climate. The rest were to quit Italy, unless before a certain day they repudiated their impious rites. Tacitus, Annals, II.85.

For some reason, the Jews were being expelled from Rome, especially those of military age. It is quite probable that the crucifixion of Judas the Galilean had started riots throughout the Roman Empire where Jewish settlements had been infiltrated by those of the Fourth Philosophy. If this were the case, then Judas/Jesus died in 19 AD. This date also conforms to the dating of the spurious Jesus passage in Josephus (See Appendix 7). This may explain why the Fourth Philosophy spread so far. In the New Testament account, Jesus died in 30-33 AD with only 120 disciples (Acts 1:15). From that pathetic beginning, we are to believe that the movement spread throughout the Roman Empire in only a few short years. If, however, Judas the Galilean were active in spreading his message afar from 6-19 AD, either personally or through surrogates, the overall reach of the movement makes sense. (See the Fourth Philosophy in Chapter Nine for further analysis.)

The march into Jerusalem for Judas and his disciples would have been exciting yet foreboding. The belief that God would deliver them from the hands of Rome was a centerpiece of their very existence. Josephus stated plainly that these followers of Judas willingly gave their lives rather than worship anyone or anything other than the one true God. Yet, even with this firm system of beliefs, doubts must have entered their minds in those times when silence reigned, in the nighttime or when negative thoughts pervaded the consciousness.

But such thoughts of failure were not mentioned aloud. Judas' mission as Messiah would not fail. And it was not at the Passover when Judas entered the city, but at the Feast of Tabernacles. Maccoby presents a convincing case that Jesus entered Jerusalem in the fall, at the Feast of Tabernacles. The conflict prophesied by Zechariah (14:16) was to take place at the Feast of Tabernacles.(2) As Jesus supposedly rode into Jerusalem on a donkey, he and his disciples must have been full aware of the time predicted by Zechariah. It was also at this time that the king was to read a portion of the law relating to his duties at the Temple. Thus, a Temple Cleansing was necessary. So when Judas entered Jerusalem as King or Messiah, he at once went to the Temple in order to prepare it. Thus, there was a second cleansing of the Temple by Judas. The first was in 5 BC in the Golden Eagle Temple Cleansing. This second cleansing was in preparation of the new Kingdom, where God would govern His people. The time for Rome was short.

After this second Temple cleansing, Judas readied himself for the fateful clash with Rome, on the Mount of Olives, as prophesied by Zechariah. Never did Judas believe that God would abandon him. But on the Mount of Olives, Judas and some of his followers were captured. These individuals were crucified under the able governorship of Pontius Pilate. Giving their approval were the High Priest, Caiaphas, and his father-in-law, Annas. These two were also central in the crucifixion of Jesus in the Gospels. (See Appendix 7)

Even with the death of Judas the Galilean, the Fourth Philosophy grew in numbers and power. Led by his second-in-command, Sadduc, the movement strengthened. I have linked this Sadduc with Cephas, and the person who replaced Judas was James the Just, the brother of Judas/Jesus. These two governed the movement from the death of Judas (19 AD) to the death of James (62 AD).

It is quite interesting to note that Judas led a Temple Cleansing at the beginning of his mission as did Jesus according to the Gospel of John. The Synoptics talk of a second Temple Cleansing of which Judas would have performed as well upon entering Jerusalem (consistent with the actions of Menahem in 66 AD). In 4 BC, there was a prisoner release. These prisoners were no doubt associated with the Golden Eagle Temple Cleansing, which was an insurrection in the city. In addition, this prisoner release occurred at the Passover. This is perfectly in-sync with the Gospel account of Barabbas. After this, Judas was proclaimed King or Messiah in Galilee, just as the Gospels portrayed the ministry of Jesus. Judas' march to Jerusalem was predicated by the census, which was convincingly conveyed to the masses by the evil High Priest, Joazar. This Joazar was replaced by Annas in 7 AD, who would then be the major opponent to Judas until his death. That is why Judas/Jesus was first taken to Annas after the arrest in the Gospel of John. For his efforts, Judas was crucified; nailed to the cross for his refusal to pay taxes to Rome and for being King, the same two charges leveled against Jesus.

Could Judas the Galilean and Jesus of Nazareth have so many things in common and be separate individuals? Appendix 1 has been compiled to detail every "coincidence" between Judas and Jesus. It is my conviction that the reader will be hard-pressed to separate the two.

THE DEATHS OF JESUS AND JUDAS THE GALILEAN

New Testament

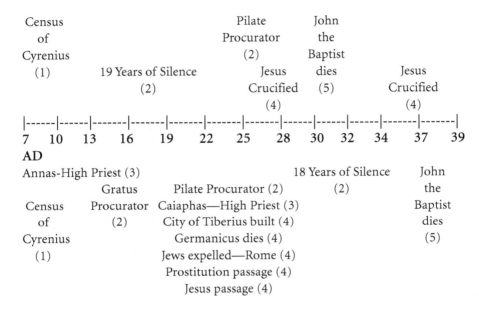

Josephus and Tacitus

1. Josephus places the census of Cyrenius at 6-7 AD. Luke also places the birth of Jesus at this very census, although it is doubtful whether or not Luke actually knew or cared about the dating of this event.

2. The Gospels have 19 years of silence, from the census to the rise of Pilate. The dating of Pilate at 26 AD is wholly dependent on Josephus, where Pilate replaced Gratus as procurator after Gratus had served <u>eleven </u>years (15-26 AD). Per Appendix 7, it was determined from the context of Josephus that Gratus served only <u>three</u> years (15-18 AD). This being the case, Pilate became procurator in 18 AD. From 19-37 AD, Josephus also has an 18 year silence. This silence is unfortunate because these were the first years of the Jewish Christian movement after the death of Judas/Jesus.

3. These two High Priests were the chief antagonists of Jesus in the Gospel accounts, somewhere between 28-39 AD. However, they fit into the time frame of Judas the Galilean (7-19 AD). Annas served as High Priest from 7-15 AD and his son-in-law, Caiaphas, was appointed in 18 AD by Gratus.

4. Matthew's chronology has Jesus being crucified in 28 AD (6 BC plus 33 years) while Luke places the crucifixion outside of Pilate's reign in 39 AD (6 AD plus 33 years). The spurious Jesus passage is squarely placed within events in 19 AD, per the accounts of Josephus and Tacitus. This was a replacement passage of the original Judas the Galilean account. Note that the 19 AD crucifixion is also consistent with the High Priests Annas and Caiaphas.

5. The death of John the Baptist was somewhere between 29-32 AD, according to the Gospel accounts. However, per Josephus, John the Baptist was executed much later, around 37 AD. This later date clearly upsets the chronology according to Matthew, where Jesus died in 28 AD. In fact, John the Baptist was a contemporary of Paul, not Jesus.

CHAPTER SIX

THE PLAYERS

Who were the other major players in the early Jewish Christian movement, and can these individuals be linked to Judas the Galilean? One would think that an analysis of the Twelve Apostles would solve all problems. The Gospels and Acts of the Apostles are filled with pertinent information about the history of Jesus and his immediate followers, known as apostles. But, as will soon become obvious, nothing is as it seems.

A good definition of apostle is one who is sent on a mission. Jesus sent out his disciples with the mission of proclaiming the Kingdom of Heaven. The first mention of any of these apostles comes from the pen of Paul.

Then after three years, I went up to Jerusalem to get acquainted with Cephas and stayed with him fifteen days. I saw none of the other apostles—only James, the Lord's brother. (Gal. 1:18-19)

Paul mentioned Cephas and James as the only apostles that he met on his first post-conversion trip back to Jerusalem, making it quite clear that he did not meet any of the other apostles, the number of apostles indeterminate. Thus the twelve apostle scheme was never confirmed by Paul. This passage also conveyed the importance of Cephas and James, the brother of the Lord. Later in Galatians, Paul recounted another visit to Jerusalem, fourteen years after the previous trip. There, he met James, Cephas and John, "those reputed to be pillars." To Paul, around the year 40 AD, the most important apostles were James, the brother of the Lord, Cephas (known as Peter to most Bible students) and John.

The Gospels also present a trio of central apostles named Peter, James and his brother, John. In the minds of most readers, it appears as if there is consistency in the infallible word of God. However, the James of Paul and the James of the Gospels were different men named James, one the brother of Jesus and the other the son of Zebedee. According to Paul, James the brother of the Lord was quite influential among the Jews of Jerusalem. This James would eventually prove to be a thorn in Paul's flesh. In the Gospels, James the brother of John, was one of the top three apostles, yet he is shadowy at best; he just tags along with John. The question to be answered is this: whose James was the historical leader known as a pillar, Paul's or the Gospels'? A closer analysis of Acts shows the overwhelming preeminence of James, the brother of the Lord. But this flesh and blood James only appeared after the mysterious James of Zebedee was eliminated from the story in Acts12. (See Chapter Six—Brothers and Chapter Eight—James, Cephas and John.)

All this proves is that the Book of Acts may impart some information but the facts are generally skewed. James, the brother of the Lord, was downplayed so that the disassociation process between Jesus and his brothers could be realized. This was just good politics for the Gentile Church considering the times. After all, Rome had just successfully defeated Israel in a war. To associate with anything Jewish was anathema to the Gospel writers. To them, the sooner Jesus could be torn from familial ties the sooner he could be made into a savior god. In this effort to make Jesus acceptable to Gentile sensibilities, all family ties were either hidden or twisted. Invariably, the truth lies conveniently buried just beneath the surface of their story.

CEPHAS

As discussed in an earlier chapter, I believe Cephas (known as Peter in the Gospels) was the Sadduc, a Pharisee chosen by Judas the Galilean to bridge the gap between Pharisees and his Fourth Philosophy, where the main difference in thought concerned sedition against Rome. This Cephas was mentioned numerously by Paul, once as one of the pillars and as the apostle to the Jews (Galatians 2). This Sadduc (Cephas) was commissioned to bring the message to all Jews throughout the Roman Empire. That is why he was mentioned so often by Paul, who also travelled throughout the Empire. In the Book of Galatians, Cephas and Paul even met on Paul's home turf. The conflict between the two was brought to a head by a letter from James, the brother of the Lord. This letter, delivered by followers of James, condemned the teachings of Paul. With this information in hand, Cephas turned his back upon Paul's ministry and led all other Jews against Paul. Obviously, Cephas must have been a powerful speaker and leader as he stood up against Paul and carried the day. (Although, to Paul, Cephas was a hypocrite. There will be more about this conflict later.)

The following passage has several interesting facts concerning Cephas.

When Jesus came to the region of Caesarea Philippi, he asked his disciples, "Who do people say the Son of Man is?" They replied, "Some say John the Baptist; others say

Elijah; and still others, Jeremiah or one of the prophets." "But what about you?" he asked. "Who do you say I am?" Simon Peter answered, "You are the Christ, the Son of the living God." Jesus replied, "Blessed are you, Simon son of Jonah, for this was not revealed to you by man, but by my Father in heaven. And I tell you that you are Peter, and on this rock I will build my church, and the gates of Hades will not overcome it. I will give you the keys to the kingdom of heaven; whatever you bind on earth will be bound in heaven, and whatever you loose on earth will be loosed in heaven." (Matt. 16:13-19)

The above passage has been used for over seventeen hundred years as a proof-text for the supremacy of Peter over all other apostles. This is quite a stretch considering what we know of the New Testament method of history; pick a few facts and create a story. So what are the facts and what are the myth-making materials? Certainly, the idea of creating a church is backwards looking. Also, the mention of John the Baptist does not derive from fact. Josephus had John being slain some short time before 37 AD, while we know that Jesus died between 30 and 33 AD from traditional dating in the time of Pontius Pilate. (See Appendix 7 for an even earlier dating for Jesus' crucifixion and Pilate's reign (19 AD)). With either dating, the reply that Jesus was the risen John cannot be true; this is pure myth-making. Even with these types of falsifications, there are two facts which can be winnowed from the story. First, Peter (Cephas) proclaimed Jesus as the Messiah. This may also have been the case with Sadduc and Judas the Galilean. Secondly, Jesus gave Peter power above all others. This also would have been true with Sadduc. This New Testament passage may be a disguised version of Josephus' Judas and Sadduc.

To complete the sham, the New Testament writers of the Gospels made Peter into a stumbling, bumbling idiot. It was Peter who tried to walk on the water but sank for <u>lack of faith</u>. It was Peter who questioned the game plan of Jesus (Matt. 16:21-23), although a good lieutenant would certainly question a faulty plan. And it was Peter who denied Jesus in order to escape persecution. This very point harkens us back to Matthias and Judas, where Matthias was martyred but Judas narrowly escaped death. Peter may have gone into hiding in order to protect the movement. Judas/Jesus knew that Cephas (Peter) must not be caught as well. After all, what were the odds of having a Roman procurator release prisoners as Archelaus had done in 4 BC. (This is the same tactic used today by Osama Bin Laden and his organization. If you get one of the leaders, you certainly will not get them all.) Thus, Peter was fashioned into a comic character, a leader of bumbling apostles so thickheaded that the plan of God had to be explained over and over again. This lessening of the apostles was in response to the letters of Paul, which denigrated Cephas, James and all others who upheld the Law.

Even though Cephas represented the weakness of man in the Gospels, none can argue his position among the apostles. With the death of Jesus, Cephas stood alone at the top. As noted earlier, the risen Jesus appeared to him first and then to James. Whether or not this really happened is a matter of faith or common sense. I believe that Judas/Jesus and the central three (Cephas, James and John) should be credited with the resurrection scenario. This scenario was to be implemented in case of failure on the Mount of Olives. They alone knew that the movement was in serious trouble, as a dead Messiah was no Messiah at all. The resurrection revived the hope in the Messiahship of Jesus and explained away Jesus' failure on the Mount of Olives. Since the earthly office of Messiah was no longer filled, an election of sorts was arranged in order to keep the balance between the Jewish sects. To undertake the responsibilities of Jesus was no easy task. Only a well-respected holy man could do it. This holy man was the second soul to witness the resurrection. Along with Cephas, James, the brother of the Lord, now became co-leader of an ever-widening movement.

Cephas, or Peter, carried out one other important task for the early second century Church as reported by Luke. He was the bridge between the wholly Jewish world of James and the anti-Law viewpoint of Paul. Cephas was the ideal candidate to distance himself from James and the earlier teachings of Judas/Jesus. Just as Nixon was able to pursue relations with the Soviet Union and China because of his anti-communist background, so could Cephas, the second-in-command to the law-abiding Jesus, turn his back upon this Law to admit those outside of the Everlasting Covenant. Acts chapter 10 details an account where Peter went to Caesarea to meet with a Gentile named Cornelius. With the help of God, in the form of dreams, Cephas concluded that this Cornelius was worthy of salvation. (Note that Paul also conversed with Jesus through dreams and revelations.) In one short episode, the writer of Acts blurred the distinction between Jews and Gentiles, using Cephas as his tool of rewriting history. Another version of this same story was related by Josephus (<u>Ant</u>. 19.332-334). In his story, Simon was escorted to Caesarea because he had preached against admitting King Agrippa into the Temple. This Simon had no intention of breaking down barriers; in fact, he wanted the barriers to be even higher. With a 180 degree turn from truth, Luke turned this pro-Law Simon into the vacillating Simon Peter. Luke's Peter helped explain how the religion of Jesus turned into the visions of Paul. Without this evolutionary bridge, the archaic Judaism of Law could never have been reconciled to the gospel of grace.

The only other bit of information concerning Cephas is the possible relationship with the successor to James in Jerusalem in 62 AD. After the death of James, Simon the son of Cleophas assumed control. This Simon would once again fulfill the dual leadership role in the movement. Beyond this date, no more information concerning Cephas or James was recorded by Josephus or by the book of Acts.

BROTHERS

The New Testament is filled with brothers, sometimes easily identifiable, sometimes lurking in the shadows. The Gospels present three sets of brothers: Peter and Andrew; James and John, the sons of Zebedee; and of course, the four brothers of Jesus: James, Simon, Judas and Joseph. The writings of Paul detail only one set of brothers, those of Jesus. Of these four brothers of Jesus, only James is named, with the other or others remaining nameless. Is this as far as the brothers' theme can go, or can an alternative framework be constructed from this paucity of information? This new framework can be built, if one only remembers that the Gospels and Acts twist occurrences and names to create a mythical world. If we take the Gospels as God-inspired unerring documents, then it is useless to go any farther. Remember the birth stories and the mistaken time frames of John the Baptist, Judas the Galilean and Theudas. These obvious errors are not isolated. There are many more, and most are purposeful.

Why would the Gospel writers alter history in regards to the brothers' theme? One only needs to examine the history of Judaism to understand their reasoning. In the second century BC, Judas Maccabee and his brothers led a revolt against the Greek occupying force, expelling that foreign influence from their holy land. A band of brothers aligned against Rome would draw unfortunate comparisons for the now mostly Gentile community of Christians. (Jewish Christianity was snuffed out during the Jewish War (66-70 AD). Most scholars agree that the three synoptics were written between 70-90 AD and some between 110-140. Per Appendix 4, I believe the date to be 105 AD for Mark and a generation later for Matthew and Luke.) In an era when Jews were singled out for their peculiar beliefs, the move away from radical Judaism was necessary. It was of paramount importance to downplay or even erase the familial ties of Jesus. If Paul had not mentioned brothers of the Lord, I doubt if the Gospel writers would have even bothered with them. But since Paul had such problems with the brothers (see Galatians), the main task of the Gospels was a slow and calculated undermining of the relationship between Jesus and his own brothers.

First, let us examine the brothers Peter and Andrew.

As Jesus was walking beside the Sea of Galilee, he saw two brothers, Simon called Peter and his brother Andrew. They were casting a net into the lake, for they were fishermen. "Come, follow me," Jesus said, "and I will make you fishers of men." At once they left their nets and followed him. (Matt. 4:18-20)

John's Gospel (1:40-42) has a slightly different story:

Andrew, Simon Peter's brother, was one of the two who heard what John [the Baptist] had said and who had followed Jesus. The first thing Andrew did was to find his brother Simon and tell him, "We have found the Messiah" (that is, the Christ). Then he brought Simon to Jesus, who looked at him and said, "You are Simon, son of John. You will be called Cephas" (which, when translated [from Aramaic to Greek] is Peter). (John 1:40-42)

In Matthew, the brothers followed Jesus without any knowledge of his mission. John at least says that Andrew had heard John the Baptist talking about Jesus, thus giving him an idea of Jesus' mission. But once again, we have the dating problem of John. John was killed <u>before</u> Jesus in the Gospels and murdered about eighteen years <u>after</u> Jesus in Josephus. This aside, the above passages do the following. Andrew was given a place among the early apostles even though he was never heard from again. His brother, Peter, was forever linked with Simon and Cephas, figures that are present in Josephus and in Paul's writings. The linking of Peter with Andrew makes it difficult to associate Peter with any other brother, such as James or Judas or Joseph, the alleged brothers of Jesus. With the brother relationship between Andrew and Peter, a possible connection with Jesus' family is severed. In addition, an explanation of the name Cephas is given; both Peter and Cephas mean rock. From this point on in the narratives, every Simon and even Cephas is read as Peter.

The second set of apostle brothers is James and John, the sons of Zebedee, also known as the Sons of Thunder. These two, along with Cephas, form the central three among the Twelve Apostles. As mentioned before, Paul asserted that the pillars of the Church were James, Cephas and John. Consistent with the modus operandi of Gospel writing, this trio was transported back into time with one huge problem. The James of Galatians 2:9 was the brother of Jesus while the James of the Gospels was the brother of John, no relation to Jesus. It is most probable that the pillars of 40 AD were the same as those following Jesus in 19 AD. (Paul even mentioned James, the brother of Jesus, and Cephas, concerning his first trip to Jerusalem, and this dated even earlier, around 20-25 AD). Thus, the Central Three of Judas/Jesus would have included the same three individuals as noted by Paul. In addition, the brotherly connection between James and John chronicled in the Gospels might also be accurate. But they are no longer the sons of Zebedee; instead they are the brothers of Jesus. If we make John the brother of James who is the brother of Jesus, then we have found one of the elusive brothers written about in 1 Cor. 9:5, which states:

Don't we have the right to take a believing wife along with us, as do the other apostles and the <u>Lord's brothers</u> and Cephas? Or is it only I [Paul] and Barnabas who must work for a living.

Placing John with James, the brother of the Lord, helps explain the power of his personage. After all, a family member with close ties to the Messiah would likely rise in an organization faster than persons from the outside.

Matthew 4:21,22 describes James and John as the sons of Zebedee, a figure not heard from again. They followed the call of Jesus and left their father behind. Curiously, their mother travelled with the small band, leaving her husband behind in the same fashion as the sons. This was strange behavior for the wife, who in most cases was tied to the husband at all times unless he wished otherwise. If Zebedee wanted to protect his two sons and wife, then why didn't he go along with them. The whole story appears fishy.

Let us logically disassociate James and John from Zebedee and the Sons of Thunder designation. If this is done, then James and John can be properly attached to Jesus as his brothers, consistent with the writings of Paul. Thus, Paul's central three pillars (James, Cephas and John) are the same three as the Gospels portray in the Transfiguration (Matt. 17:1-13). The sons of Zebedee and the Sons of Thunder designation can now be placed on two or possibly four apostles: James the Younger, Simon the Zealot, Judas and Joseph. These four will be examined further in the following section: the Sons of Judas the Galilean.

The actual brothers (?) of Jesus are listed in Matthew 13:55,56:

Isn't this the carpenter's son? Isn't his mother's name Mary, and aren't his brothers James, Joseph, Simon and Judas? Aren't all his sisters with us?

Why were these brothers included in the New Testament? The answer is twofold: it was done to help create an antagonism between Jesus and his own family, and it also followed the mention of brothers in 1 Cor. 9:5 as noted above. It is my belief that these supposed brothers were actually the sons of

Jesus (Judas the Galilean), and that the only possible brothers mentioned in the New Testament were James and John, the brothers of Jesus as opposed to the Gospel James and John, the sons of Zebedee.

The Gospels pitted the brothers against Jesus, just as James and the brothers tormented Paul. Thus, the treatment of the brothers is backwards looking. In reality, Jesus and his brothers had very similar views while Paul's view of grace was not supported by James (See the Epistle of James). When this is understood, the whole early Christian movement comes into focus. Christianity was not an other worldly religion to the founding Jewish faithful, but rather a movement of liberation and equality. Paul's message to the Gentiles was totally opposed to this liberation theology. It was Paul, not Jesus, who exhorted his disciples to obey the government and to dutifully pay their taxes. Remember, Judas the Galilean/Jesus the Galilean died on the cross because of his stand against Rome and their taxes.

THE SONS OF JUDAS THE GALILEAN

Brothers were mentioned in the New Testament but sons were not, a shell game with the reader as the victim. Paul wrote plainly in 1 Cor. 9:5 that Cephas and the brothers of the Lord (Jesus) had believing wives. It would logically follow that these unions produced sons and daughters. A closer look at the Gospels and Acts may help us discover these sons.

Matthew 13:55 states: "Isn't this the carpenter's son? Isn't his mother's name Mary and aren't his brothers James, Joseph, Simon and Judas?" The parallel passage in the earlier Gospel of Mark is somewhat different: "Isn't this the carpenter? Isn't this Mary's son and the brother of James, Joses, Judas and Simon?" (Mark 6:3) First, Jesus is called the carpenter in Mark while he is demoted to the carpenter's <u>son</u> in Matthew. This may be an innocent statement of truth. After all, if Jesus' father was a carpenter then there was a good chance that this would be Jesus' profession as well. Or, the switch may have been a way to further distance Jesus from his wife and children. Maybe the original undoctored passage said, "Isn't this the carpenter? Isn't this Mary's <u>husband</u> and the <u>father</u> of James, Joses, Judas and Simon?" This all boils down to the age of Jesus. As already noted, the birth scenarios of Jesus were unhistorical and that the timing of these narratives corresponded to the era of Judas the Galilean, whose age would have been twenty five years older than the traditional age of Jesus. How unlikely would it have been for a fifty-five to sixty year old man to be followed around the countryside by his elderly mother and grown brothers? The probability favors that those following Jesus were his wife and children. This interpretation would jibe with the passage in 1 Cor. 9:5

where Paul said the brothers of the Lord and Cephas travelled with their believing wives. One must also remember that the Pharisees respected the elderly and coupled age with wisdom. A Messiah figure would more likely be fifty than thirty. (Per Chapter Nine, Judas the Galilean's reign lasted from 4 BC to 19 AD. His age during this span would have ranged from 30 to 53.)

The passages above may have named the sons, not the brothers of Jesus. But to work upon this hypothesis, the sons must be hidden within the pages of Acts? In Acts 12:1-19, James, the brother of John, and Simon Peter were captured by Herod around the years 44-49 AD. In the New Testament account, James was beheaded and Peter miraculously escaped. Now, every time an unbelievable miracle occurs, we should look much closer for signs of tampering. This passage is curiously timed to the passage in <u>Antiquities</u> 20:102 concerning the sons of Judas the Galilean.

...and besides this, the sons of Judas of Galilee were now slain; I mean of that Judas who caused the people to revolt, when Cyrenius came to take an account of the estates of the Jews, as we have shown in a foregoing book. The names of those sons were James and Simon, whom Alexander commanded to be crucified. [46-47 AD]

Is this pure coincidence that a James and Simon were captured? True, in Josephus, both James and Simon were crucified, while the James and Simon of Acts were treated differently: James was beheaded and Simon Peter escaped. Before we go farther, once again recognize the working pattern of Acts: take a truth and twist it into a story.

The Gospels and Acts routinely used Peter as a catchall for anyone named Simon. We know that one of Jesus' sons (or brothers) had the name Simon. Also, one of the sons of Judas the Galilean was named Simon. And Simeon Bar Cleophas (son of Cephas), also a popular figure in early Christian literature, replaced James, the brother of the Lord at James' death in 62 AD. Thus, there were many Simons in the early Jewish Church and Peter represented them all. In the above passage, the author of Acts placed Peter in prison in the same time frame that Josephus had Simon, the son of Judas the Galilean, in prison. This was not just another unbelievable coincidence. This was a premeditated alteration of history.

Another passage from Matthew may shed some light upon the above confusion.

Then the mother of Zebedee's sons came to Jesus with her sons and, kneeling down, asked a favor of him. "What is it you want?" he asked. She said, "Grant that one of these two sons of mine may sit at your right and the other at your left in your kingdom."

"You do not know what you are asking," Jesus said to them. "Can you drink the same cup I am going to drink?" "We can," they answered. Jesus said to them, "You will indeed drink from my cup, but to sit at my right or left is not for me to grant. These places belong to those for whom they have been prepared by my Father." When the ten heard about this, they were indignant with the two brothers. (Matt. 20:20-23)

First, the mother of two of the twelve asked Jesus for a favor. As noted above, the association of Zebedee with James and John is suspect. Let's assume that the James and John were really the brothers of Jesus. If this were the case, then their mother was petitioning Jesus for two grown men. According to tradition, James the brother of Jesus was ninety-six at his death in 62 AD.(1) Thus, in the year 19 AD, James would have been fifty-three and his mother approximately eighty years old. It's hard to believe that an elderly woman would be traveling with the apostles and even harder to swallow that James the Just, the most prominent figure in Jerusalem from 19-62 AD, would be hiding behind his mother's skirt. So the association of the two with Jesus' brothers or to the Gospel James and John is not at all logical. But there is another clue in the passage which points us in another direction. Jesus asked if the two could drink the same cup as he. This same cup was death at the hands of Rome by crucifixion. Note that Josephus only singled out three individuals by name as dying by crucifixion: Jesus and the sons of Judas the Galilean, James and Simon. In Acts 12, Luke acknowledged two captured men named James and Simon. However, his history had James being beheaded, and his Simon was the Gospel Peter, who miraculously escaped death. Note that the passage in Josephus preceding the one about the sons of Judas concerned Theudas, a magician beheaded by the Romans. Luke simply had James beheaded, thus eliminating a fictitious James. (There were two James: James the brother of the Lord, known as James the Just and James the son of Judas the Galilean, known as James the Less or James the Younger. Most New Testament scholars equate James the Just with James the Younger, even though James was an old man of fifty-three at this time.) Luke's James, the son of Zebedee, was inserted into the book of Acts to confuse. How convenient to remove this James at the same time he introduced the other James, the brother of the Lord (Acts 15). As for Peter, he took the place of anyone named Simon. Thus, it was imperative to have Peter escape, for Peter (or Cephas) was central to other events detailed in the book of Acts (Acts 15). Even though the real person captured and crucified was Simon, the son of Judas, Luke has us believe in miracles and escapes. Certainly, Luke's version interests and entertains, but his disregard for fact is truly awe inspiring. Luke removed two major players without even acknowledging them (James and Simon, the sons of Judas the Galilean), beheaded a fictional character (James, son of Zebedee) and replaced Simon with Peter, who magically escapes.

We have examined two of the sons of Jesus, but what about Joseph and Judas. Interestingly, there are individuals named Joseph and Judas hidden in the book of Acts. In Acts 1:23-26, there was an election to replace Judas Iscariot. However, per Eisenman, this election was called to replace Jesus.(2)

So they proposed two men: Joseph called Barsabbas (also known as Justus) and Matthias. Then they prayed, "Lord, you know everyone's heart. Show us which of these two you have chosen to take over this apostolic ministry, which Judas left to go where he belongs." Then they drew lots, and the lot fell to Matthias; so he was added to the eleven apostles.

As mentioned earlier, Cephas and James, the brother of the Lord, established control of the movement after the death of Jesus. This James was also known as Justus or James the Just. Luke placed this nickname on the loser, Joseph. Luke's winner was none other than Matthias, a man never heard from again. This twisted history has James the Just losing and Matthias, the martyred teacher from the early days of Judas the Galilean, as winning. Other than this intentional misstatement of history, one other point must not be missed. The stand-in for James is Joseph, called Barsabbas.

One other person is named Barsabbas in Acts: Judas Barsabbas in Acts 15:22. Thus, we have two individuals named Barsabbas, Joseph and Judas. Remember, there were four sons listed as "brothers" of Jesus. These "brothers," or more likely sons, were named James, Simon, Joseph and Judas. James and Simon were crucified, leaving Joseph and Judas. These two were code named Barsabbas. Barsabbas may mean son of bather, an Essene designation.(3) However, this may have been a corruption of Barabbas, meaning, Son of the Father,(4) or Barrabbas, meaning son of the rabbi. These two were either identified with bathers (Essenes) or with the son of the rabbi or son of the Father, all terms relating directly to Jesus. (They may also have been the sons of James, as they appear in Acts along with the mention of James the Just.)

One further possibility exists: Judas may have been the twin brother of Joseph. Both are surnamed Barsabbas, thus establishing a close link between the two. To an ultra religious couple like Jesus and Mary, the naming of twins could be symbolic: to Judas or Judah the scepter was promised and Joseph was heralded as a prince among his brothers. (Gen. 49:10,26) These names also would represent the Northern and Southern kingdoms, the twelve tribes of Israel. Also note that Judas, Thaddaeus and Thomas are intertwined in the apostle lists. Thomas means twin and this nickname may have been attached to Judas. The commingling of names would result in Thaddaeus or even Theudas. A Theudas was mentioned in Josephus as being a miracle worker.(Ant. 20.97,98) He was put to death with the sword just before the two sons of Judas the Galilean were crucified. So it is possible that Josephus recorded the deaths of three of the four sons of Jesus.

It seems likely that the four brothers were really four sons and that Mary was really the wife, not the mother of Jesus. Of the references to Mary, Mark has her as the mother of James the Just (Mark. 6:3) and to James the Younger (Mark 15:40). As James the Just is reported as an old man of ninety-six at his death, he could not have been known as James the Younger.(5) (See Appendix 3) Remember, in Chapter Two, almost every point in the birth narratives was suspect. It appears that Mary can now join this list.

As the church transformed from a Jewish movement to a Gentile one, after the destruction of Israel in 70 AD, the character of Jesus changed from a Jewish rabbi to a Gentile man-god. While the rabbi would be expected to be married, the man-god could hardly sully himself with sex. Also, in Paul's view, the unmarried man could better follow God (1 Cor. 7:32), and this attitude was present in many ascetic groups reaching to our own time (Catholic priesthood). The Gospel writers simply changed the wife of Jesus into the mother of Jesus, thus preserving the virginity of Jesus and assuring his holiness. Catholics even went further and claimed that Mary was exempt from original sin, thus saving Jesus again from the folly of mankind.

Once we have accepted that many of the Gospel and Acts characters are sons and not brothers, certain individuals take on different backgrounds. John Mark, mentioned in Acts 12:12, 13:13 and 15:37 lived in Jerusalem and travelled on and off with Paul in the late 30's. Such a travel schedule was more in line with a younger, more vigorous man. While there were no direct links to Cephas in the Acts, tradition has John Mark as a helper of Cephas. In the early chapters of Acts, John is the main helper of Cephas. Therefore, it is not too much of a stretch to assign John Mark as the son of either John or Cephas.

Barnabas was first mentioned in Acts 4:36: "Joseph, a Levite from Cyprus, whom the apostles called Barnabas (which means Son of Encouragement)..." He also travelled with Paul and was a trusted follower, or perhaps a monitor for the apostles in Jerusalem. Note that Barnabas and Paul were designated Zeus and Hermes by the people at Lystra (Acts:14:12). Paul was called Hermes as he acted as chief speaker and Barnabas Zeus because he directed Paul. This slightly changes the traditional relationship between the two, giving Barnabas much more influence, making him a more important player. In Galatians 2:11-13, Barnabas left Paul and sided with Cephas after receiving information from Jerusalem, sent by James the brother of Jesus. It follows that James, Cephas,

John Mark and Barnabas were all working together, making sure that their prized convert, Paul, was really on the up and up. It is likely that Barnabas was the son of one of the brothers, either James or John or possibly even Cephas. Regardless, he was probably related to Jesus in some way. We will never know for sure.

The sons theme becomes much more likely if Jesus is a generation older than traditionally believed. From the above arguments, Jesus of Nazareth and Judas the Galilean are simply different names for the same person. That is why so many names are the same, with some individuals known by nicknames. Paul referred to James as the brother of the Lord. If there were only one James, then this would not be necessary. But at the time frame referenced by Paul, there were two James alive and well: James the brother of Jesus and James the son of Jesus. James, the son of Zebedee of Gospel fame, was a individual created to confuse, and it has worked for two thousand years. (Since Judas/Jesus was code-named Zebedee, there really were sons of Zebedee. But it was James, the son of Judas/Jesus who was the son of Zebedee.)

JUDAS ISCARIOT AND JESUS BARABBAS

Other than Adolph Hitler, no other name conjures up as much loathing as Judas Iscariot. Think about how many children are named Adolph or Judas. Hitler was a mass murderer of epic proportions and Judas Iscariot the man responsible for the death of Jesus Christ, the son of God. Nothing good can be ascribed to Hitler (except maybe the Volkswagon and the autobahn), but what about Judas? Was he too a monster or just misguided? "Jesus Christ Superstar" portrayed Judas as a well-meaning follower of Christ, but one who could not go the last mile, one who had a better idea of the future. As we read the pages of the Gospels, the conflict of Judas must touch us. Can we figure him out; can we even begin to know him?

As with our other players, the first stop on our road of discovery begins with Paul, as his writings predate the Gospels by sixty-five to eighty-five years. (See Appendix 4) Paul never mentioned the name of Judas Iscariot but only that Jesus was betrayed.

For I received from the Lord what I also passed on to you: The Lord Jesus, on the night he was betrayed, took bread, and when he had given thanks, he broke it and said, "This is my body which is for you; do this in remembrance of me." (1 Cor. 11:23,24)

This passage is very instructive in how Paul's gospel took shape. Paul received information from "the Lord," but it was not from earthly contact; Paul had never met Jesus in the flesh. Paul encountered Jesus through visions, and Gentile Christianity is built upon these revelations. Today, such a man would be locked away for the public's safety. Two thousand years ago, such visions were not common, but rather the sign of a holy man. It is through this lens that we must search for Judas Iscariot.

Was it a vision which formed Paul's version of betrayal? Or had Paul heard the stories from other followers, possibly Barnabas or even Cephas? It is most likely that the story of betrayal was an early one. After all, to find Jesus unattended in the surrounds of Jerusalem seems unlikely. Even with all our (USA) highly sophisticated surveillance equipment, we could not capture Bin Laden in Afghanistan. The Romans were probably tipped off; but by Judas Iscariot? The traitor in all likelihood did not possess the same feelings for the poor as did Jesus and was probably pro-establishment, one who could be bought for a price. Undoubtedly, Jesus may have been betrayed for some silver, but not from the hands of Judas Iscariot. (It has come to light that the U.S. special forces had many successes in Afghanistan because they paid off the clan leaders with millions of dollars. Betrayal does have a price.)

Paul had a genuine hatred for the Jews after the run in with Cephas, portrayed in Galatians. To Paul, the Jews were the enemy, the race who betrayed God by not listening to him (Paul). They had the law, but Paul possessed grace, a much more powerful gift from God. The law was temporary, but grace began with the death of Jesus and would last forever. So in Paul's eyes, it was the Jews with their unswerving dedication to the law who actually betrayed Jesus. The name Judas simply has the same root as Jew. Paul did not invent Judas Iscariot, but he fostered the environment where a later writer could transfer the guilt of a nation upon the head of one man, Judas Iscariot.

The name Iscariot is similar to the Roman sicarios, meaning curved dagger. From this term comes the naming of a group of assassins, the Sicarii. The Sicarii were much hated by Rome and by their Jewish historian, Josephus. Josephus blamed the Sicarii for the agitation in Judea and to the eventual war with Rome, and finally the very destruction of the temple (Ant.18:4-10). This was well known to the Gospel writers, who fused Paul's hatred of the Jews and Josephus' contempt for the Sicarii. From this mixture emerged Judas Iscariot, a fictional character for sure. This is made certain as Josephus did not mention the Sicarii until the late 50's and early 60's AD. Judas Iscariot was supposed to be a 20's and 30's AD figure. This tampering with history created a figure which has been hated for centuries.

The tragic tale of Judas Iscariot ended with Judas returning the thirty pieces of silver to the chief priests. "I have sinned," he said, "for I have betrayed innocent blood." He then went out and committed suicide. (Matt. 27:3-5; Acts

1:15-19) It may be a telling sign that this story was not included in the earliest Gospel, that of Mark. Regardless, the authors of Matthew and Acts must have sensed the irony of their betrayer committing suicide. In the Jewish War, one man named Eleazar convinced his Sicarii followers to commit suicide en masse at a site called Masada. This Eleazar was a grandson of Judas the Galilean. (War 7.253) Once again, the stories of Judas and Jesus intersect.

Alongside Judas Iscariot and sharing in his infamy stands the bandit Jesus Barabbas, the man released by an unwilling Pilate, prompted only by the Jewish mob's demand. Note that the name Jesus Barabbas means Jesus, Son of the Father, the same name as could be attached to Jesus of Nazareth. Like Jesus of Nazareth, Barabbas was accused of sedition, a "notorious prisoner" thrown in prison for leading "an insurrection in the city and for murder." (Matt. 27:16; Luke 23:19) Matthew states that it was the custom at the Feast to release a prisoner chosen by the crowd. This too may be another lie to further the story line as nowhere else in the Empire was the ruthless, efficient Roman government guilty of releasing political prisoners. So it appears that the Pilate-era Barabbas was fabricated in the same way as Judas Iscariot.

The Gospel writers were inspired by Josephus' account of how Archelaus pacified the crowds after his father, Herod the Great, had died.

Some clamoured for a lightening of direct taxation, some for the abolition of purchase tax, others for the release of prisoners. He promptly said Yes to every demand in his anxiety to appease the mob. (War 2.4; Ant. 17.204,205)

The release of Barabbas in the Gospel story was modeled after this prisoner release in 4 BC by Archelaus. It never had anything to do with the Roman procurator Pilate in 19 AD. In all probability, Judas the Galilean was an important prisoner at this time (4 BC), as the release came shortly after the Golden Eagle Temple Cleansing. Since Judas was so popular, it is easy to see why the crowd may have clamoured for the release of Barabbas or "son of the Father." Consistent with the Gospel story, Judas also had led an insurrection in the city. Coincidentally, this was timed with the Passover. (Ant. 17.213)

Both Barabbas and Judas Iscariot were stand-ins for the real Jesus or Judas the Galilean. Barabbas had a similar name (son of the Father), was referred to as Jesus Barabbas in some early manuscripts and had led an insurrection in the city. This was identical to Jesus of Narareth. As noted above, the released Barabbas was none other than the captured Judas the Galilean in 4 BC. In the Gospels, Barabbas was used to emphasize the Jews' hatred for Jesus. The Jewish crowd preferred Barabbas over Jesus, the bad Jesus over the good Jesus.(6) Judas Iscariot represented Judas the Galilean, the founder of the Fourth

Philosophy which spawned the Sicarii. That Judas the Galilean and Jesus of Nazareth were one in the same is further strengthened by the above revelations. In fact, Jesus was Judas the Galilean, who was Judas Iscariot, who was Jesus Barabbas. They were all the same.

JOHN THE BAPTIST

In the Gospels, John the Baptist was the prophet who readied the Jewish nation for the arrival of the Messiah. He preached a baptism of repentance for the forgiveness of sins. This baptism was done with water while the baptism of Jesus was with the Holy Spirit. (Mark 1:1-8) According to Josephus, the water baptism itself did not wash away sins but represented the purification which was performed by God after the individual had repented of his sins. In this history, John preached that forgiveness was obtained only through righteousness. (Ant. 18.117) Even Jesus was baptized by John in the Gospels, not for forgiveness of sins but to fulfill all righteousness. This connects with Josephus' version for all participants, not just Jesus. But the Gospel writers believed Jesus to be without sin, and therefore, his baptism could not be for forgiveness of sins.

The difference between the Gospels and Josephus might seem minor to us, but the relevance would have shaken the Gentile Church. Per Josephus, John preached that God would forgive if only the Jews would practice righteousness. This is diametrically opposed to Paul's theology, where forgiveness was only possible through the sacrifice of Jesus. That John preached this after the death of Jesus proves that Paul did not follow the message of Jesus.

The first mention of John the Baptist in the Gospels occurs in the birth narratives, which have been found devoid of truth (see Chapter Two). In the birth narratives, John was the cousin of Jesus and acknowledged the savior while still in the womb. This, of course, is mere nonsense, written only to set the stage for John's part in the Jesus narrative. From birth, John would be subservient to his master, Jesus.

Luke 3:1-20 describes the ministry of John. He began preaching in the desert, around the Jordan River, in the fifteenth year of the reign of Tiberius Caesar. This dates the beginning of John's ministry at 29 AD., a good ten years after the death of Jesus (19 AD), per our earlier calculations. John's message centered on repentance, sharing and good deeds. He stated, "Produce fruit in keeping with repentance." This is more in line with Jewish thought than with the Pauline notion of Grace. He also condemned Herod the Tetrarch (Antipas) for marrying Herodias, the wife of his brother, Herod, and the daughter of his brother, Aristobulus. Herod the Tetrarch (Antipas) had John arrested and locked up in prison. The date of this arrest was not recorded in Luke.

Josephus gives us more information concerning John the Baptist in <u>Ant.</u> 18.116-19. About the same time as Philip's death, who was Herod's and Antipas' brother, Antipas became involved with Herodias. This was dated by Josephus as 34 AD, the twentieth year in the reign of Tiberius. If this dating is correct, then John the Baptist lived at least until 34 AD. This is fifteen years beyond the earliest date for the death of Jesus in the Pilate era (19 AD) and a few years beyond the traditional date of the crucifixion (30-33 AD). Thus, the Gospels may be building a relationship between John and Jesus which did not really exist.

Josephus then tells us the reason why Antipas (Herod the Tetrarch) had John put to death.

Now, when [many] others came to crowd about him [John], for they were greatly moved by hearing his words, Herod [Antipas], who feared lest the great influence John had over the people might put it into his power and inclination to raise a rebellion, (for they seemed ready to do anything he should advise), thought it best, by putting him to death, to prevent any mischief he might cause.... (<u>Ant.</u> 18.118)

It is safe to say that Josephus dated John's death at 37 AD. This occurred after the crucifixion of Jesus by at least eighteen years if Jesus died during the early tenure of Pilate and by four to seven years if Jesus died in the later Pilate era (30-33 AD), per the traditional view. It appears as if John also competed with the early church for the affections of the crowds, a competitor rather than a follower of Jesus and his movement. From what we have seen so far, the Jesus movement concentrated upon communal living and the eventual removal of Rome while John seemed more interested in righteousness and less interested in Rome. However, when we systematically examined the Fourth Philosophy in Chapter Nine, John the Baptist's methods fell easily within the bounds of the movement. It should be noted that although Josephus did not specifically state this, John may have also rallied the people against Rome. His criticism of the Herodian leadership was also a criticism of Rome. Regardless, the John of Josephus' history is not the John of the Gospels.

Paul also claimed that a John was one of the Pillars of the Church, along with Cephas and James. Some scholars have suggested that this John was John the Baptist. But this does not make sense as Paul met the three Pillars on his second trip to Jerusalem in the late 30's to early 40's (Gal. 2:9). Since John the Baptist was imprisoned for a while and then executed by Antipas in 37 AD, there is no possibility that he was in Jerusalem in 40 AD. As noted earlier, the John in question was probably the brother of James and Jesus.

Why would the Gospel writers twist the history of John the Baptist? The answer may be found in 1 Cor., chapters 1-3, where Paul addressed divisions amongst his followers. He claimed to have planted the seed of the Gospel while Apollos watered it. In Acts 18:24-19:7, Apollos was described as a follower of Jesus who knew only the baptism of John. Acts then makes it clear that Apollos lacked full knowledge of the proper Gospel (Paul's baptism of the Holy Spirit). Apollos was corrected by Paul's followers which then made him the perfect disciple. Just as Apollos became subservient to Paul, the Gospel writers thought it necessary to make John the servant of Jesus, even if they had to stretch the truth.

John the Baptist was not a contemporary of Jesus; he preached and died during the ministry of Paul. This flies in the face of traditional dating, but in the following section, the time frame of Paul will be moved forward from 35-58 AD to 22-45 AD. This being the case, the first letter to the Corinthians may have been written shortly after the Baptist's death. That Apollos knew only of John's baptism would make more sense with this dating. In the traditional picture, we are expected to believe that Apollos knew only of John's baptism, nearly twenty-three years after John's death. (The traditional dating of 1 Cor. is approximately 55 AD while John supposedly died a year or two after his introduction in 29 AD, or about 32 AD). One must wonder: was Apollos totally out of touch for twenty years? In reality, this Apollos preached the message of John only a short time after the Baptist's death.

John the Baptist was just one more victim of the creative writing exercise called the Gospels. A powerful speaker who excited the crowds and threatened Antipas was transformed into a preacher whose only purpose was to introduce Jesus to the world. The dating proves the Gospels to be wrong, just pure fabrication. John the Baptist died at the hands of Antipas and Herodias in 37 AD while Jesus was crucified by Pilate in 19 AD.

PAUL

Paul was the transitional player who consciously transformed Judas the Galilean into Jesus Christ the Savior. This is not to say that Judas was not hailed as the Messiah, but his kingship was of this world, not in the heavenly realm. (The Jewish Christians hoped for the imminent return of Jesus from the heavens to establish an earthly kingdom). It was Paul's genius (or madness) which attached an other-worldly garb upon the Jewish Messiah, much in the tradition of the mystery religions prevalent in those days. Paul did not create the elaborate stories of the Gospels, but his influence made possible an environment ripe for such tinkerings with history, where a Jewish, anti-Roman Messiah figure could be transformed into a pro-Roman god of the Gentiles.

Understanding Paul is the key to unraveling the many mysteries and contradictions contained in the New Testament. In Chapter Two, we did a credible job debunking the birth narratives. This was done to illustrate how the Gospel writers combined myth, facts and Scripture to create a framework for the person named Jesus. The most important question behind the Gospel effort is this: why would anybody change history in such a way as to totally misrepresent a person and a movement? Unfortunately, we have little information of the time, only Paul and the memories and inquiries of Josephus. From two separate episodes, one from Paul and one from Josephus, we will attempt to answer the above question.

Before we examine the passage from Paul, it is imperative to better understand his working method. Although the passage on love in 1 Cor. 13 is believed to properly define Paul, I think the passage from 1 Cor. 9:19-23 best describes the apostle to the Gentiles.

Though I am free and belong to no man, I make myself a slave to everyone, to win as many as possible. To the Jews I became like a Jew, to win the Jews. To those under the law I became like one under the law (though I myself am not under the law), so as to win those under the law. To those not having the law I became like one not having the law (though I am not free from God's law but am under Christ's law), so as to win those not having the law. To the weak I became weak, to win the weak. I have become all things to all men so that by all possible means I might save some. I do this for the sake of the gospel, that I may share in its blessings.

Ask yourself: would I teach my children to behave in such a manner. The working method of Paul was not at all honorable, but rather, two-faced. He pretended to be a Jew to impress the Jews, but from his writings we know he despised their worship, from their eating customs (the weak) to their devotion to the old prophet Moses and the Old Covenant. How could such a man be trusted? Truly, I would never trust such a man, if I were privy to his ways. It will soon become clear that the Jewish Christian leaders did not trust him either, and this as soon as they understood his game.

In the book of Galatians, Paul described an encounter with Cephas which had weakened the community's faith in Paul. Cephas apparently (we have only Paul's side of the story) was in the habit of eating with the Gentiles. To the Jew, this would only be permissible if the foods were proper (vegetables) and had not been offered to another god. Thus, Cephas could have properly dined with the Gentiles.

[However], he began to draw back and separate himself from the Gentiles because he was afraid of those who belonged to the circumcision group. The other Jews joined him in his hypocrisy, so that by their hypocrisy even Barnabas was led astray. (Gal. 2:12,13)

The men from the circumcision had been sent by their leader in Jerusalem, James the brother of Jesus. This message must have contained information about Paul's <u>true</u> teachings—his gospel. Cephas received information which now made it impossible to fellowship with Paul's disciples. Note that Paul even admitted that all the other Jews and Barnabas took the side of Cephas. Today, this argument over the law seems so petty, but to the Fourth Philosophy, the law had to be followed at all costs, even to the point of death. This whole episode perfectly demonstrates the risks involved in Paul's modus operandi, to "be all things to all men." To the Fourth Philosophy, one either followed God and the law or he did not. Paul's trickery, once discovered and exposed, sealed his fate with Jewish Christianity. If not for the Jewish War and the utter destruction of Jerusalem and countless followers of Judas, Paul's gospel would have been long since forgotten.

Galatians 1:6-8 and 11,12 state:

I am astonished that you are so quickly deserting the one who called you by the grace of Christ and are turning to a <u>different</u> gospel—which is really no gospel at all. Evidently some people are throwing you into confusion and are trying to pervert the gospel of Christ. But even if we or an angel from heaven should preach a gospel other than the one we preached to you, let him be eternally condemned!...I want you to know, brothers, that the gospel I preached is not something that man made up. I did not receive it from any man, nor was I taught it; rather, <u>I received it by revelation from Jesus Christ.</u> (emphasis mine)

Paul was acting the part of a Gentile to win Gentiles. Here he compared his gospel to the inferior gospel of Cephas and James. He even goes farther, stating that such teachers should be eternally condemned. The same is echoed in 2 Cor.11:13-15:

For such men are false apostles, deceitful workmen, masquerading as apostles of Christ. And no wonder, for Satan himself masquerades as an apostle of light. It is not surprising, then, if his servants masquerade as servants of righteousness. Their end will be what their actions deserve.

Like the book of Galatians, 1 and 2 Corinthians deal primarily with those of the circumcision, namely Cephas and James. In this passage, the Jewish apostles are now said to be servants of Satan. Is it no wonder that the later Gospel of John used the same theme; the father of the Jews was the devil! (John 8:42-47) It is amazing at how much hatred emanated from the author on the prized chapter on love. But this should not surprise us. Paul was fighting for his ideas, his very career. Using the same methods practiced by preachers of today, he framed the whole argument as good versus evil, his gospel against the <u>false</u> gospel of Cephas and James.

To make Paul look even worse in our eyes (but not in the eyes of his Gentile audience of the time), he claimed that his gospel came directly from Jesus Christ through revelations. In short, Paul invented his gospel from dreams and visions, where he had direct talks with the Risen Christ. This was his convincing argument to his naive audience. Today, his only listeners would be therapists at the mental ward. Paul not only claimed inspiration here but in the passage describing the last supper and communion. (1 Cor. 11:23-26) Obviously, today's Christian churches owe much to the revelations of a man with little moral authority. The next time the word hypocrite crosses your mouth, remember who really acted the part in the early church.

Galatians details an earlier meeting between Paul and the Jewish leaders, James, Cephas and John. From Paul's rendering, the three "pillars" gave him full reign to preach to the Gentiles as Cephas had been commissioned to preach to the Jews. (Gal. 2:1-10) Paul said this concerning the Jewish leaders, "All they asked was that we should remember the poor, the very thing I was eager to do." (Gal. 2:10) Paul did not mention whether or not the "Pillars" instructed him to preach the Jewish law and to try to convert the Gentiles if they were willing. In fact, Paul walked away from this meeting with the impression that he was authorized to teach anything he wanted to the Gentiles. Is that what the Jewish apostles intended?

Acts chapter 15 details the meeting. There are two main points which come from this chapter. The first is from Acts 15:19-21 which details the decision of James concerning the Gentile question:

"It is my judgment, therefore, that we should not make it difficult for the Gentiles who are turning to God. Instead we should write to them, telling them to abstain from food polluted from idols, from sexual immorality, from the meat of strangled animals and from blood. For Moses has been preached in every city from the earliest times and is read in the synagogues on every Sabbath."

In saying this, James preferred that the Gentiles convert to Judaism, but if all the trappings were too much (circumcision for instance) then they should follow the Noahic Covenant.(7) This was acceptable to the Jews in general. Gentiles following such requirements would not be considered full Jews, but rather, God fearers, a group included under God's covenant with Noah. Thus, there is nothing in James' speech which would denigrate the law or even de-emphasize it. He was just not requiring Gentiles to become full Jews in order to follow the movement. Paul took this and simply told his followers that the law was dead and that if you followed the law than Christ had died for nothing. (Gal. 5:1-6) Surely, Paul had perverted the decision of James!

The second point of Acts 15 illustrates Act's working method: take from Josephus and twist into an acceptable story. In Acts 15:7-11, Peter explained to the Jews his meeting with Cornelius, where God told them that the law was unnecessary for the Gentiles saying, "We believe it is through the grace of our Lord Jesus that we are saved, just as they [Gentiles] are." The author of Acts had Peter mouthing Paul's doctrines to the Jews. He not only had Peter saying that the law was unnecessary for the Gentiles but also for the Jews. Taken to its logical conclusion, Peter was really denying the beliefs of Jesus who said, "For if you forgive others their trespasses, your heavenly Father will also forgive you." (Matt. 6:14) While Jesus believed God could and would forgive sins, the Pauline doctrine of grace, supposedly adopted by Peter, linked forgiveness to belief in the crucified Jesus. Therefore, this meeting was meant to be a passing of the torch from a primitive Christianity, based upon Jewish law, to the final version, based upon Paul's revelations of God's grace.

The meeting with Cornelius took place in Acts 10, before the capture of James and Simon, which is dated around 46 AD. Here, Peter was summoned by Cornelius' servants and soldiers, who escorted him from Joppa to Cornelius' home in Caesarea. Cornelius was known as a "righteous and God-fearing man, who is respected by all the Jewish people." Once there, Peter was convinced by the Holy Spirit that even the Gentiles could attain eternal life through faith in Jesus Christ. Thus, the law was unnecessary.

Compare this to Josephus' version in <u>Ant.</u> 19:332-334:

However, there was a certain man of the Jewish nation at Jerusalem, who appeared to be very accurate in the knowledge of the law. His name was Simon. This man got together an assembly, while the king was absent at Caesarea, and had the insolence to accuse him as not living holily, and that he might justly be excluded out of the temple, since it belonged only to native Jews. But the general of Agrippa's army informed him that Simon had made such a speech to the people. So the king sent for him; and, as he was then sitting in the theatre, he bade him sit down by him, and said to him with a low and gentle voice,—"What is there done in this place that is contrary to the law?" But he had nothing to say for himself, but begged his pardon. So the king was more easily reconciled to him than one could have imagined, as esteeming mildness a better quality in a king than anger; and knowing that moderation is more becoming in great men than passion. So he made Simon a small present and dismissed him.

Note that in both cases a Simon was sent for, accompanied by soldiers to Caesarea. Luke transformed this Simon into Peter, while I think it was probably Simon, the son of Judas the Galilean, who was crucified shortly after this meeting with Agrippa (44 AD). In both cases, Simon at first was adamant that nothing unclean or unholy should be admitted to the movement or temple. Then, after talking with Cornelius or Agrippa, Simon changed his tune. In Acts 10, Peter wanted to admit Gentiles into the movement. In Josephus, Simon grudgingly accepted Agrippa into the temple for fear of his life. Reminiscent of Jesus, Simon had nothing to say and was at the mercy of the king. For now, Simon's life was spared as a show of kindness and generosity. However, upon release, Simon must have continued preaching against the Herodians and Romans, for he was crucified with his brother James in 46-47 AD.

The purpose of twisting this particular story is to give the Pauline notion of grace equal footing with the law, so that the fateful meeting in Acts 15 could decide the question once and for all, and in Paul's favor. In reality, Paul was rejected by the Jews, once they found out what he was truly teaching. The Jews never abandoned their Covenant with God or would ever teach others to downplay their law. This abrogation of the law was unique to Paul. His standing in the movement sunk to its lowest in Acts 21 and 22 where the Jewish Christian mob (Fourth Philosophy) tried to kill him. After this, Paul languished in prison for awhile and was then lost to history. And so ends the life story of Paul as reported by the author of Acts.

However, there may be several references to Paul in Josephus, right after the murder of James, the brother of Jesus.

Costobarus, also, and Saulus did themselves get together a multitude of wicked wretches, and this because they were of the royal family; and so they obtained favour among them, because of their kindred to Agrippa: but still they used violence with the people, and were very ready to plunder those that were weaker than themselves. (<u>Ant</u>. 20.214)

How fitting that Paul (Saulus) might gain revenge against James and the citizens of Jerusalem. The Saulus mentioned by Josephus was a member of the Herodian family, just as Paul was. (See Appendix 6 for Paul's roots.)

This same Saul was again mentioned by Josephus in the War as a representative of the Jerusalem "Peace Party." (War 2.418 and War 2.556-558)(8) Again, the Peace Party would have been antagonistic towards the anti-Roman Fourth Philosophy. These passages have not traditionally been assigned to Paul the Apostle because Josephus spent little or no time exploring Christianity. However, I believe that Josephus was obsessed with Jewish Christianity, but it was designated the Fourth Philosophy. So the thought of Paul playing a role against the Fourth Philosophy is quite plausible. If this is so, then it overturns the time frame set forth by Acts. The Peace Party went to Agrippa in 66 AD while Acts placed Paul in prison in Rome.

This claim is further bolstered by the negative references to Paul in the Pseudo-clementines. These writings were a history of the early church with a different twist than Acts. In this literature, Paul was the "Liar" and an apostate, while James was the hero.(9) With the festering hatred of Paul for James and James' distrust of Paul, the chasm between Jewish Christianity (Fourth Philosophy) and Gentile Christianity grew so wide that no bridge could ever connect them again. So is it possible that these references by Josephus were attributed to Saul, one-time persecutor of the church? I would not bet against it. (Appendix 6 fully explores the life and teachings of Paul. In this study, the case will be made that Saul actually was a participant in Jerusalem political affairs from 62-66 AD. This completely contradicts Acts which placed Paul in prison, safely away from Jerusalem and any ties which could tarnish his mythical image.)

If the end of Paul's life as recorded by Acts is false, then what about the beginnings? All we know for sure comes from the pen of Paul. In Galatians, Paul stated that he went to Jerusalem three years after his conversion and returned there fourteen years later. After this, he and Cephas had their falling out in Antioch. This sequence of events probably occurred over the span of twenty years. The question is this: when did this twenty year period begin and when did it end?

Traditionally, Paul converted to Christianity around 35 AD, a few years after the death of Jesus. By using Paul's numbers, he must have visited Jerusalem in 38-39 AD after his conversion (Acts 9:26-30; Gal. 1:18). Paul did not return again to Jerusalem for another fourteen years. This would have placed the Council of Jerusalem in the year 52 AD (Acts 15; Gal. 2:1). The argument with Cephas occurred after this Council meeting or around 53-54 AD. Finally, Paul's last entrance into Jerusalem was in 58 AD, at the time of the Egyptian (Acts 21).

Just as Winston Smith (1984) discovered mistakes in the party's rewriting of history, we can also do the same. In Acts 11:27-30, Paul and Barnabas were sent to Jerusalem to provide help to the poor. This was done in response to the famine which occurred between 44-48 AD. Note that this event was not mentioned by Paul in Galatians. There can only be two explanations for this omission. First, it is possible that Paul did not see the necessity of relating the incident to his church in Galatia. This is the position of the traditionalists. My viewpoint is very different. I believe Paul did not mention the famine relief trip to Jerusalem because it had not yet occurred.

There are three reasons why I believe Paul's career with the Fourth Philosophy lasted from 22-45 AD. First, the argument with Cephas in Galatians is the same argument which occurs twice in Josephus: Simon and Agrippa (<u>Ant</u>. 19.332-334) and the story of the conversion of King Izates (<u>Ant</u>. 20.34-46). Both events happened in the early 40's. In the case of Izates, a Pauline figure converts him to a form of Judaism without the need of circumcision. Consistent with the circumcision group sent by James to Cephas, a Jew from Galilee was sent to persuade Izates to undergo circumcision. Certainly, the Jewish Christians were clamping down upon the unauthorized teachings of Paul and his disciples.

The second point of interest concerns the famine of 44-48 AD. In Galatians, Corinthians and Romans, Paul was collecting money for the poor in Jerusalem. This activity makes perfect sense if it were in response to a real need, such as the shortage of food in Jerusalem. This same response was made by Queen Helena and King Izates (<u>Ant</u>. 20.49-53).

Another possible connection comes from a secondary source. The Pseudoclementine Recognitions claimed that Paul attacked James in Jerusalem in the 40's. Such an attack would have been impossible by the traditional dating scheme. However, if Paul had been excommunicated by James and Cephas in the Antioch showdown, then the motive for attack becomes clear. Paul did his best to convince his disciples that his gospel was superior to that of Cephas and James. This was necessary because the famine collection had not yet been completed. Paul then took whatever money had been collected and left for Jerusalem. Who received the money? Obviously, the Fourth Philosophy did not partake in the wealth. This may have been the reason why a fight ensued between the followers of Paul (Herodians) and the disciples of James (Jewish Christians). The Recognitions say that James was badly injured in the fight, but he was not killed. It should not be missed that the murder of James in Jerusalem in 62 AD curiously comes right before Josephus' mention of Saul persecuting those weaker than himself (Jewish Christians).

THE PLAYERS

New Testament

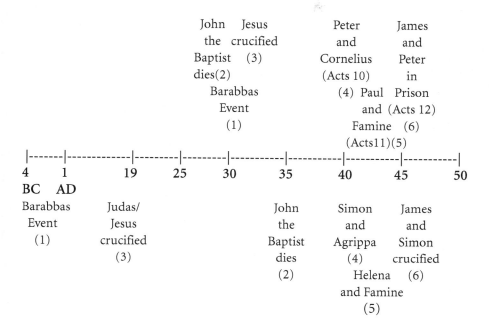

Josephus

1. The original Barabbas event occurred in 4 BC when Archelaus released Herod the Great's prisoners because he was afraid of the mob. One of the prisoners was Judas/Jesus, known as Barabbas, or son of the father. This same story was repeated by the Gospel writers concerning the trial before Pontius Pilate (traditionally 33 AD). In the Gospel story, Pilate replaced Archelaus, and Barabbas was a murderer who had been imprisoned for leading a rebellion in the city of Jerusalem. In the Gospels, Barabbas the murderer was preferred over Jesus by the Jewish crowd, the bad son of the father over the good.

2. The Gospels place John the Baptist before Jesus. John became subservient to Jesus saying that he (John) baptized with water but one greater (Jesus) would baptize with the Holy Spirit. This actually had more to do with John and Paul than John and Jesus. In reality, John the Baptist was murdered by the Herodians in 37 AD, some five or so years after the Gospel version. The later date places John into the time frame of Paul and not Judas/Jesus.

3. In Appendix 7, it was proved that Pilate became procurator in 18 AD. Shortly thereafter, Judas/Jesus was lured to Jerusalem, captured and then crucified. The Gospels place the capture, trial and crucifixion of Jesus in 28-33 AD. It is interesting that the High Priests who questioned Jesus were Annas and Caiaphas. Annas was High Priest from 7-15 AD and was responsible for supporting the taxation of Rome. His main adversary was Judas the Galilean. Caiaphas was High Priest in 18-19 AD. Together, Annas and Caiaphas solved the taxation problem; they had Judas/Jesus crucified.

4. In Acts 10, Peter was escorted by representatives of Cornelius to the city of Caesarea. With the help of God, through dreams and visions, Peter learned that the Gentiles were worthy of the same gift belonging to the Jews. This discovery bridged the gap between the Judaism of Jesus and the gospel of grace, as preached by Paul. In Josephus, a Simon was escorted to Caesarea by soldiers sent by Agrippa. It seems as though Simon had been preaching that only Jews were to be allowed into the Temple. He stated that even the Herodians should be barred. This did not sit well with Agrippa, so he sent for Simon. Like Jesus before Pilate, Simon was silent before Agrippa. Clearly, the Gospel writers twisted this story of exclusion into a fantastic tale of inclusion.

5. Josephus wrote that Queen Helena and King Izates sent aid to Jerusalem during the famine (44-48 AD). In Acts chapter 11, Paul also travelled to Jerusalem with monies for the poor in Jerusalem. This too was timed with the famine. In Galatians, Paul never mentioned this trip to Jerusalem. This is due to the fact that the famine relief trip had not yet occurred. The famine relief is why Paul collected money from his congregations in Galatia and Corinth.

6. In Acts 12, Luke wrote that James and Peter (Simon Peter) were imprisoned. In his story, James was beheaded and Peter miraculously escaped. Josephus' story concerned the two sons of Judas the Galilean, James and Simon. They were imprisoned and then crucified. These two were the only two who drank of the same cup as Jesus—crucifixion.

THE PROBLEM OF PAUL

Acts (1)

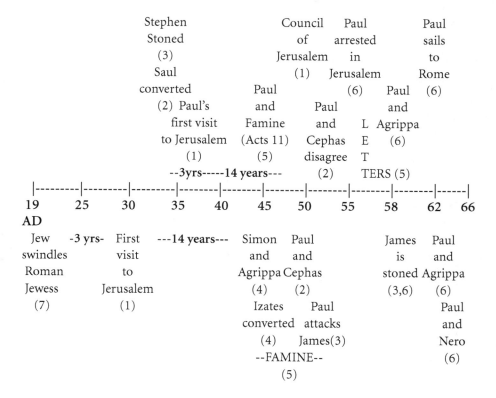

Josephus and Pseudoclementine Recognitions (1)

1. Both the New Testament and Josephus timelines incorporate the two meetings in Jerusalem as detailed by Paul in Galatians: 3 years after his conversion and then 14 years later. Note that Paul never mentioned a visit to Jerusalem during the famine. This is due to the fact that the letters to the Corinthians, Galatians and Romans preceeded his eventual trip to Jerusalem for the famine relief.

2. Since the actual crucifixion of Jesus occurred 14 years earlier than traditionally thought (19 AD vs. 33 AD), the beginning story of the Church would have also been 14 years earlier. Thus, it is possible that Paul persecuted the Church in 19 AD and converted to the faith in 20-24 AD. If this scenario is true, then Paul would have been excommunicated by Cephas and James around 40-44 AD.

3. The Book of Acts claims that Saul persecuted the early Church and approved of Stephen's stoning around 35 AD. In Josephus, Saul persecuted those weaker than himself after the stoning of James, around 62-64 AD. This description of Saul was used by Luke to invent his own version of history. Also, the Pseudoclementine Recognitions claims that Paul attacked James in Jerusalem in the 40's. This could not have occurred based upon the chronology of Acts, but it does fit with the earlier positioning of Paul within the movement.

4. The two passages from Josephus concerning Simon and Agrippa as well as King Izates, Ananias and Eleazar, show that a struggle was underway for the hearts and minds of Jewish <u>converts</u>. In the early 40's, Jewish Christians were being sent out from Galilee to ensure converts were accepting full conversion, which included circumcision. This is the exact argument described by Paul in Galatians. This helps prove that Paul's career with the Fourth Philosophy (Jewish Christians) was nearing an end by 40-45 AD.

5. Scholars date 1 and 2 Corinthians, Galatians and Romans at 57 AD, based upon the chronology of Acts (which is absolutely useless in dating events). According to the early placement of Paul within the movement, these letters were written shortly after Paul's excommunication (early 40's). Note that Paul was collecting monies for those in Jerusalem. This effort probably related to the famine which Josephus placed between 44-48 AD. If Paul travelled to Jerusalem at the time of the famine, he may have come in contact with James, and a struggle may have ensued (Ps. Rec.). In any event, the monies probably went into the Herodian coffers and not to the Fourth Philosophy (Jewish Christians).

6. The story of Paul's later career in Jerusalem is dated a few years earlier in Acts than in Josephus. This earlier dating of Acts (58-62 AD) helps to distance Paul from the following: the stoning of James in 62 AD; Saul's petition for an army from Agrippa in 66 AD; and Saul's appeal to Nero in 66 AD, two years <u>after</u> Nero massacred Jewish Christians in Rome. In short, Acts sent Paul to Rome before the Saul of Josephus could do his dirty deeds in Jerusalem and beyond. This being the case, the entire ending chronology of Paul's life is bogus. It is therefore possible to shift Paul's career with the Fourth Philosophy to an earlier time.

7. In full circle, the beginnings of Paul's career may be traced back to an unnamed Jew who extorted money from a wealthy Jewess in 19 AD Rome. This unnamed Jew worked with others, professed to be knowledgeable in the Law and convinced converted Jews to send monies to Jerusalem. All this fits in nicely with Paul's methods as described by himself in Galatians, Corinthians and Romans. Paul's anti-Law attitude may have actually preceeded his "conversion" to Jewish Christianity. The "conversion" for Paul was the synthesis of anti-Law teachings

with the death and resurrection of Jesus. It was through this "grace" that Paul could soothe his own conscience.

CHAPTER SEVEN

THE DEAD SEA SCROLLS

Can any book claiming to identify the flesh and blood Jesus ignore the wealth of information derived from the Dead Sea Scrolls? The answer is no! Although the Scrolls do not identify anyone by name, there are a few individuals who attract our attention. In The Cairo Damascus Document (1.9-11), three figures are introduced: the Root of Planting, the Righteous Teacher and the Wicked Priest. The dating range of interpretations for these three vary widely, from the times of Judas Maccabee (approximately 180-150 BC) to that of James, the brother of Jesus (19-62 AD). Therefore, hypotheses on the composition of the Scrolls differ by over two-hundred years. These different viewpoints are examined below.

Robert Eisenman's hypothesis represents the later time frame, claiming Jesus to be the Root of Planting, James as the Righteous Teacher and Ananas as the Wicked Priest. He equates the Liar or Spouter of Lies of the Dead Sea Scrolls with Paul.(1) Eisenman claims that the internal evidence of the Scrolls (their content) should be weighed more heavily than the external evidence (carbon dating, etc.) which may point to an earlier date. The support for his position is impressive as non-Biblical information concerning James and Paul is quite abundant. By reading his book, James, the Brother of Jesus, one must be impressed by his dogged determination in associating James with the Righteous Teacher and Paul with the Liar. The Liar designation was routinely denied by Paul in his letters when he would promise his listeners, "I do not lie." So it is possible that Eisenman has contributed much to the debate about the characters named above. But the only question I have is this: was James the first Righteous Teacher or was Judas/Jesus?

The orthodox view of the Scrolls is based primarily upon external evidence such as carbon dating and paleographical dating. With these as a starting point, the internal evidence must not vary from the established dating parameters. For instance, if Paul is the Liar, then the Scrolls concerning the Liar must have been written about 40 AD. According to Geza Vermes, author of The Complete Scrolls in English, the Commentary on Habakkuk, which "is one of the main sources for the study of Qumran origins," has a paleographical dating range from 30-1 BCE and a radiocarbon range from 120-5 BCE.(2) To the orthodox, the views of Eisenman are fringe at best. In their view, the Commentary on Habakkuk is backwards looking. They associate the Wicked Priest with Jonathan who assumed the leadership of the Maccabean rebels in 161 BC and became High Priest in 152 BC.

Thus, the early date looking backwards to 150 BC is supported by some of the external evidence while the later date of 19 AD (death of Judas/Jesus in the Pilate era) is supported by much of the internal contents. It is very easy to be sympathetic to each argument, but both cannot be correct.

Over two and a half centuries, many coins were dropped and hopelessly lost in the Qumran area. A distribution of 476 recovered coins by dates is as follows:(3)

135 BC-104 BC	2	
103 BC-76 BC	143	
75 BC-4 BC	20	
4 BC-68 AD	281	
68 AD-132 AD	30	Roman Coins

Note that there are two main date ranges for the occupation of Qumran, from 103 BC-76 BC and from 4 BC-68 AD. The earlier date has at most 145 possible coins (all coins later than 76 BC) while the later date has at least 301 coins (all coins from 75 BC-68 AD.) And it is quite possible that some of the earlier coins were also lost in the later period, for coins stay in circulation for centuries.

As an avid U.S. coin collector, I have often asked for and received $25 of pennies from the bank, which are randomly rolled. Of these 2,500 pennies (a very large sample), I usually find 5 or 6 wheat pennies (pennies dated from 1909 to 1958). Thus, out of every 500 pennies, one is a wheat. Considering that wheat pennies have been hoarded since 1959 and almost completely out of circulation by now (2003), 1 in 500 is not too bad a find. If the coins were not being removed from circulation, then the odds of finding a wheat would be wholly dependent on mintage, the number of coins made in a particular year. So it is very possible that a man living in Qumran in 4 BC could have had in his possession coins dating from 76-135 BC. But no man living in 76 BC could have had a coin minted in the future. Thus, our table above probably understates the coins in the latter period and overstates the earlier period.

The second period was definitely the most active time at Qumran. Coincidentally, the beginning date of 4 BC corresponds with Herod's death and the release of Judas the Galilean via the "Barabbas" event, which occurred not long after the Golden Eagle Temple Cleansing. The coin data is probably more important than the other external evidence championed by the orthodox view. Carbon dating can be relevant but the range of possible years was 125 in the case of the Commentary on Habakkuk, and even this is questioned by Eisenman. But the coin data cannot be questioned. The heaviest activity occurred between 4 BC and 68 AD, and this corresponds perfectly with the movement of Judas the Galilean. Eisenman is right in asserting that the internal evidence points towards Jesus and James but his dating is wrong. He, like most scholars, believes that the Christian era began with Jesus and his death, post 27 AD. This later date does not correspond with most external data and is not a perfect fit for the coin distribution as well. I have moved the Christian era back to 5 BC with the Temple Cleansing of Judas and Matthias. This will still fit with much of Eisenman's arguments, although his Righteous Teacher (James) and Liar (Paul) were second generation players in this drama. It will also quiet the critics of the later date because it falls within the range of the external data.

THE ROOT OF PLANTING

The following passage has been reproduced from The Damascus Document, where the Root of Planting is described.

For when they were unfaithful and forsook Him, He hid His face from Israel and His Sanctuary and delivered them up to the sword. But remembering the Covenant of the forefathers, He left a remnant to Israel and did not deliver it up to be destroyed. And in the age of wrath, three hundred and ninety years after He had given them into the hand of King Nebuchadnezzar of Babylon, He visited them, and He caused a plant root to spring from Israel and Aaron to inherit His Land and to prosper on the good things of His earth. And they perceived their iniquity and recognized that they were guilty men, yet for twenty years they were like blind men groping for the way.

And God observed their deeds, that they sought Him with a whole heart, and He raised for them a Teacher of Righteousness to guide them in the way of His heart. And He made known to the latter generations that which God had done to the latter generation, the congregation of traitors, to those who departed from the way. This was the time of which it is written, *like a stubborn heifer thus was Israel stubborn* (Hos. iv.16), when the Scoffer arose who shed over Israel the waters of lies. He caused them to wander in a pathless wilderness and removing the boundary with which the forefathers had marked out their inheritance, that He might call down on them the curses of His Covenant and deliver them up to the avenging sword of the Covenant. Damascus Document 1.2-19 (4)

I have quoted a lengthy passage which describes the plant root, the Teacher of Righteousness and the Scoffer. Each will be discussed in the following pages. The Damascus Document begins by giving a brief historical sketch: 1) Israel forsook God; 2) God punished Israel by delivering them up to the Babylonians and King Nebuchadnezzar in 586 BC; 3) three hundred and ninety years later (586 - 390 = 196 BC), God caused a plant root to spring from Israel so that they could once again inherit the land.

First, The Damascus Document made clear that an evil, unrepentant Israel would be punished by God. This same sense can be observed in the writings of Jeremiah and Isaiah, where the powers (Assyria and Babylon) would punish Israel for their sins against God. Thus, the attitudes and actions of the people of Israel were very important to the writer(s). A Law loving people would be safe while an impertinent, selfish country would be punished.

Secondly, God would remember his Covenant with His people and a remnant would survive. So even after the destruction of Israel by King Nebuchadnezzar of Babylon, some remnant lived on to eventually reassert themselves in the name of God. The Babylonian captivity occurred in 586 BC and the return of God to His people happened three hundred and ninety years later, in the year 196 BC. This approximates the date (197 BC) when Judea became a province of the Selucid Empire.(5)

Thirdly, because someone else was ruling the land, God would plant a root which would grow and eventually overtake the land for Israel and God. This would be accompanied by the remnant of Israel exhibiting right behavior: recognizing their sins and repenting. And even after this, it would take a generation to oust the foreigners, for the document says, "yet for twenty years they were like blind men groping for the way."

From the above, it is obvious that the prototype for the present movement (latter generation) was the liberation movement of the Maccabees, whose main players were named Judas and Mattathias. It was Mattathias who led the revolt against Antiochus Epiphanes, the king who tried to destroy the Jewish religion in 169 BC.

And king Antiochus wrote to all his kingdom that all the people should be one: and every one should leave his own law. And all the nations consented to his service, and they sacrificed to idols and profaned the sabbath.... <u>And that whoever would not do according to the word of king Antiochus should be put to death</u>. (1 Maccabees 1:43-52)

It was this king who profaned the Temple and transformed it into a temple for the Greek god, Zeus. From this period, the concept of religious martyrdom developed, becoming part of the literature of the Maccabees and the forerunner of the nationalism of Judas the Galilean.(6)

Chapter two of 1 Maccabees describes how Mattathias (the father of John, Simon, Judas Maccabee, Eleazer and Jonathan) led a rebel force into the hills in order to fight for their God and for His Law against Antiochus. Thus, the struggle for Israel moved from Jerusalem to the mountainous hiding places, where Mattathias organized his resistance movement. Upon his death bed, Mattathias said this to his sons:

O my sons, be ye zealous for the law, and give your lives for the covenant of your fathers. And call to remembrance the works of the fathers, which they have done in their generations: and you shall receive great glory and an everlasting name. (2 Maccabees 2:50-51)

He then named Judas Maccabee as the leader with Simon as his counselor. (2 Maccabees 2:65-66) (Note that this plea to give their lives for the Law of God was reproduced by Matthias and Judas in the Golden Eagle Temple Cleansing (see Chapter Three). In addition, the reward of great glory for their deeds was also promised by the latter Matthias and Judas.)

The original Root of Planting was the resistance movement of Mattathias which was carried on by his sons, most notably Judas Maccabee and his brother Simon. Now Eisenman claims that Jesus was the Root of Planting for a most obvious reason: he is believed to have originated the Christian religion. As already discussed, the death of Jesus can be ballparked to 19 AD if the crucifixion occurred in the early Pilate era. Thus to Eisenman, the Root of Planting occurred during the reign of the Roman procurator, Pontius Pilate. Eisenman's arguments are solid, but there is an individual a generation earlier whom he has overlooked because scholars have not linked Jesus to Judas the Galilean. That person is none other than Matthias, the co-teacher with Judas.

Although Matthias was not necessarily older than Judas, his martyrdom in 5 BC is 31-37 years earlier than the traditional dating of Jesus' death (27-33 AD). (In Appendix 7, an argument will be put forth which moves the death of Judas/Jesus back towards the census of Cyrenius, during the early governorship of Pilate (19 AD). If this is true then the space of time between the deaths of Matthias and Judas would be twenty-three years.) It was with Matthias' life and death that a movement sprang forth. Note that the Fourth Philosophy did not begin with the death of Judas the Galilean. A movement was already coalescing when the census of Cyrenius brought Judas to the forefront. Therefore, Judas the Galilean, or rather Jesus, could not have been the Root of Planting.

Matthias' martyrdom is reminiscent of the death of the earlier Mattathias. Both led men zealous for the law and both aimed at Cleansing the Temple by removing the impurities which polluted the site. And at their deaths, two individuals carried on the movements: Judas Maccabee and Simon at the time of Antiochus Epiphanes and Judas the Galilean and Sadduc (Jesus and Cephas) after the death of Herod the Great. In addition, both movements had the same goals: to rid the land of the occupying force and to be zealous for the law of God. Also, note the eerie similarities in names: Matthias, Judas and Simon. For the time in question, 4 BC-68 AD, no other movement is closer to that of the original Root of Planting than that of Matthias and Judas the Galilean. (It should also be noted that the New Testament does mention a Matthias. He is the one who replaced Judas Iscariot as the twelfth apostle in Acts 1:23-26. Eisenman proves without a shadow of a doubt that the election of Matthias was really an election to replace Jesus.(7) Two things must be remembered. First, Judas Iscariot is only code for Judas the Galilean or Jesus (See Chapter Six). Secondly, the election of a replacement leader coincidentally refers back to Matthias and his passing on of leadership to Judas the Galilean.)

One other point should be made concerning the twenty years where the followers of God were like blind men groping for the way. It is after these twenty years that God raised up a Teacher of Righteousness. So if our focus is upon the Golden Eagle Temple Cleansing, where Matthias and Judas removed the Golden Eagle from the Temple in 5 BC, then there must have been an event twenty years earlier which led to this action. In Ant. 15.267-268, Josephus described how Herod introduced foreign practices to Israel, from celebrating athletic games every fifth year in the honor of Caesar to the building of a theater in Jerusalem and an amphitheater in the plain. At this, the Jews were outraged at the change to their customs. (Ant. 15.274-276) The crime was so great in their eyes that ten men conspired to kill Herod. Their means of assassination was a precursor to the Sicarii: "[they] took daggers with them under their garments for the purpose of killing Herod." (Ant. 15.282) Unfortunately for the conspirators, Herod found them out and had them executed. To those opposing Herod:

...the conspiracy they had sworn to was a holy and pious action...[done for] those common customs of the country, which all the Jews were obliged to observe, or to die for them. (Ant. 15.288)

Per the dating by Josephus, this occurred in 25-24 BC.

The Root of Planting was a movement which arose because of the foreign practices which were introduced to Israel. Herod was the individual who championed the pagan influences, just as Antiochus Epiphanes had done during the days of Mattathias and Judas Maccabee. The twenty years of groping for the way ended when Matthias and Judas Cleansed the Temple. Herod had Matthias killed but Judas escaped immediate sentence to death and was later released by Archelaus in the "Barabbas event". It is at this point that Judas became the Righteous Teacher.

THE RIGHTEOUS TEACHER

Like the Root of Planting, there was an original Righteous Teacher who sprang from Mattathias. His name was Judas Maccabee, the man responsible for the Cleansing of the Temple in the days of Antiochus Epiphanes (164 BC). To Judas and the rebels, the Cleansing of the Temple and strict adherence to the law overrode all other things (2 Maccabees 15:6-24). Not only was Judas faithful to the Law but his bravery (1 Maccabees 9:5) and faith in God (1 Maccabees 4:6) set him apart from all others. He would be the prototype for all other Righteous Teachers.

I use the plural of Teacher because I believe there were two from 4 BC to 62 AD, Judas the Galilean and his brother James. Judas the Galilean was obviously the first Righteous Teacher, leading the rebels as Judas Maccabee had done 160 years earlier. Josephus called Judas the Galilean a wise man, beloved by the people, and a rabbi of his own sect. After the death of Matthias at the hands of Herod and the release of Herod's political prisoners by Archelaus, Judas fled to Galilee and armed himself for battle. Like Judas Maccabee, Judas the Galilean would become a rebel leader, a hero to his own kind but a thorn in the flesh to the ruling authorities.

When Jesus was baptized by John in Matthew 3:15, he replied to John, "Let it be so now [Jesus being baptized by John]; it is proper to fulfill all righteousness." In Chapter Six, we discovered that John the Baptist came after Jesus, not before. So what does the above passage mean? Even without the mention of John the Baptist, the washing in water was a way to symbolically wash away sin. Since the Righteous Teacher was placed upon a pedestal, this washing was a way to show the others that he too was a man and that all hearts needed cleansed to approach righteousness. Jesus also used righteousness often in his preaching: "those who hunger and thirst for righteousness" (Matt. 5:6); "who are persecuted because of righteousness" (Matt. 5:10); and to "seek first His kingdom and His righteousness" (Matt. 6:33). To Jesus, righteousness was the centerpiece to a relationship with God.

Following the death of Jesus (or Judas the Galilean as I believe), the mantle of Righteous Teacher was thrust upon James. This is consistent with the Maccabean example where Jonathan, the brother of Judas Maccabee, assumed control after Judas' death. Unlike Jonathan, James had a dual role: he carried on the duties of the Righteous Teacher in Jerusalem while Cephas preached in other lands; and both preached the resurrection of Jesus, the former Righteous Teacher. This was necessary because Jesus had been proclaimed Messiah, the great liberator. If Jesus were dead, then the movement might also die. So James assumed the leadership on a wait and see basis.(8) This balancing act continued from the death of Jesus (19 AD) to his own death (62 AD), an amazing forty-three years. Like Jonathan before him, James made a name for himself and removed himself from the long shadow of Judas/Jesus.

The Righteous Teacher was a man who taught the people to follow the Way of God, to follow His laws and commands. That the movement of Judas the Galilean/Jesus patterned itself after Judas Maccabee should be instructive in how to interpret the Dead Sea Scrolls. The orthodox view paints Jonathan, the brother of Judas Maccabee, as the Wicked Priest, not the Righteous Teacher. This means that the orthodox theory considers the Dead Sea Scrolls as anti-Maccabean. But knowing that the majority of the activity at Qumran occurred between 4 BC and 68 AD should lead us to the logical conclusion. Since the caves were manned by the Fourth Philosophy disciples of Judas, starting around 4 BC, it is extremely unlikely that they would have preserved anti-revolutionary material. The simple fact that the Scrolls exist point towards a pro-Maccabean interpretation.

THE WICKED PRIEST

Consistent with the Root of Planting and the Righteous Teacher, the Wicked Priest of Judas the Galilean's time had a forerunner in the era of Judas Maccabee. The original Wicked Priest was named Alcimus.

And there came to him [Demetrius the king] the wicked and ungodly men of Israel: and Alcimus was at the head of them, who desired to be made high priest.... And Judas saw all the evils that Alcimus, and they that were with him, did to the children of Israel, much more than the Gentiles. (1 Maccabees 7:6,23)

This illustrates the character of the Wicked Priest, in that he desired power and wealth at the expense of the people and the law. Alcimus conspired with the Gentiles and was a traitor to his people. The modern day equivalent would be the Vichy government in France during World War II, where some ambitious locals backed the Nazi invasion against the wishes of the majority.

In the time frame of Judas the Galilean, the Wicked Priest was named Joazar, a prominent player in the Temple Cleansing of 5 BC and the census of 6 AD. It is not certain if Joazar was deemed wicked by the populace at the time of the Temple Cleansing. He replaced the existing high priest and presided over the murder of Matthias. (Ant. 17.164) However, this same Joazar was removed temporarily from the high priesthood by Archelaus for "assisting the seditious." (Ant. 17.339) But again he appeared as the heavy by persuading the people to pay taxes to Rome, this time at the census of Cyrenius. (Ant. 18.3) Against Joazar and his supporters, Judas the Galilean led a revolt "and exhorted the nation to assert their liberty."(Ant. 18.4) Thus, there is no doubt that Joazar was bought and paid for, a tool of Rome and an instrument of the ruling class against the poor.

A passage from the Commentary on Habakkuk perfectly fits Joazar.

Interpreted, this concerns the Wicked Priest who was called by the name of truth when he first arose. But when he ruled over Israel his heart became proud, and he forsook God and betrayed the precepts for the sake of riches. He robbed and amassed the riches of the men of violence who rebelled against God, and he took the wealth of the peoples, heaping sinful iniquity upon himself. And he lived in the ways of abominations amidst every unclean defilement. (8.9-14)(9)

To the orthodox, this passage applies to Jonathan, the brother of Judas Maccabee, who became high priest. However, the Book of Maccabees has nothing but good to say about him, and he was a national hero to the people. As mentioned before, if this were written against the Maccabees, the followers of Judas the Galilean would not have preserved it. With the orthodox paleographical external dating of 30-1 BC, the odds of this passage looking backwards 150 years is extremely unlikely. Instead, the dating only confirms my claim that the Wicked Priest was Joazar, a person living at the time of the composition.

Eisenman then takes the ball and makes extensive arguments concerning James, Paul and Ananas as the Teacher of Righteousness, Liar and Wicked Priest, respectively. He is simply reading the same good versus evil struggle into a different time frame. After the death of Jesus, James became the reigning Teacher of Righteousness and against him was aligned the forces opposing the Law. Paul even confirmed his feelings about the Law by saying the Law was dead (Romans and Galatians). So Eisenman is quite right in applying the Liar label to Paul. After all, we cannot assume that the Scrolls were not evolving literature.

Passages would be interpreted differently depending on the situation. Certainly, by the year 50 AD, a passage written about Joazar would equally apply to the current high priest and to the Liar, Paul.

This being said, there was one other character in the life of Judas/Jesus who may have held the title of Wicked Priest. Annas was named High Priest in 7 AD, replacing Joazar. This Annas reigned until 15 AD and still retained power through his son and son-in-law who were appointed High Priests between 15-19 AD. Annas was originally installed by the Roman procurator Coponius, at the time of the census. His role would have been in <u>support</u> of the Roman occupation and <u>against</u> Judas the Galilean. This same Annas interrogated Jesus after his arrest, <u>before</u> Jesus was sent to the current High Priest, Caiaphas (19 AD). Even though Annas was not the current High Priest, there was an understanding that the power still resided with him. The death of the Righteous Teacher (Judas/Jesus) was on his hands. Undoubtedly, the Fourth Philosophy would have considered Annas as a Wicked Priest.

THE COMMUNITY RULE

Perhaps the Community Rule (CR) is the oldest of the Dead Sea Scroll documents, dating from 100 BC. Per Geza Vermes, there was no type of literature quite like it, from either Jews or the early first century Christians.(10) A reading of this document is a must because it really illustrates the fanaticism of this particular sect. Like the other Scrolls, this one also speaks of light versus darkness, the elect versus the "men of perdition". Thus, this document could have spoken to any group who viewed themselves as the light, whether it be from 100 BC or 4 BC. Although it is an early Essene writing, it could have also been used by the fledgling Fourth Philosophy as well. What I am saying is this: The Community Rule was not written by the followers of Judas and Matthias in 4 BC, but it most certainly was absorbed or incorporated into their philosophical outlook.

Although Vermes sees no comparable literature from either the Jews or earliest Christians, a few passages do stand out as "familiar". First, the Community Rule said this concerning property:

[if he is deemed acceptable to the Community] his property shall be merged and he shall offer his counsel and judgement to the Community.... If one of them has lied deliberately in matters of property, he shall be excluded from the pure Meal of the Congregation for one year and shall do penance with respect to one quarter of his food. (CR 4.20-26)

Like the early followers of Judas the Galilean and the early Christians of Acts, this Community also believed in pure communism.

Listen closely to this passage from the Book of Acts.

All the believers were one in heart and mind. No one claimed that any of his possessions was his own, but they shared everything they had.... There were no needy persons among them. For from time to time those who owned lands or houses sold them, brought the money from the sales and put it at the apostles' feet, and it was distributed to anyone as he had need....Now a man named Ananias, together with his wife Sapphira, also sold a piece of property. With his wife's full knowledge he kept back part of the money for himself, but brought the rest and put it at the apostles' feet. Then Peter said, "Ananias, how is it that Satan has so filled your heart that you have lied to the Holy Spirit and have kept for yourself some of the money you received for the land? Didn't it belong to you before it was sold? And after it was sold, wasn't the money at your disposal? What made you think of doing such a thing? You have not lied to men but to God." When Ananias heard this, he fell down and died. (Acts 4:32-5:5)

Note that the Essenes and Jewish Christians shared all things in common, and it was not acceptable to hold anything back from the Community. Today, a man who would sell land and give 25% to the Church would be deemed a saint; then he would be excluded and punished. (Remember, communism is easier to implement if most or all are poor; what do they have to lose? Such an economic practice is extremely unpopular in an affluent society.)

In the Council of the Community there shall be twelve men and three Priests, perfectly versed in all that is revealed of the Law, whose works shall be truth, righteousness, justice, loving-kindness and humility. They shall preserve the faith in the Land with steadfastness and meekness and shall atone for sin by the practice of justice and by suffering the sorrows of affliction. (CR 8.1-4)

Two points must be made here. First, this movement was so unlike the Gentile Christian Church of Paul in that personal actions or works were emphasized. To Paul, only the death of Christ could atone for sin, but here the practice of justice does the trick. However, this understanding of God's mercy would be in-line with the Fourth Philosophy of Judas. In addition, Jesus quoted the Old Testament prophet Hosea, "I desire mercy, not sacrifice." He meant that mercy is a way of life by which one is righteous before God.

Secondly, the early church may have patterned their apostle scheme after this passage. Although Paul does not place a definite number to the apostles, using only a plural when designating them, the move towards the number twelve was very early, established at least by 105 AD (my dating of the earliest Gospel—see Appendix 4). However, it is the three priests which most intrigue me. Remember that the Fourth Philosophy was governed by a pair of teachers: first, Matthias and Judas, then Judas and Sadduc (Cephas) and finally, Cephas and James. So where does the third priest fit in? According to Paul, in Galatians 2:9, the three leaders or pillars of the church were Cephas, James and John. We know that James was located in Jerusalem, a powerful figure of his day (Acts 21:20). Cephas travelled throughout the Empire, bringing more Jews into the Way of Righteousness (Gal. 2:7). But what about John? Although Paul claimed that John was a pillar, he expressly omitted him from the Jerusalem fold during his first visit there, meeting only Cephas and James (Gal. 1:18). It is possible that John was in charge of the desert community. After all, the movement started there and the caves were a safe breeding ground for the Fourth Philosophy's message. This is mere speculation, but Paul did go to the desert for three years after his conversion (Gal. 1:17,18). So it is very likely that new converts were trained in the desert before returning to their "normal" lives in whatever city they lived. However, the new converts in Jerusalem may have been directly under James, passing up the trip to the desert.

"He shall conceal the teaching of the Law from men of injustice, but shall impart true knowledge and righteous judgement to those who have chosen the Way." (CR 9:17) In Acts 24:14, the followers of Jesus were referred to as the Way. This term was also used among the Fourth Philosophy of Judas the Galilean.

Although the Community Rule was written well before the Fourth Philosophy of Judas, it did serve his movement as well. The organization and discipline put forth in this Scroll certainly helped mold those of the Fourth Philosophy just as it had served the Essene community. The genius of Judas was his willingness to include others, to absorb their ideas and to create a new philosophy with a healthy hatred of Rome. In fact, if there was a competition for souls, the Fourth Philosophy had the upper hand; they preached a message which encompassed the beliefs of the Pharisees and Essenes but also gave their followers a glimmer of hope concerning their present lives—liberation from Rome.

CONCLUSION

The dating of the Scrolls will be debated and argued for the next hundred years and beyond. The identity of the Root of Planting, Righteous Teacher and Wicked Priest will also depend upon one's guess concerning the dates. If the orthodox belief is true and the Wicked Priest was originally Jonathan, then it goes to show that early readers of the Scrolls also saw different things in the vague writings. The Fourth Philosophy of Judas the Galilean rose at the exact time when the caves of Qumran saw their busiest use (4 BC-68 AD). And the movement of Judas the Galilean was based upon the liberation movement of Judas Maccabee. They would not have interpreted the Wicked Priest as Jonathan. Like today, the movements of the past interpreted history based upon their time and circumstances. In short, the very existence of the Scrolls show that the Fourth Philosophy believed the documents supported their movement. If it were not so, then the documents would have been destroyed.

But it is possible that the dating of many Scrolls could be within the Fourth Philosophy's time frame (4 BC-68 AD). Many external pieces of evidence point this way; the coins establish the dates of the caves' heaviest use and the paleographical dating of the Commentary on Habakkuk (30—1 BC) fits closer to the Fourth Philosophy then to the anti-Jonathan theory. Although no one will ever know for sure, the Scrolls have a very good chance of following my hypothesis.

THE FOUR PHILOSOPHIES

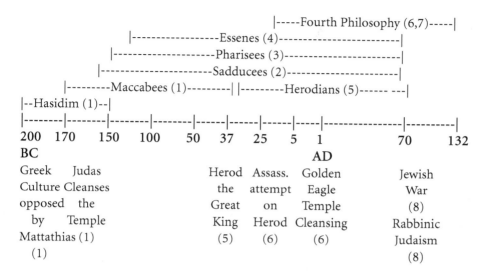

1. From 196-142 BC, Israel was occupied in varying degrees by the Seleucid Kingdom. They were Greek in culture and ruled as absolute monarchs. The most famous of their kings was Antiochus Epiphanes, who in 167 BC established an idol in the Temple and desired all Jews to follow Greek customs. Mattathias organized a resistance movement to this Greek presence, and he and his five sons were successful in eventually driving the Greeks out of Israel. Mattathias' five sons were named Judas, Simon, John, Jonathan and Eleazar. The most famous of these sons was Judas Maccabee, the one who cleansed the Temple and who is still celebrated by Jews today in the Jewish feast of Hanukkah. The Maccabean rule lasted until 37 AD, the year that Herod the Great assumed power.

   The holy men of that time, the Hasidim (meaning godly), supported the movement led by Mattathias. "Many of those attracted to the cause came from the poorer elements of society, so that the rebellion assumed the aspect of class warfare."(11) This aspect of revolt was repeated during the days of Judas the Galilean.

2. The Sadducees were a small group of aristocratic priests who originally opposed the Maccabean rule. This group was much more comfortable with the Greek rulers before Judas Maccabee. However, in time, the Sadducees aligned themselves with the Maccabean movement, where they could better influence policy.(12) In the time of Judas/Jesus, the Sadducees sided with Rome and the Herodians, those

invested with power. Needless to say, they were very much against the popular movement of Judas/Jesus and were instrumental in having him crucified.

3. The Pharisees represented the masses and were opposed to the Sadducees. They were of middle class origins, and their rise dates from the Hasidim's break with the "Hasmonaean regime because of its secular character."(13) Pharisees believed in an evolving relationship between God and man and were much more likely to be nationalistic. They were also the social critics of the time. Many of the early Jewish Christians came from the ranks of the Pharisees. Jesus criticized a number of Pharisees for being self-righteous. As critics of the ruling elites, they could only perform their jobs if they concentrated on the will of God. Jesus only lashed out at those who loved themselves more than their fellow man.

4. The Essenes may have been a reactionary group opposed to Jonathan who ruled after Judas Maccabee, from 160-143 BC. Many Dead Sea Scroll scholars claim that the Essenes framed this Jonathan as the Wicked Priest. There may be some truth in this as Jonathan was constantly making alliances with different kings and may have been untrustworthy to a number of people. Even if this is true, I believe the purpose of the Essenes was to place Israel on the right path before God, back to the good old days of Mattathias and Judas Maccabee.

They also were an offshoot of the Hasidim and had contempt for the Hellenizers and worldly Sadducees. They felt that they were the true representatives of the high-priestly tradition.(14) Their method was the pursuit of righteousness. Just as the Essenes desired to go back to the ideals of Mattathias and Judas, later Essenes saw this same spark in Matthias and Judas the Galilean. That is why there seems to be so much in common between Essenes and followers of the Fourth Philosophy (Jewish Christians). According to Josephus there were two types of Essenes: those who married and those who practiced a chaste lifestyle. Judas and his movement would have been closely associated with those who married; after all, to marry and have children was the will of God as told by Genesis.

5. The Herodians came into power in 37 AD and replaced the Maccabeans. Their first king was Herod the Great. According to Josephus, Herod introduced foreign (Greek) ways to Israel and was vehemently opposed by the more Law abiding citizens. In a sense, the whole Maccabean movement was swept aside by Herod. The Maccabees had been successful in stemming the Greek culture from overtaking Judaism; now Herod was intent on reintroducing Greek culture to the Jews. An important symbol of this Hellenization was the Golden Eagle, which was placed in the Temple. This act was reminiscent of Antiochus Epiphanes, who had placed an idol in the Temple some 150 years earlier.

6. In 25 BC, a group of ten men attempted to assassinate Herod using short swords hidden in their tunics. They were found out and executed. This may have been the first act against Herod and was followed twenty years later by the Temple Cleansing of Matthias and Judas. This Temple Cleansing marked the beginnings of the Fourth Philosophy. This movement had the same aim as the Maccabees: to overthrow the foreign invaders. The beauty of Judas' genius was his ability to take the best from the Essenes and Pharisees and fuse them together with extreme nationalism, creating a movement of fanatics. The majority of these members were slaughtered in the Jewish war.

7. The nationalism of the Fourth Philosophy survived even though the Jamesian wing had been discredited. After 70 AD, nationalists were drawn to other rabbis and this eventually led to a second Jewish war, led by Bar Kochba in 132 AD. Rome also won this second war. The remnants of the Jamesian wing of the Fourth Philosophy became known as the Ebionites or the Poor. This group was excluded from both Judaism and Gentile Christianity and was eventually lost to history.

8. After 70 AD, the Jewish nation was destroyed. The Sadducees, Pharisees and Essenes perished from view, to be replaced by a unified Rabbinic Judaism. Prior to the destruction of Jerusalem, a Pharisee named Johanan Ben Zakkai escaped the seige by being smuggled out to the Romans. He later received permission to create a synod at Jamnia which eventually replaced the Sanhedrin. This Rabbinic Judaism was pro-Roman and discouraged further attempts to find the "Messiah". In fact, to this day, the Books of the Maccabees (rebels from authority) are absent from the Jewish Scriptures.

CHAPTER EIGHT

THE LIFE OF JESUS —A LOGICAL APPROACH

Thomas Jefferson, one of the Founding Fathers, was far ahead of his time in the search for truth concerning the person named Jesus.

Of Jesus himself, he [Jefferson] pointed out that his parentage "was obscure: his condition poor; his education null; his natural endowments great; his life correct and innocent....His message was offered under numerous disadvantages: he wrote nothing of himself; the elite of his country, 'entrenched in power and riches', strongly opposed him; and 'unlettered and ignorant men', writing long after the events had taken place, provide our only source of information about him. His death at 33, before he had attained the height of his reasoning power, was a result of the conspiracy between 'the altar and the throne.'"(1)

Jefferson's assessment of Jesus, based upon the information of his time, was given before scholars tried to isolate the historical Jesus from the spiritual one. Jefferson "did not believe in mysteries, miracles, incomprehensible 'logomachies', the divinity of Jesus, nor the doctrine of the atonement."(2) In fact, Jesus could be discovered, if that were possible, by applying logic and scientific inquiry. Thus, Jefferson dismissed all miracles and the like, because such literary tools were just that, not real events in history.

So in our search, we will follow in the footsteps of Jefferson. We will question the traditional picture of Jesus, from his miraculous birth to his atoning death. Note from the above passage, Jefferson questioned the birth narratives and the veracity of the Gospel authors. He bolstered our Fourth Philosophy claim by insisting that Jesus was opposed by the wealthy and powerful. And finally, Jefferson noted that Jesus died at an early age, before men reached their highest intellectual abilities. This too ties with the Judas the Galilean theory, where Jesus was not thirty-three at the crucifixion but closer to fifty-five, an age of respect and wisdom, based upon accumulated knowledge.

THE AGE OF JESUS

The Gospel of Luke claimed that Jesus was thirty years old at the start of his ministry (Luke 3:23). Many scholars believe that the ministry lasted for three years, thereby ending his life at the tender age of thirty-three. However, this dating depends entirely upon our understanding of his birth. In Chapter Two, we noted that the two birth scenarios given in Matthew and Luke were eleven to twelve years apart, one in 6 BC and the other in 6-7 AD. The dating of these two births coincided with the two accounts of Judas the Galilean, as told by Josephus (Chapters Three and Four). In addition, the date of Jesus' death may have occurred in 19 AD, not 30-33 AD. (See Appendix 7) This would nullify not one but both birth narratives. With these large discrepancies, the idealized picture of a youthful Jesus may be more wishful thinking than hard fact. Ask yourself this question: Could a thirty year old man accomplish the deeds ascribed to Jesus?

First, let us examine the predecessors of Jesus mentioned in the Old Testament. The patriarch of the Jewish race was Abraham. In Genesis 17:1-10, God established an everlasting covenant with Abraham when Abraham was ninety-nine years old. Obviously, God was not One to promise everlasting covenants with untested youths. The prophet Moses, the one through whom God gave Israel the Law, led the Israelites out of Egypt at the age of eighty. Moses had been thoroughly tested before God commanded him to lead His people. For forty more years, Moses led the Israelites in the desert until his death at the age of one-hundred and twenty (Deut. 34:7). Following Moses in the desert was the prototype for Jesus, that is Joshua. Assuming an early apprenticeship of twenty, Joshua would have been sixty when relieving Moses of his spiritual duties. And Mattathias, father of Judas Maccabee, was an older man when he began the revolt against Antiochus Epiphanes. So it seems that God and the Jewish people chose wisdom over the powers of youth.

But what about David, the youth who slew Goliath. God recognized the heart and soul of David at an early age, but the greatness of the man came with time. He endured the guilt associated with the murder of Uriah and the stealing of Uriah's wife, Bathsheba. His own son, Absalom, rebelled against him and desired the kingdom. So the daily struggles of life, the ups and downs, were what made David. It can be argued in his case and many others that only with age does wisdom spring forth. It is also recorded that his son Solomon agonized for years over the purpose of life. After much troubles, he concluded,

"Fear God and keep his commandments for this is the whole duty of man. For God will bring every deed into judgment, including every hidden thing, whether it is good or evil." (Eccl. 12:13,14) Only a wise man, whose years were tempered by struggle, could conclude this.

So in every case, the greatness of the man came with age, from Abraham down to Matthias. How then could a young man of thirty garner the necessary respect from the elders and the masses? In the Gospels, Jesus sent out seventy-two disciples ahead of him to every town, proclaiming the message of the coming kingdom (Luke 10:1-24). How on earth could this succeed unless the groundwork was already laid? What I am saying is this: the seventy-two were simply alerting the already converted. Judas the Galilean had followers in every city, in every corner of Israel. This call to arms among the zealous followers of Judas seems much more likely than people accepting a call to action from the thirty year old Jesus, an unknown quantity. Thus, the age of Judas the Galilean fits in with the Jewish concept of acquired wisdom while the Gospel Jesus would find little or no support among the elders of each and every city.

In Chapter Nine, I argue that Judas the Galilean/Jesus was crucified in an earlier time, after the tax revolt which began around 6-7 AD. His career ended under Pontius Pilate in 19 AD. If this is true, then Judas the Galilean would have been a seasoned man of fifty-five when captured and crucified. On top of this, his qualifications for leadership would have been greatly enhanced by his earlier association with Matthias. It is quite likely that Matthias was the elder statesman, the father figure to the younger Judas. After the death of Matthias, Judas carried on the mission, and the respect for Matthias would have been transferred to Judas. So even if Judas were crucified in 19 AD at the age of fifty-five, his background would have been similar to that of Joshua or Judas Maccabee. In any case, Judas the Galilean was well respected by the people and was a known national figure. Certainly the people knew of his stand against Herod the Great, his struggle in Galilee and his position against Rome and the High Priest, Joazar, concerning the census tax. Judas the Galilean was famous in his time, and the success of the seventy-two going from town to town only rings true with such a man as Judas.

THE WEDDING AT CANA

The wedding at Cana can be dismissed as an attempt by the Gospel writer, John, to put Jesus on an equal footing with the Greek god, Dionysis. Each could produce wine with a simple hand gesture. However, if we remove the pagan influence of a miracle which flies in the face of modern science, we are left with a simple marriage with two main characters, Jesus and Mary. Putting aside the wine miracle, the only other point in the story concerns those in charge of the wedding feast. (See John 2:1-11) With the wine supply exhausted, Mary was quick to point this fact out to Jesus. Together, they fixed the situation by providing more wine. The logical question is this: would not the bride and groom be responsible for their own wedding feast (or at least the families of the bride and groom)? According to the story, there was no relative being married. So it seems very possible that the wedding celebration was for Jesus and Mary, husband and wife, not son and mother.

First, let us go back to the important Jewish historical characters: Abraham, Moses, Joshua, Mattathias, David and Solomon. Not only did their age secure wisdom but each was married, at least once. Obviously, in Jewish history, it was no sin to be married. In fact, this was the preferred state as God commanded:

So God created man in his own image, in the image of God he created him; male and female he created them. God blessed them and said to them, "Be fruitful and increase in number; fill the earth and subdue it."...The man said, "This is now bone of my bones and flesh of my flesh; she shall be called woman for she was taken out of man." For this reason a man will leave his father and mother and be united to his wife, and they will become one flesh. (Gen. 1:27,28; 2:23,24)

It is easy to see why Jewish religious leaders practiced marriage instead of celibacy. To marry and reproduce were commands in the above stories of Adam and Eve. And those zealous for the Law would be inclined to follow the Word of God over the mistaken traditions of a certain group. For instance, the Essenes in general did not marry but devoted themselves entirely to prayer and following the Law to the letter. However, Josephus did write that a segment of the Essenes did marry in order to fulfill God's command to multiply. I am of the opinion that Jesus fit into this second category.

The ascetic view concerning marriage and sexual relations was put forth by Paul:

I would like you to be free from concern. An unmarried man is concerned about the Lord's affairs—how he can please the Lord. But a married man is concerned about the affairs of this world—how he can please his wife—and his interests are divided.... I am saying this for your own good, not to restrict you, but that you may live in a right way in undivided devotion to the Lord. (1 Cor. 7:32-35)

Although Paul did not forbid marriage, he made clear that celibacy was preferable, the only way to perfectly please the Lord. However, this thinking contradicts God's commands in Genesis.

Paul defended his life compared to that of the other apostles using marriage as an example.

> Am I not an apostle? Have I not seen Jesus our Lord? Are you not the result of my work in the Lord? Even though I may not be an apostle to others [Jewish Christians], surely I am to you. For you are the seal of my apostleship in the Lord. This is my defense to those who sit in judgment on me. Don't we have the right to food and drink? Don't we have the right to take a believing wife along with us, as do the other apostles and the Lord's brothers and Cephas? Or is it only I and Barnabas who must work for a living? (1 Cor. 9:1-6)

The above quote tells us much about the situation in the early Church. First, Paul was fighting for legitimacy from his own converts since the Jewish Christians obviously questioned his credentials. One of Paul's chief defenses was that he worked harder than the other apostles. Note that he and Barnabas did not have the luxury of a believing wife as did the other Jewish apostles, including the brothers of Jesus and Cephas as well. Thus, Paul inadvertantly gave us the evidence that the Pillars of the Church (James, Cephas and John) were married. It is only logical to assume that Jesus, like his brothers and Cephas, was also married.

With the destruction of the Jewish Christian movement in 70 AD, the majority of the Jewish followers of Judas the Galilean, James and Cephas were dead, and so too their teachings. It is only at this point that the mythical Jesus became dominant. This Jesus did not marry or sully himself in any ways of the flesh. He became like Paul, completely devoted to the Lord's affairs. As such, Jesus could not have been married. The Catholics have taken the verse from 1 Cor. 7:32 as a proof-text for their insistence of celibacy within the priesthood. And this is practiced today even though their first Pope, Cephas (Peter), was married.

The real Jesus was married and had many children. His wife was Mary and his sons named Simon, Judas, James and Joseph. This acknowledgement of marriage puts Jesus into our world, exactly where God wanted us all. The forced celibacy was unnatural then and is so today. Jesus was like the other Jews, like his brothers and Cephas; he married and had children. The wedding feast in Cana may be a dim reflection of this fact. And if he were married, then he comes one step closer to Judas the Galilean.

THE EVIL STEPBROTHERS

The orthodox Christian doctrine states that Jesus was the son of Mary and Joseph and his four brothers (or stepbrothers) were James, Judas, Simon and Joseph. Many Christians, particularly Catholics, contend that Mary bore only Jesus and the other sons were to an earlier wife of Joseph. From Chapter Two, the birth narratives have been seriously challenged. Thus, Mary and Joseph may not be historical. But what about the brothers?

It is important to list out the relevant passages concerning the brothers. First, in Mark 3:20-35, the family of Jesus either did not understand Jesus or was against him.

Then Jesus entered a house, and again a crowd gathered, so that he and his disciples were not even able to eat. When his family heard about this, they went to take charge of him, for they said, "He is out of his mind."...Then Jesus' mother and brothers arrived. Standing outside, they sent someone in to call him. A crowd was sitting around him, and they told him, "Your mother and brothers are outside looking for you." "Who are my mother and my brothers?" he asked. Then he looked at those seated in a circle around him and said, "Here are my mother and my brothers! Whoever does God's will is my brother and sister and mother."

Here Jesus de-emphasized familial relationships in favor of a family of like-minded individuals. In all likelihood, the Fourth Philosophy would have had a close bond amongst themselves. But even this would not have superceded his love for his wife and children, who were also members of the group. The Gospels portray Mary and the children as unbelievers.

The most damning indictment of the brothers is found in John 7:1-11.

After this, Jesus went around in Galilee, purposely staying away from Judea because the Jews there were waiting to take his life. But when the Jewish Feast of Tabernacles was near, Jesus' brothers said to him, "You ought to leave here and go to Judea, so that your disciples may see the miracles you do. No one who wants to become a public figure acts in secret. Since you are doing these things, show yourself to the world." For even his own brothers did not believe in him.

The brothers were either jealous of Jesus or wanted him captured in Jerusalem. Their flattery reminds us of the devil (Matt. 4:1-11) and was intended to force Jesus into an unwise decision. In short, these brothers had as much love for Jesus as did the ten brothers for Joseph (Gen. 37).

John played one last trick upon the brothers.

When Jesus saw his mother there [at the cross], and the disciple whom he loved standing nearby, he said to his mother, "Dear woman, here is your son," and to the disciple, "Here is your mother." From that time on, this disciple took her into his home.(John 19:26,27)

According to John, Jesus' own mother was entrusted to John (son of Zebedee) instead of her own sons. This once again separates Jesus from his family in a most startling way: to trust non-family more than flesh and blood would be strange today but even more so in that particular culture. This would have been a monumental slap in the face of James, the brother of the Lord. However, like much of the New Testament, this scene was added for effect. First, there was no John, the son of Zebedee (see next section); the only John was the brother of James, the brother of Jesus. Thus, Jesus was really entrusting his mother (or wife) into the hands of his own flesh and blood brother. Second, if Mary were his wife, it would be common practice to have a brother look after her. And considering the times, the wife and sons would be targets of Rome as well. If the year were 19 AD, then Mary's sons would have been teenagers or young adults and in need of male guidance, such as a strong uncle. With this sad scene at the cross, the Gospel of John ended its campaign of libel against the family of Jesus.

Their treatment at the hands of Luke is not as severe, but likewise, misleading. Luke recorded that the mother and brothers of Jesus were together with the Apostles right after the death and resurrection of Jesus (Acts 1:12-14). However, Luke minimized the brothers' impact on the early Church, not mentioning James the Just until Acts Chapter 15. Thus, according to Luke, the brothers had been turned into believers but their importance to the Church was secondary to the other apostles.

If the brothers were late converts to the Jesus movement and then minor players, why then did Paul lavish so much attention to James, the brother of the Lord? In Galatians, Paul stated that he first met with Cephas and James, the brother of the Lord, three years after his conversion (anywhere from 23-37 AD). Thus, according to Paul, James was already a leader in Jerusalem. Later in the same book, Paul called James, Cephas and John the reputed pillars of the Church. (Note that John is probably the other brother of Jesus and James). Obviously, Paul's version gave preeminence to the brothers while the Gospels and Acts demonize them or marginalize their impact upon the Church. (See Galatians 1:18,19 and 2:9).

This difference was due to the time when Paul wrote his letters versus the dating of the Gospels. When 1 Corinthians and Galatians were written, James and the Jewish Church were powerful forces in Judea and throughout the world. Note that Paul's writings can be dated from 40-55 AD, some fifteen to thirty years before the destruction of the Temple. The Gospels were written a full generation after the Jewish War, where no viable vestige of Jewish Christianity remained. Therefore, the denigration of Jesus' family was a way to separate Jesus from the failed policy of the Jews during the War. And such a separation was intended to deflect criticism away from the Gentile Church. This Gentile Church did not want to repeat the Neronian persecutions of 64 AD, where the Jewish Christians were mercilessly tortured and killed.

In reality, there were no evil stepbrothers of Jesus. His flesh and blood brothers were James and John (named the Sons of Zebedee in the Gospels). These two were also the Pillars as reported by Paul. The stepbrothers of the Gospels were really the sons of Mary and Jesus (see Chapter Six). In short, the family structure of Jesus was much like that of Judas Maccabee and his brothers. And just as Judas Maccabee was a rebel, so too was Judas the Galilean, the Jesus of the Gospels.

CEPHAS, JAMES AND JOHN—THE PILLARS

We have already touched upon these "Pillar" Apostles in other segments of this book, but I feel it is imperative to fully understand their true relationship to Jesus. Therefore, we will once again compare the "Pillar" Apostles of Paul to the Central Three of the Gospels. In Galatians, Paul named the "Pillar" Apostles as James, Cephas and John. (Gal. 2:9) The date of this writing falls within the range of 40-55 AD. In the first chapter of Galatians, Paul stated that he met with Cephas and James, the brother of the Lord, nearly fifteen years earlier or around 25-40 AD. (Fourteen years separated Paul's first two visits to Jerusalem and some time, perhaps a year, had expired after his second trip.) (Gal. 1:18—2:1) So to Paul, the "Pillar" Apostles in our range of years (25-40 AD) would have been Cephas, James the brother of Jesus and John, the brother of James, who was also the brother of Jesus. This is further solidified by the passage in 1 Cor. 9:5 where Paul again named the "Pillars" as Cephas and the Lord's brothers.

The Gospels and Acts also designated the Central Three or "Pillar" Apostles as Peter, James and John. However, this James and John brother combination was different, being the sons of Zebedee and not the brothers of Jesus. In addition, James was martyred in Acts 12, around the year 47 AD. Note the overlap between the James of Paul's version and the James of Acts. Each would have been one of the "Pillars" if we believe both accounts. But that is impossible! Therefore, one account is a purposeful lie, and that fabrication is contained in the Gospels and Acts.

All the apostle lists name two Simons, two James and one John. According to my Judas the Galilean hypothesis: the two Simons were Cephas (Sadduc) and Simon the Zealot, the son of Jesus; the two James were James, the brother of Jesus and James, the son of Jesus; and John was the brother of Jesus and James. In these five individuals, we have the "Pillar" Apostles and the two sons of Judas the Galilean/Jesus, who were crucified in the year 47 AD. When Paul designated James as the brother of the Lord, he did so because there was also a James, the son of the Lord, alive at the same time.

In the last section, the family members were denigrated to help shift Jesus from Jewish history into a spiritual realm, apart from the Jewish Law and the politics of the time (Jewish War). The same process was utilized in the handling of the "Pillars" in the Gospels and Acts. Peter, James and John (the sons of Zebedee) were not as they seemed but were composites of actual people. The formulas are below:

1. Peter represented two individuals: Cephas and Simon, the son of Jesus.
2. James, the son of Zebedee was a composite of James, the brother of Jesus and James, the son of Jesus.
3. John, the son of Zebedee was simply John, the brother of James and Jesus.

First, the Gospel writers removed all familial relationships from the Three "Pillars" so that the brothers and sons were not even considered in the Jesus story. Also, note from the previous section that the brothers were portrayed as nonbelievers before the resurrection and minor players after the resurrection. So in one fell swoop, the brothers and sons were written out of the Gospel accounts, replaced by Peter and the sons of Zebedee.

The passage which helps unravel this confusion is Acts chapter 12, where Peter and James were arrested. Per Josephus, this corresponds exactly to the time when Simon and James, the sons of Judas the Galilean, were arrested and crucified (47 AD). (Ant. 20.102) In Acts 12, the composite James (son of Zebedee) was put to death, which coincides with the death of James, the son of Judas the Galilean. So the only James left was James, the brother of Jesus. And the composite James was killed just in time, as James, the brother of Jesus, was revealed to be the leader of the Church (Acts 15 and Galatians). The composite James played the part of James, the brother of Jesus in the early Church and James, the son of Jesus in the crucifixion of said James. With the removal of the composite James, the real James, the brother of Jesus, could then be introduced.

So the composite James hid the real movers of the early Church, James the brother and James the son of Jesus.

The same process occurred with Peter. However, in this case, Peter is a composite but is identified as Cephas. In the Gospels and early chapters of Acts, the composite Peter was everywhere, doing the job of two men: Cephas and Simon, the son of Jesus. (Note that the Simon of Acts 10 was most likely Simon, the son of Jesus, not Cephas). In the arrest scenario (Acts 12), Peter miraculously escaped even though the real Simon was crucified. This was necessary because Cephas was still alive and kicking. After Acts 12, Peter represented only Cephas. So the crucifixions of James and Simon removed three individuals from the story: James and Simon, the sons of Judas the Galilean, were removed but only as composites of James, the son of Zebedee and Peter; James, the son of Zebedee, passed from the story to make room for the real James, the brother of Jesus.

As mentioned earlier, Josephus cited the crucifixions of only three individuals: Jesus and the two sons of Judas the Galilean, James and Simon. That these three were highlighted should not surprise us, for they were prizes to the Roman authorities. And it is quite likely that the early Jewish Church played upon this in the story of two brothers (the sons of Zebedee in Matt. 20:20-28) who wanted to sit next to Jesus in his glory. Jesus prophesied that they would drink of the same cup as he (crucifixion). Thus, the mother who requested help from Jesus was his own wife, Mary, and the two sons were his own. It could not have been the sons of Zebedee as James was beheaded and John lived a long life according to tradition.

The final bait and switch concerns John, the son of Zebedee. He also was removed from Jesus' family by giving him a fictitious background. Note that if James, the son of Zebedee, was a sham, then so too John. John was simply the brother of James and Jesus. The genius of the Gospel writers is fully displayed in this name game. For two thousand years, people assumed that Jesus was a virgin and had no children; his family was antagonistic towards him; and that the sons of Zebedee were real.

THE TEACHINGS OF JESUS

Using just his intellect and the scientific inquiry of the time, Thomas Jefferson whittled the teachings of Jesus down to three:

1. That there is only one God and He all perfect. 2. That there is a future state of rewards and punishments. 3. That to love God with all thy heart and thy neighbor as thyself, is the sum of religion.(3)

Along with these three, one must also add the love of the Law. Jefferson omitted this as he was a man of his time, not privy to all the research done over the past two-hundred years. For we learn from the writings of Paul that the Jerusalem Apostles, represented by James, Cephas and John, followed the Law to the letter, and it was Paul who taught against the Law. Religious people tend to place the beliefs of Paul onto Jesus while it is much more likely that the views of James and Jesus would coincide.

These four teachings are touched upon in the following passages. As for the Law, Jesus said:

I tell you the truth, until heaven and earth disappear, not the smallest letter, not the least stroke of the pen, will by any means disappear from the Law until everything is accomplished. Anyone who breaks one of the least of these commandments and teaches others to do the same will be called least in the kingdom of heaven, but whoever practices and teaches these commands will be called great in the kingdom of heaven. (Matt. 5:17-19)

Christian commentators have downplayed this love of Law as being transitory, soon to be replaced by the gospel of grace, as described by Paul in Galatians. However, Paul gave us indisputable documentation concerning the group led by James, the brother of Jesus. This group, known derisively as the circumcision, followed the Law on every point, especially the command of circumcision, the physical sign of the Everlasting Covenant between God and His people. This circumcision group existed <u>after</u> the death of Jesus. Therefore, the death did <u>not</u> nullify the Law as most Christians today would argue. James and his circumcision group were simply obeying the precepts of the Everlasting Covenant, just as Jesus had practiced before them. It should be noted that James' disciples were called "zealous for the Law." (Acts 21:20) This is the exact behavior described by Josephus concerning the followers of Judas the Galilean. (<u>Ant</u>. 18.4-10)

The passage which supports two of Jefferson's three teachings of Jesus is found in Matthew 22:37-40:

Jesus replied, "'Love the Lord your God with all your heart and with all your soul and with all your mind.' This is the first and greatest commandment. And the second is like it: 'Love your neighbor as yourself.' All the Law and the Prophets hang on these two commandments."

The first part of the passage was quoted from Deut. 6:5. Most likely, Jesus would have also quoted Deut. 6:4, "Hear, O Israel: The Lord our God, the Lord is one. [One God]" So the essence of Jesus' message was that there was but one God, not three as Christians declare. Also, the love of God was the most important commandment. But to love God, one had to obey God. Therefore, following every aspect of the Law was paramount in the minds and hearts of Jews. And it would follow that if one loved his neighbor, he would also be fulfilling the Law concerning relationships with others. These two commands do <u>not</u> nullify the Law but are a result of obeying the Law. Josephus described the pain and torture the Fourth Philosophy and Essenes would endure rather than accepting another Lord. This love of God was central to Judas and his disciples.

The final teaching concerns rewards and punishments. In Chapter Three, Josephus described what the followers of Matthias and Judas expected in return for their martyrdom. Also, the Pharisees believed in the resurrection of the dead and rewards to those who obeyed God. The passage which most plainly states Jesus' view is Matthew 7:15-23.

...Thus, by their fruit you will recognize them. Not everyone who says to me, "Lord, Lord," will enter the kingdom of heaven, but only he who <u>does</u> the will of my Father who is in heaven. Many will say to me on that day, "Lord, Lord, did we not prophesy in your name, and in your name drive out demons and perform many miracles?" Then I will tell them plainly, "I never knew you. Away from me, you evildoers."

Thus, Jesus placed all emphasis on <u>doing</u> the will of God. Belief or faith is inadequate if it is not supported by deeds. This is completely opposite from Paul's teachings concerning grace and is fully supported by James, the brother of Jesus. According to James, "faith without deeds is dead." (James 2:14-26)

In essence, the teachings of Jesus would be comparable to the teachings of Judas the Galilean and the Fourth Philosophy. The only teachings which would separate Jesus from Judas the Galilean were not truly part of his message but were transferred to him from the teachings of Paul. For example, the Gospels contend that Jesus declared all foods clean. Thus, the purity laws were no longer in effect. This in itself would contradict Jesus' own statement on following the Law (Matt. 5:17-20). But upon further analysis, this belief was held by Paul, not by any of the Jewish apostles. Paul claimed that James, Cephas and those of the circumcision were weak minded in their slavish attention to the purity laws (1 Cor. 8). However, to the Jews, this observance of dietary law was not only healthy but showed respect for God and His Law.

These four doctrines of Jesus were synonomous with the Fourth Philosophy and not with the Gentile mission of Paul. It should be noted that a corollary of the "love thy neighbor" command concerns the sharing of wealth. Jesus wanted people to store up wealth in heaven instead of the accumulation of goods on earth. He said, "You cannot serve both God and Money." (Matt. 6:24) The story of the rich young man also confirmed the importance of sharing.

Jesus answered, "If you want to be perfect, go sell your possessions and give to the poor, and you will have treasure in heaven. Then come, follow me." When the young man heard this, he went away sad, because he had great wealth. Then Jesus said to his disciples, "I tell you the truth, it is hard for a rich man to enter the kingdom of heaven. Again I tell you, it is easier for a camel to go through the eye of a needle than for a rich man to enter the kingdom of God." (Matt. 19:21-24)

If this is true, then most of us are in trouble.

THE TRANSFIGURATION

Jefferson would have had a good laugh while reading the story of the Transfiguration. On the surface, the events appear to be wholly invented, a mad desire to make Jesus other worldly. And of course, this is the case. To place stock in the literal Transfiguration is akin to believing in Santa Claus. In Mark, Jesus picked Peter, John and James to accompany him onto a mountain to pray, six days after Peter proclaimed Jesus the Messiah. As Jesus prayed, a bright light shone upon him, and he conversed with Moses and Elijah. This scene surprised the sleepy apostles, and Peter made the ridiculous comment of building three shelters for Moses, Elijah and Jesus. Just then a cloud enveloped them and God spoke, claiming Jesus as His Son.

It is hard to imagine that there may be some truth behind this ghost story. Hyam Maccoby described this mystical event with perfect clarity as being a Coronation account. The specific six day interval came after the Salutation, where Peter proclaimed Jesus the Messiah. In Near Eastern coronation rites, a full ceremony would come one week after the Proclamation. And these Near Eastern coronation rites often occurred on a mountain. The tabernacle statement by Peter now makes sense because a tabernacle was used to enthrone the king in these coronation rites. The announcement by God was taken from the Coronation Psalm (Ps. 2) which was recited for every Jewish king. And the transfiguration itself signified that the king was being reborn (1 Sam. 10:6).

Luke recorded that the seventy-two were sent out after this to announce the coming of the Messiah. The king or Messiah would tour his kingdom after his coronation, but Jesus needed to take care of business in Jerusalem first. After his success there, Jesus planned to make a triumphant tour of his whole kingdom. That Jesus contemplated this makes the crucifixion a surprise and not a planned event as the Gospels declare.(4)

If Jesus did assume the Messiahship, then this put him on a collision course with Rome. As I have mentioned before, the network built by Judas the Galilean would have had cells of disciples in every town. The seventy-two went forth to alert these elements and to proclaim the eventual overthrow of Rome. So this story, when stripped of its miraculous overtones is nothing more than a political statement.

THE MESSIAH

The Transfiguration was the official coming-out party for the new Messiah. This Messiah was the Anointed One of God or the King, but what else did that title represent to the Jews? Certainly, this title of Messiah conferred upon its owner a status somewhere between God and man.(5) Terms such as the Son of God, the Son of Man, the Son of David and the Jesus/Joshua all represented power beyond the capabilities of mere mortals. Did this make the Messiah God? No, but the Messiah was empowered by God, and God could and would perform miracles through him.

Son of God is an extremely powerful title, linking the Messiah to God as a son is linked to his father through blood. In the Coronation Psalm, God said, "You are my Son; today I have become your Father. <u>Ask of me</u>, and I will make the nations your inheritance, the ends of the earth your possession." (Ps. 2:7,8) Here the Son of God is not divine but has access to the power of God through prayer (also see James 5:16-18).

The Son of Man title began humbly enough but gained in prestige and power as the times demanded. The early version of the Son of Man looks back to the creation of Adam and Eve:

...what is man that you are mindful of him, the son of man that you care for him? You made him a little lower than the heavenly beings and crowned him with glory and honor. You made him ruler over the works of your hands; you put everything under his feet: all flocks and herds, and the beasts of the field.... (Ps. 8:4-8) (Also see Gen. 1:28)

But as time passed, the concept of the Son of Man also grew and this in response to foreign invaders. Now the Son of Man must have dominion over nature and the nations as well. During the time of the Maccabees, the Book of Daniel was written. In it is the more powerful Son of Man.

In my vision at night I looked, and there before me was one like a son of man, coming with the clouds of heaven. He approached the Ancient of Days [God] and was led into his presence. He was given authority, glory and sovereign power; all peoples, nations and men of every language worshipped him. His dominion is an everlasting dominion that will not pass away, and his kingdom is one that will never be destroyed. (Dan. 7:13,14)

If the Messiah were blessed with this type of power, then not even Rome could stand against him. It is understandable why Jesus and his disciples gladly marched into Jerusalem. They had nothing to fear; God would lead them to victory.

While the Son of God and Son of Man terminology verged on transforming the Messiah into a secondary god, the Son of David and Jesus/Joshua designations concerned this world. David and Joshua were both Old Testament heroes, prototypes for all who aspired to greatness. David was the most noted King in Israel's history. As a young man, he slew Goliath, a Herculean feat, and his military career was filled with conquests over the Amalekites, the Philistines, the Moabites and the followers of Saul, the former King. After the coronation ritual (Transfiguration), Jesus set off for Jerusalem, to claim the city as David had once done. As he entered, the crowds cried out, "Hosanna to the Son of David! Blessed is he who comes in the name of the Lord." (Matt. 21:9) His opponents, the chief priests and their Herodian bosses, were indignant that the crowd supported this Messianic claimant. Their association of Son of David with Messiah was unmistakable.

The last designation applied to the Messiah may be the most important, and that is the name Joshua or its variant, Jesus. According to Robertson:

The Book of Joshua leads us to think that he [Joshua] had several attributes of the Sun-god, and that, like Samson and Moses, he was an ancient deity reduced to human status. This would explain why he is put on a level with Moses as an institution of the Passover rite and circumcision, and credited with the miracle of staying the course of the sun—a prodigy beyond any ascribed to Moses. In Exodus [Ex. 34:11] it is prophesied that an Angel in the name of Yaweh, would lead Israel to triumph against the Amorites, Hittites and Jebusites—the very list (lacking one) of the conquests effected by the Lord through Joshua. By virtue of his possession of the magical name he is identified in the Talmud with the mystic Metatron, who is in turn identified with the Logos. Thus, the name Joshua/Jesus is already associated in the Pentateuch with conceptions of the Logos, Son of God and Messiah.(6)

In Robertson's point of view, the name Joshua/Jesus was a Messianic title. He reasoned that the Jesus of the Gospels was not real but rather a story told to give the belief system an historical background. This makes sense when viewing just the Gospels. But we know through Paul's writings that the Lord had a brother. Thus, the Lord was flesh and blood. From the writings of Josephus, the only man who could have possibly worn the title of Messiah was Judas the Galilean. At the Coronation, Judas became the Messiah, the Son of God, the Son of Man, the Son of David and Joshua/Jesus. The name Jesus was a title that Judas the Galilean accepted and one that all followers gladly proclaimed, for the name Jesus meant Messiah, the Coming of the Kingdom of God and the establishment of a new Jerusalem, where the invaders would be destroyed. (See Revelation)

THE LAST SUPPER

Most Christians believe that Jesus initiated the Last Supper, the night of his arrest.

While they were eating, Jesus took bread, gave thanks and broke it, and gave it to his disciples, saying, "Take and eat; this is my body." Then he took the cup, gave thanks and offered it to them, saying, "Drink from it, all of you. This is my blood of the covenant, which is poured out for many for the forgiveness of sins." (Matt. 26:26-28)

This indeed was a confusing moment for the Apostles as they believed Jesus to be the Messiah, the one to lead Israel into the kingdom of God. But now Jesus was predicting his own death and inviting his co-workers to dine upon his symbolic flesh and blood, knowing this seeming disaster would ultimately turn to triumph as his death would lead to the forgiveness of sins.

There are several problems with the above account. It was not unusual for the disciples to break bread together as many passages show (Acts 2:42; Luke 24:30), but the meaning attached to the Last Supper meal was shocking in that a Jew uttered it and his disciples partook in it. Jesus likened the bread and wine to his body and blood. To the observant Jew, this would have been abhorrent, as God officially discontinued human sacrifice with Abraham and Isaac (Gen. 22:1-19), and the prophets railed against the nations for this practice. In addition, Jesus said that this was the new covenant for the forgiveness of sins. In one fell swoop, Jesus was replacing God's <u>Everlasting</u> Covenant with his own. Obviously, the word everlasting was not a focal point of Jesus' message. And to top it off, this sacrifice would forgive sins, thus removing this messy job from God. What I am saying is this: a good Law observing Jew like Jesus would not have said such things. Also, from the discussion of the Transfiguration, Jesus believed himself to be the deliverer, the Messiah, the Anointed One of God. In reality, Jesus did not believe that his mission would end in death.

If the Last Supper dialogue did not come from the mouth of Jesus, then where did it originate? The answer is in your Bible.

I want you to know, brothers, that the gospel I preached is not something that man made up. I did not receive it from any man, nor was I taught it; rather I received it by revelation from Jesus Christ. (Gal. 1:11,12)

Even though Paul had never met Jesus in the flesh, he claimed that Jesus had given him a gospel. This is amazing considering the Jewish Apostles were teaching a different gospel. Paul even admitted that his gospel did not come from any man, whether that be Cephas or James. This mindset is delusional. So we must question whether the following passage actually came from the Jesus of history. In fact, it came from the Risen Christ, the Jesus of Paul's imagination.

For I [Paul] received from the Lord [through revelations] what I passed on to you: The Lord Jesus, on the night he was betrayed, took bread, and when he had given thanks, he broke it and said, "This is my body, which is for you; do this in remembrance of me." In the same way, after supper he took the cup, saying, "This cup is the new covenant in my blood; do this, whenever you drink it, in remembrance of me." (1 Cor. 11:23-25)

This revelation is almost word for word inserted into the Gospel accounts of the Last Supper. Thus, a long-held sacrament of the Church is nothing more than a Law-hating Herodian's vision. Such a celebration did not originate with Jesus and was never practiced by his Jewish disciples, including Cephas, James and John, the Pillars of the Jewish Church.

So where did Paul's revelations come from? An early Church writer, Justin Martyr, said this concerning the Christian's Lord's Supper, "The wicked devils have imitated [the Lord's Supper] in the mysteries of Mithra, commanding the same thing to be done."(7) He also stated that the demons anticipated the Christian mysteries [Lord's Supper] and prepared parodies of them beforehand.(8) The Lord's Supper revelation of Paul was simply a borrowing of the Mithraic Lord's Supper. It is also from Mithra where Gentile Christians stole the idea of "washed in the blood of the lamb."(9)

After this is understood, the picture of Jesus going willingly to his death must be reassessed. Judas the Galilean had become the Jesus at the Coronation (Transfiguration), and he was bent on liberating Israel from Rome, just as

Joshua conquered Palestine. The Last Supper may have been filled with prayer but these were confident prayers. God would not forsake them.

One other element which supposedly occurred during the Last Supper was the foretelling of the betrayal by Judas and the denial by Peter. Jefferson would have questioned the veracity of these stories, as <u>prophecy</u> was unscientific and could not be proved with empirical data. It is quite possible that a betrayal did occur and that Cephas denied knowing Judas/Jesus after the arrest, but the <u>prediction</u> by Jesus cannot be supported. Most likely, these stories were circulated by Jesus' disciples after the events to excuse the failures of Jesus and Cephas. With a Messiah figure in Jerusalem, the chief priests and Roman authorities would have paid at least 30 pieces of silver for information about Jesus' schedule. However, any tie to the mythical Judas Iscariot must be questioned. As already noted, Paul did mention a betrayal but did not name Judas as the guilty party. (1 Cor. 11:23) The Judas Iscariot story simply made for interesting reading. This betrayal also helped explain why Jesus was arrested. As for the denial by Peter, the <u>prediction</u> by Jesus helped insulate Cephas from criticism after Cephas disassociated himself from Jesus right after the arrest. Certainly, Cephas may have saved his own skin by denying his allegiance to Jesus. From what we know of the Fourth Philosophy, this was extremely unusual. A good disciple would have died with his master. But the denial by Cephas may have been <u>ordered</u> by Judas/Jesus beforehand, in order to keep the movement going in case of the unthinkable—arrest and crucifixion.

THE ARREST OF JESUS

When the Last Supper had ended, Jesus and the disciples prepared to leave for the Garden of Gethsemane. "The disciples said, 'See Lord, here are two swords.' 'That is enough,' he said." (Luke 22:38) Now it seems astonishing that Jesus planned to confront the Roman soldiers with only two swords in hand. Surely, he could have mustered quite an army of followers, equipped with all types of weapons. Why then did he act in this way? The traditional view is that Jesus had accepted the fact that he was to die for the sins of humanity. But if that were the case, then why take any swords?

After leaving the house, Jesus took Peter, James and John to the Garden of Gethsemane for a night of prayer. Again, if all were already decided, then why the need for constant prayer? Perhaps this vigil was a final push to gain access to the power of God. Remember the two swords. Jesus and his few disciples were to start the battle and God would finish it. Jesus had plenty of Biblical precedents to support this idea. Gideon was asked to fight the Midianites even though his clan was the weakest in Manasseh and he was least in his clan. Even so, Gideon raised an army of 30,000 men. God said the number was too great because if they defeated the Midianites with such an army, then Israel might boast in its own strength. So Gideon sent 20,000 men home and proceeded with 10,000 men. Still, God said there were too many soldiers.

So Gideon took the men down to the water. There the Lord told him, "Separate those who lap with their tongues like a dog from those who kneel down to drink." Three hundred men lapped with their hands to their mouths. All the rest got down on their knees to drink. The Lord said to Gideon, "With the three hundred men that lapped I will save you and give the Midianites into your hands."(Judges 7:5-7)

At first, Gideon believed his 30,000 men would not suffice, but God led him to victory with only 300 men. As Jesus saw it, this miracle would be reproduced on the Mount of Olives with God leading the way. In fact, the battle and the results had already been prophesied.

When Jesus entered Jerusalem, newly anointed Messiah or King of Israel, he rode into the city on a donkey, as prophesied by Zechariah.

Rejoice greatly, O Daughter of Zion! Shout, Daughter of Jerusalem! See, your king comes to you, righteous and having salvation, gentle and riding on a donkey, on a colt, the foal of a donkey.(Zech. 9:9)

Surely, Jesus and his advisors knew of this passage as they prepared to enter Jerusalem. Like any competent politician, Jesus was placed on a donkey to fulfill this prophecy. So if this were fulfilled, why then not the Oracle by Zechariah.

Then the Lord will go out and fight against those nations as he fights in the day of battle. On that day his feet will stand on the Mount of Olives.... This is the plague with which the Lord will strike all the nations that fought against Jerusalem: Their flesh will rot while they are still standing on their feet, their eyes will rot in their sockets, and their tongues will rot in their mouths. On that day men will be stricken by the Lord with great panic. Each man will seize the hand of another, and they will attack each other. Judah too will fight at Jerusalem. (Zech. 14:3,4,12-14)(10)

From this passage, one can sense why Jesus believed two swords were enough.

The prayer in the Garden of Gethsemane was designed to access the power of God. Listen to the words of James, the brother of Jesus:

Elijah was a man just like us. He prayed earnestly that it would not rain, and it did not rain on the land for three and a half years. Again, he prayed, and the heavens gave rain, and the earth produced its crops. (James 5:17,18)

If the prayers of men could change the course of Mother Nature, then these prayers could also defeat Rome. So why did the prayers of Jesus go unanswered? Reading the passage in Matt. 26:36-46, we note that although Jesus prayed with fervor, his favorite three disciples (James, Peter and John) could not help themselves; they napped through the entire prayer vigil. On the night of God's deliverance of Rome into their hands, these three (the Pillars) could not stay awake. This would be like running for President and not staying up for the election results. Such an idea is absurd but absolutely necessary in order to retain the Messiahship for Jesus. You see, the arrest was not Jesus' fault but that of the Apostles.(11)

All this appears ridiculous to our twenty-first century ideas of sane behavior. But this happened two thousand years ago when miracles were everywhere. All acts of nature and events of chance which could not be explained were attributed to God: from floods, to earthquakes, to plagues to dreams. And it helped that Jesus was well versed in the Scriptures. He believed in the prophecy of Zechariah so much that common sense would appear as an affront to God. That is why only two swords were taken to confront the Roman soldiers. It should not be missed that Judas the Galilean had already participated in a disastrous conflict with the authorities in the time of Herod the Great. In the Golden Eagle Temple Cleansing, the followers of Judas were no more prepared than the followers of Jesus. And Judas was well acquainted with Scripture too, being called a wise man by Josephus, well respected by the people for his knowledge of the Law. So in this blind, foolhardy devotion to God, Judas the Galilean and Jesus were inseparable.

This rush to confront Rome may have been precipitated by Pilate's first acts as procurator in 18 AD. Judas/Jesus had been careful in avoiding the long arm of the law, having evaded Herod and Pilate's predecessors since 4 BC. In fact, the last time Judas had been in Jerusalem was during the Golden Eagle Temple Cleansing in 5 BC. That sedition ended tragically with the deaths of Matthias and many of their young disciples. But a funny thing happened as a result of this debacle: the movement grew. The blood of the martyrs fueled a mighty expansion. (See Chapter Three.) This lesson was not lost upon Judas. Although he believed mightily in the power of God to defeat Rome, he nevertheless had a fall back position. I believe that Judas/Jesus and his close advisors (Cephas, James and John) had already worked out the Suffering Servant scenario based upon Isaiah 53. If Judas/Jesus were captured and killed like Matthias, then his death would serve the movement as well.

In Chapter Seven, the ability to fashion Scripture was an important aspect of the evolving Fourth Philosophy. Judas/Jesus had become the Righteous Teacher and now assumed the role of Suffering Servant. This was absolutely necessary to connect the Fourth Philosophy with God's ultimate plans. If Judas/Jesus had succeeded on the Mount of Olives, such an interpretation would have been unnecessary. In the Gospel story, this alternative plan was put into Jesus' own words <u>before</u> he entered Jerusalem. Jesus clearly told his disciples that he had to suffer and die. Note that this prophecy was no different than the prophecy explaining away the crucifixions of Judas' own sons, James and Simon, and the one where Jesus forewarned the disciples about the false prophets. (See Chapters Nine and Ten.) These obvious failures by the Fourth Philosophy were made into triumphs by showing that the deaths were planned by God and known to Judas/Jesus.

THE CRUCIFIXION

Paul claimed that righteousness was gained through the death of Jesus on the cross, not in the vain act of following the Law.

I have been crucified with Christ and I no longer live, but Christ lives in me. The life I live in the body, I live by faith in the Son of God, who loved me and gave himself for me. I do not set aside the grace of God, for if righteousness could be gained through the Law, Christ died for nothing. (Gal. 2:20,21)

This is the same letter where Paul claimed personal revelations from God, a gospel obviously different than that of the Jewish apostles. (Gal. 1:11,12) These personal revelations had much to do with the pagan religions of the time. Paul absorbed these into his subconsciousness and combined the practice and beliefs of Mithraism into his vision of Jesus. In Mithraism, "the doctrine was that resurrection and eternal life were secured by drenching or sprinkling with the actual blood of a sacrificial bull or ram...or lamb."(12) To be "washed in the blood of the lamb" was the same for the followers of Mithra, Paul and most Christians today.(13) So the Crucifixion to Paul was not only necessary but a good thing as well. For outside of this blood of Christ, there could be no forgiveness.

We have already discovered that Jesus had no intention of being a blood sacrifice for the forgiveness of sins. Such an idea of human sacrifice had long since been discredited by the story of Abraham and Isaac (Gen. 22) and by

God's words to Moses, "Any Israelite or any alien living in Israel who sacrifices any of his children to Molech must be put to death. The people of the community are to stone him." (Lev. 20:2) So the Crucifixion was not a God-ordained sacrifice but rather a cruel punishment of death, ordained by the power of Rome.

Rome had used crucifixion as a punishment for political crimes since the first century BC. The most famous political prisoner crucified was Spartacus (died 71 BC), who led a slave revolt of 70,000. The 1960 movie starring Kirk Douglas shows the crushing power of mass crucifixions, where six-thousand rotted in the sun for three months for all to witness. Such an execution was meant to send a message to the <u>living</u>: follow Rome or follow these poor creatures to the cross.

So the question is this: what crime would you have to commit to warrant a death sentence by crucifixion? The orthodox answer is that Jesus spoke and acted against the Jewish Law and the Jews <u>forced</u> Pilate to crucify him. The Gospels claimed that Jesus supported Roman taxation and did not proclaim an earthly kingdom for himself. At this, Pilate could see no need to crucify him. But the Jews blackmailed Pilate, and he was forced to "wash his hands" of the whole affair. And that is the Gospel portrayal of Roman justice.

That Pilate "washed his hands" of the whole affair does not ring true. After all, it was his job to keep peace in the name of Caesar. And beyond this, Pilate was reported as offering a prisoner release to the Jewish mob. Only an incompetent ruler, unsure of himself and his supporters, would have released a dangerous prisoner in such a manner. Remember, Pilate had the power of Rome behind him. So this was <u>not</u> Roman justice, but it did happen in the life of Judas the Galilean. At the Golden Eagle Temple Cleansing, the high priest stepped down because of a dream where he had sexual relations with his wife. (<u>Ant</u>. 17.166) In the Gospels, Pilate was much troubled by a dream his wife had concerning Jesus (Matt. 27:19), causing him to step down or to "wash his hands". Also, after the Golden Eagle Temple Cleansing and the death of Herod the Great (4 BC), Archelaus did release prisoners to the mob. He did this to appease the people. Thus, our story of Pilate and the release of Barabbas was really the story of Judas the Galilean in 4 BC. (<u>War</u> 2.4)

In reality, Rome accepted all types of religions as long as those religions were not used against Rome. For instance, the religion of Paul would have been perfectly fine with the Roman authorities.

Everyone must submit himself to the governing authorities, <u>for there is no authority except that which God has established.</u> The authorities that exist have been established by God.... He [ruler] is God's servant, an angel of wrath to bring punishment on the wrongdoer. Therefore, it is necessary to submit to the authorities, not only because of possible punishment but also because of conscience. That is also why you pay taxes, for the authorities are God's servants, who give their full time to governing. (Romans 13:1-7)

It is no wonder that Gentile Christianity thrived in Roman lands and eventually captured the government as well. We can take Paul's reasoning even further, to the absurd: God condoned Hitler and the massacre of Jews. Therefore, all men should have submitted to Hitler's desires as he was established by God. (Remember, Paul wrote this when Nero was Emperor.) Can this Pauline dribble be considered anything but utter nonsense? Unless, of course, you belong to the ruling elite, and then it is just good politics. (Paul had Herodian connections—see Appendix 6). Certainly, the Jewish Christians or Fourth Philosophy had a different viewpoint. They had no sympathy for Rome or any other foreign occupying power (remember Judas Maccabee). So the idea of Pilate intervening in purely Jewish religious affairs is not supported by the facts. Pilate and other Roman procurators did, however, have a stake in squashing dissent, and Jesus and his rabble were seen as a dangerous threat. (In Chapter Nine, a case will be made where Judas/Jesus was crucified earlier, in 19 AD).

Now there were two charges leveled against Jesus which would have netted him a crucifixion penalty: refusal to pay taxes and claiming to be a king. "We have found this man subverting our nation. He opposes payment of taxes to Caesar and claims to be Messiah, a king." (Luke 23:2) These two charges are supported by Jesus' popular arrival in Jerusalem (Matt. 21:6-11). The people would support a Messiah who could free them from foreign occupation and taxation. What type of Messiah would support the Roman tax system?

On the tax issue, both Jesus and Judas the Galilean were strongly opposed to foreign taxation. In Chapter Four, we saw that the Fourth Philosophy coalesced around the tax issue during the census of Cyrenius. On the side of the Roman government were the powers-to-be, namely the Herodians and their High Priest. During the census of Cyrenius, Joazar, the High Priest, stood with Rome against Judas the Galilean and the Jewish people. Coponius replaced Joazar in 7 AD with Annas, who officially ruled as High Priest until 15 AD. This Annas also supported the taxation and would have been the archenemy of Judas the Galilean. During the trial of Jesus (19 AD), the High Priest, Caiaphas, and his father-in-law, Annas, accused Jesus of opposing the Roman taxation. As noted above, Paul would have been on the side of Joazar, Annas and Caiaphas. So it was the tax issue which brought Jesus to the cross. Anyone standing in the way of revenues would be crucified as an example.

The second charge of being Messiah, a king, would also have brought swift retribution. Judas the Galilean's disciples would never have accepted Roman rule, since God was their only master. The introduction of Pilate and his overt confrontational style must have maddened the Fourth Philosophy. Not only did Pilate bring effigies into the Temple Courts, but he siphoned off Temple funds for his own building projects. Each of these acts goaded the Fourth Philosophy into action, and it is at this point that Judas accepted the mantle of Messiah or king. He would cleanse the Temple just as he and Matthias had done some twenty-three years earlier. Judas may have been crowned Messiah earlier in Galilee, but the nationwide attention had brought the movement to new heights. By fighting the greatest power in the world, Judas/Jesus would be savior to all people.

Unfortunately, Jesus was crucified with the main charge against him posted upon a placard above his head. "This is Jesus, the king of the Jews." (Matt 27:37). Crucified on each side of him were "robbers". Now from the writings of Josephus, robbers and innovators were designations for Judas' followers. So in reality, Jesus was crucified amongst his own captured followers. (Cephas was careful to escape using Judas' capture in the Golden Eagle Temple Cleansing as an example). Even this is twisted by the Gospels. "In the same way, the chief priests, the teachers of the law and the elders mocked him....In the same way the robbers who were crucified with him also heaped insults on him." (Matt 27:41-44) It is understandable that Jesus' enemies would insult him. These enemies were Rome and those who enjoyed privilege from the hand of Rome: Herodians, chief priests and those sympathetic to the upper classes. But fellow rebels would not have heaped abuse on Jesus. In Chapter Four, we learned that the bandits would suffer all types of tortures without cursing God. It is hard to believe that these bandits were so atypical.

When Jesus had had time to reflect upon the whole situation and the failure that had overtaken him, he cried out, "My God, my God, why have you forsaken me?" On the Mount of Olives, Jesus was assured by his faith that God would rescue Israel as foretold by Zechariah. But now the realization of defeat deafened his senses. Why had God forsaken him? Orthodox Christians believe this is a reference to his being momentarily separated from the Father. But I think it is much simpler: Jesus was questioning the only One possible who knew the answers. And as he died, his followers looked on, not knowing if God would ever answer their prayers.

One other point should be made. The Gospels claimed, "At that moment [the ninth hour] the curtain of the temple was torn in two from top to bottom." Josephus also described an event which happened at the ninth hour.

At the ninth hour of the night, so great a light shone around the altar and the Temple, that it appeared to be the brightness of midday. This light continued for half an hour...and was interpreted by the sacred Scribes as a portent of events that immediately followed upon it. (War 6.290-291) (14)

The Gospel writers took the ninth hour theme from Josephus and made their version say that Judaism was forever charged with the death of Jesus. Josephus said that the sign meant that God was leaving the Temple, and it was to be destroyed. Once again, the Gospel writers "borrowed" an idea and applied it to Jesus.

RESURRECTION

The disciples must have been crushed at the loss of their leader. The words, "My God, my God, why have you forsaken me?" must have terrified and even paralyzed many of them. It was out of the despair that the idea of resurrection occurred to the remaining leadership. Without a resurrection, the Fourth Philosophy would be seriously damaged. After all, would you be attracted to a political party whose king or Messiah had already been defeated in grand fashion? The answer is no. It was only with the resurrection of Jesus that the movement could go forward.

Those credited with the resurrection are Cephas and James, the brother of the Lord. Paul gave them preeminence in the first sightings of Jesus after his death (1 Cor 15:3-8) and the account on the road to Emmaus also happened to a pair of disciples (undoubtedly Cephas and James).(Luke 24:13-35) Thus, the purpose of the resurrection was twofold: to maintain the cohesion of the Fourth Philosophy behind an undefeated Messiah and to use this as a recruiting tool. It is also possible that Judas/Jesus had a fall back position in case of defeat. The "clever rabbi" may have instructed his inner circle to preach the Suffering Servant of Isaiah 53 as well as the resurrection. In this way, confrontation with the Romans was a win-win proposition.

This resurrection was viewed differently by Paul. As a late-comer to the Fourth Philosophy, he did not personally meet the living or "resurrected" Messiah. His only meetings with Jesus came through visions and dreams. Not surprisingly, his interpretation of the resurrection was much different from the Jerusalem Apostles. In fact, the resurrection was the cornerstone of his faith.

If there is no resurrection of the dead, then not even Christ has been raised. And if Christ has not been raised, our preaching is useless and so is your faith....And if Christ has not been raised, your faith is futile: you are still in your sins. (1Cor 15:13-17)

To Paul, everything was useless without the resurrection; there was no forgiveness of sins. Jews on the other hand had the Law (a purpose), and they already believed that God could and would forgive sins. So the viewpoints of resurrection were wildly different between the Jewish Christians of James and Cephas and the Gentiles of Paul. Today, Christianity follows the interpretation of Paul. This is done even though <u>any</u> resurrection is scientifically impossible. It is here that we return to Jefferson. This great man knew that truth went beyond the supernatural, beyond the miracles and superstitions that most hold dear to their hearts. Truth can often be discovered by testing the facts, to see what can pass and what will ultimately fall. The traditional story of Jesus is based upon some actual events, but when the miracles and name games are discarded, we are left with a different view of Jesus. This new Jesus looks much like another man from his own time. That man, that "clever rabbi" is Judas the Galilean.

CHAPTER NINE

THE FOURTH PHILOSOPHY

We have mentioned the Fourth Philosophy in relationship to Judas the Galilean, but further analysis is needed to sort out various problems, such as the incompatibility between the love of God as espoused by Jesus and the assassinations carried out by the Sicarii. Using Josephus as a road map, we will trace the Fourth Philosophy from its beginnings to its tragic ending. This movement was evolving, even during the lifetime of Judas and surely afterwards. But every movement changes, primarily to meet new challenges or to bend to the whims of new leadership. The passage in Chapter Four may be confusing because Josephus described the Fourth Philosophy in terms of the census of Cyrenius (6-7 AD) and continued to the year 70 AD, where the "followers" of Judas helped bring down Jerusalem and the Temple itself. The telescoping of sixty-five years does not let us appreciate the Fourth Philosophy as it developed during the first century.

But perhaps this can be better understood by studying a more recent philosophical movement: communism. In 1848, Karl Marx published <u>The Communist Manifesto</u>, believing that the final crisis of capitalism was at hand. Marx preached an economic communism based upon the workers owning the "means of production". With all ownership in the hands of the workers, Marx envisioned a utopian society with economic equality. This revolution was to occur in the industrialized Western world, not in Russia's backward agrarian society.

Marx had expected this final [economic] crisis in 1848. When it failed to happen, he continued to hope that the next crisis would do the trick. An economic crisis duly occurred in 1857. It had no political consequences at all.(1)

And capitalism continued on, with power becoming more and more entrenched in the hands of a few.

The followers of Marx came to believe that communism would be ushered in with a great war between the industrial powers. In this they were partly correct. The First World War helped create the Russian communist experiment. However, this was inconsistent with Marxist economic doctrine. The industrialized nations were the ones on whom Marx pinned his hopes. According to the Gospel of Marx, Russia had no chance of becoming communist as its industrial production was meager at best. But even this contradiction was explained away by Lenin, who saw Russia as just the beginning. He believed that the rest of Europe would soon fall. In this he was dead wrong.

By the 1920's Stalin had replaced Lenin, and it was through this madman that all nations suffered. He purged his own country of anyone remotely opposed to him. Millions died in the purges and millions more during the Second World War, where Stalin and Hitler combined to reduce the world's population by at least 40 million.

So the dream of equality in 1848 became a nightmare of persecution and death seventy years later. The name communism was attached to both Marx and Stalin. The economic system of communism was tossed aside in favor of a totalitarian political communism, with no freedoms and no real equality. Is it accurate to paint Marx and Stalin with the same brush; one wanted equality for the workers; the other desired power at the expense of the masses? In the same way, we must not sully Judas the Galilean with all that happened forty to sixty years after his death. Times change, people change, and movements change.

THE BELIEF SYSTEM

The Fourth Philosophy did not create new beliefs but merged existing ones. Other philosophies predated it in Jewish society: the Essenes, the Pharisees and the Sadducees. The genius of Judas the Galilean was his ability to combine the best of competing movements to his own advantage. Of the three earlier philosophies mentioned above, Judas intertwined the beliefs of the Pharisees with the practices of the Essenes. Since the Sadducees were few in number, opposed to the belief system of the Pharisees and supported foreign invaders, they were left out of this strange mixture, termed the Fourth Philosophy by Josephus.

Such a combination of beliefs, though not standard practice, can be found in other movements as well. The New Democrats, headed by Bill Clinton, combined the economic policies of the Republican Party (welfare reform and trade policies) with the social programs spearheaded by the most liberal of the Democratic Party (gay rights and abortion rights). Thus, Clinton was tolerated by the middle and had some support from the old Republican right and the far Democratic left. If it were not for his personal life, the New Democrats would have been landslide winners in 2000 and 2002. However, his affairs turned off more people than his policies recruited.

The new philosophy of Judas the Galilean may have had its beginnings before the Golden Eagle Temple Cleansing (5 BC). For Judas and Matthias exhibited behavior which could have been associated with either Essenes or Pharisees. And the later passage by Josephus concerning the census of Cyrenius (6-7 AD) also leaves us with a mixed picture of Judas' movement. To pinpoint the exact date of the Fourth Philosophy's birth may be impossible, but to examine the beliefs and practices is well within our abilities. (Per Chapter Seven, the Fourth Philosophy may have traced their beginnings to the anti-Herod movement of 25 BC, where a group of rebels tried unsuccessfully to murder Herod.)

The Essenes had several practices which were also common to the Fourth Philosophy. Josephus claimed that the Essenes were "contemptuous of wealth [and] communists to perfection."(War 2.122) This fits in perfectly with the picture of Judas fighting the taxation and with later Sicarii burning the debt records to "enable the poor to rise with impunity against the rich."(War 2.427) This love of perfect communism is also found in the Dead Sea Scrolls (Community Rule). Jesus preached the same message and his disciples practiced this in Acts 2:44, "All the believers were together and had everything in common."

Although the Essenes were not a majority party, having only four thousand men (Ant. 18.20), they had colonies in every city.(War 2.124) Thus, the movement of the Fourth Philosophy had possible adherents throughout Israel. When Jesus sent the seventy-two out to proclaim his kingdom, surely each city had an Essene community which either supported him or had sympathy for him. So the spread of the Fourth Philosophy was made possible by an already existing network.

It was no easy task to join the Essenes. In the first year, the initiate was excluded from the group and his temperance was tested. If he passed the test, two more years of character testing occurred within the community. If he was worthy, then he was accepted into the fold.(War 2.137,138) This is consistent with the Community Rule (Chapter Seven) which also had some similarities to early Christian practice. In addition, Paul claimed to have had at least three years between his conversion and his first meeting with the Pillar Apostles. This three year absence may have been his testing period. (Gal. 1:18)

To the Essenes, "Obedience to older men and to the majority is a matter of principle: if ten sit down together one will not speak against the wish of the nine."(War 2.146) I bring this point up because it emphasizes the place of elders in Jewish society. Unlike our own society, where the elderly are often ignored or shipped away to nursing homes apart from the everyday troubles of this world, the elders of Jewish society were the teachers and well-respected by all. That is why I think it very unlikely that Jesus was only thirty years old as he led his revolution. It is much more probable that the masses would have followed an older, more seasoned rabbi, such as Judas the Galilean who would have been at least forty-five in 10 AD. (His younger brother, James, would have been forty-four in 10 AD if he died at the age of ninety-six in 62 AD.)

"They neglect wedlock, but choose out other persons' children, while they are pliable, and fit for learning; and esteem them to be of their kindred, and from them according to their own manners."(War 2.120) The Essenes were so dedicated to following the Law that they viewed sex and marriage as a stumbling block. However, to perpetuate their own views, they had to indoctrinate other peoples' children and raise them up to be Essenes. This may explain why Matthias and Judas taught young men at the Temple. These men were "well-beloved by the people, because of their education of their youth; for all those that were studious of virtue frequented their lectures every day." (Ant. 17.149) This may sound more Pharisee and less Essene, but the concentration on teaching young men may have had Essene roots.

[For there was another sect of Essenes] which agrees with the other in its way of life, customs and rules, and differs only in its views on marriage. They think that the biggest thing in life—the continuance of the race—is forfeited by men who do not marry, and further, if everyone followed their example mankind would rapidly disappear....When conception has taken place intercourse ceases—proof that the object of the marriage was not pleasure but the begetting of children. (War 2.160,161)

The above passage illustrates a huge difference between these two Essene groups. To have wives and children places the religious members in the same boat with everyone else. It is my belief that the Fourth Philosophy attached itself to this more liberal interpretation, consistent with Genesis and the Pharisaic beliefs. In 1 Cor. 9:5, Paul complained that Cephas and the brothers of Jesus had believing wives. Obviously, the inclusion of women in the movement helped it absorb the Essene followers. Which group would you choose?

There is one other close relationship between the Fourth Philosophy and the Essenes: both groups would undergo pain, torture and death before forsaking their God. And both believed that God would reward them accordingly. As for the Fourth Philosophy:

They also do not value dying any kind of death, nor indeed do they heed the deaths of their relations and friends, nor can any such fear make them call any man Lord;...nor am I afraid that anything I have said of them should be disbelieved, but rather fear, that what I have said is beneath the resolution they show when they undergo pain. (Ant. 18.23,24)

Compare this to the description of the Essenes:

Our war with the Romans gave abundant evidence what great souls they had in their trials, wherein, although they were tortured and distorted, burnt and torn to pieces, and went through all kinds of instruments of torture, that they may be forced either to blaspheme their legislator, or to eat what was forbidden them, yet could they not be made to do either of them, no, nor once to flatter their tormentors, or to shed a tear; but they smiled in their very pains, and laughed those to scorn who inflicted the torments upon them, and resigned up their souls with great alacrity, as expecting to receive them again. (War 2.152,153)

There are two possibilities concerning the above account from Josephus. The most probable scenario is that the Essenes and Fourth Philosophy shared a similar view of the afterlife and were willing to undergo all sorts of torture for God and His Law. Note that the Essenes would rather die than eat forbidden foods. This is the same obsession which Paul condemned in James and his followers (1 Cor. 8; Gal. 2:11-13). Or, it may be that Josephus confused Essenes and Judas' followers in the War. Unlike Antiquities, the War had little mention of Judas the Galilean, not explaining or even naming the Fourth Philosophy. It is possible that Josephus corrected his earlier version by attaching the torture passage to the Fourth Philosophy and omitting it from his account of the Essenes. The same can also be said for the number of Essenes as discussed above. In the War, Josephus said, "They possess no one city but everywhere have large colonies." (War 2.124) This implies that the Essenes were a very large group. However, in Antiquities, he numbered them at just four thousand. Again, the inflated numbers in the War may be a confusion between the Essenes and the Fourth Philosophy. Any way we look at it, there was a correlation between the Essenes and the Fourth Philosophy.

In describing the Fourth Philosophy, Josephus compared them with the Pharisees.

But the fourth sect of Jewish philosophy, Judas the Galilean was the author. These men agree in all other things with the Pharisaic notions; but they have an inviolable attachment to liberty; and say that God is to be their only Ruler and Lord. (Ant. 18.23)

So although they had many things in common with the Essenes, their beliefs were essentially Pharisaic.

[The Pharisees were] esteemed most skillful in the exact explication of their laws....[They] ascribe all to fate, and to God, and yet allow, that to act what is right, or the contrary, is principally in the power of men, although fate does cooperate in every action...[and] the souls of good men are only removed into other bodies,—but that the souls of bad men are subject to eternal punishment. (War 2.162,163)

When Jesus prayed in the Garden, he believed it was within the power of men to assist God in His triumph over Rome. Although God was the ultimate force in the universe, men were not mere pawns to be moved against their own free will. In addition, Jesus taught that the evil man would be punished forever in the fires of hell.(Matt. 5:27-30 and 7:15-23) Certainly, the Fourth Philosophy owed much to the Pharisees concerning these beliefs.

[The Pharisees] live meanly, and despise delicacies in diet;...and what they prescribe to them as good for them, they do....They also pay a respect to such as are in years; nor are they so bold as to contradict them in anything which they have introduced....[They believe that] souls have an immortal vigor in them, and that under the earth there will be rewards and punishments, according as they have lived virtuously or viciously in this life; and the latter are to be detained in an everlasting prison, but that the former shall have power to revive and live again. (Ant. 18.12-14)

The diet prescribed by James and his followers was very strict, as noted by Paul in 1 Cor. 8. In this respect, Jesus' followers adhered to the dietary laws, opposed to Paul's more liberal (non-Jewish) stance. So we have specific teachings which tie together the Fourth Philosophy, Pharisaic teachings and Jewish Christianity. In addition, these groups all respected their elders and had similar views concerning the rewards and punishments accorded to the good and bad. Unlike Paul's concept of grace, Pharisees and the Fourth Philosophy counted heavily upon one's righteousness. As James said, "faith without deeds is dead."(James 2:26) To top it off, the early followers of Jesus were known as the "Way"(Acts 24:14) or the "Way of Righteousness".

So there was a solid link connecting the Pharisees, the Fourth Philosophy and Jewish Christianity. Note that both Judas the Galilean and Jesus were called Rabbi or teacher, a Pharisaic designation. Josephus called Judas the Galilean a "clever rabbi" (War 2.433) and Peter referred to Jesus as rabbi in Mark 9:5 (the Transfiguration) and Mark 11:21 (the withered fig tree). We also know that Jesus taught through the use of parables, as did many of the other

Pharisees. And Judas the Galilean's second-in-command (Sadduc) was denoted as a Pharisee by Josephus. Thus, the tie between Judas and Jesus becomes more evident.

An interesting New Testament passage may help solidify this strange mixture of beliefs.

"Master," said John, "we saw a man driving out demons in your name and we tried to stop him, because he is not one of us." "Do not stop him," Jesus said, "for whoever is not against you is for you." (Luke 9:49-50)

Such a saying by Jesus is <u>not</u> consistent with traditional Christian beliefs as espoused by Paul. "But even if we or an angel from heaven should preach a gospel other than the one we preached to you, let him be eternally condemned!" (Gal. 1:18) Yet the attitude by Jesus fits perfectly with Judas the Galilean, that teacher who brought all types of men together. In terms of the Fourth Philosophy, anyone with the desire for freedom from Rome was an ally.

It was the unifying factor of foreign occupation which made the Fourth Philosophy so powerful and widespread. Both Essenes and Pharisees were drawn to this belief system because it took the best of their practices and added a touch of hatred for Rome, popular to the masses and to the teachers as well. Judas the Galilean must have been a very charismatic teacher to keep disparate groups together, but he was helped in his cause by continual Herodian and Roman oppression. Every time the Romans stepped near the Temple or displayed their standards, Judas had a ready made disturbance at hand. And these unifying actions helped solidify his new philosophy amongst the masses. In Acts 21:20, James and the elders said, "You see, brother, how many thousands of Jews have believed, and all of them are zealous for the law." These followers of James were of the Fourth Philosophy. This will be further proved in the following sections which will describe the movement's growth through the writings of Josephus.

PHASE 1—THE BEGINNINGS

The Fourth Philosophy did not mystically arise from a vacuum. The enemies were in place long before the movement officially began. A hatred of Herod the Great helped formulate the resistance, but although people yearned for freedom, there was no unified opposition.(2) This changed at the Golden Eagle Temple Cleansing, where Matthias and forty students were slain for their part in the sedition. This event can be linked to the Root of Planting as described in the Dead Sea Scrolls (see Chapter Seven). This slaughter by Herod brought people together as the Alamo did for Texas independence.

Shortly after the Temple Cleansing, Herod the Great died (4 BC). His son Archelaus replaced him as Ethnarch of Judea (4 BC-7 AD).

> This promise [of Archelaus to be kinder than his father, Herod the Great] delighted the crowds, who at once tested his sincerity by making large demands. Some clamoured for a lightening of direct taxation, some for the abolition of purchase-tax, others for the release of prisoners. He promptly said Yes to every demand in his anxiety to appease the mob. (War 2.4) (see also Ant. 17.204,205)

Archelaus sensed that he had a potential disaster on his hands as the mob's hatred of his father was transferred to him. To avoid a bloody coup, he attempted to appease the crowd by reducing their tax burden and by releasing political prisoners jailed by his father. This short-term effort may have placated some, but the followers of Matthias and Judas were not going to stop their protests.

> At this time also it was that some of the Jews got together, out of a desire of innovation. They lamented Matthias, and those that were slain with him by Herod. The people made a great clamor and lamentation hereupon, and cast out some reproaches against the king also, as if that tended to alleviate the miseries of the deceased....[And out of revenge they wanted Archelaus to] deprive that high priest whom Herod had made, and would choose one more agreeable to the law, and of greater purity, to officiate as high priest. (Ant. 17.206-207)

The followers of Matthias and Judas were incensed at the murders but still their concern was directed towards the Temple and the high priest. Obviously, this opposition group was centered on God and His Law, not just "robberies" as Josephus would have us believe.

Within the year, at the Passover, another disturbance began (4-3 BC).

> But those that were seditious on account of those teachers of the law, irritated the people by the noise and clamors they used to encourage the people in their designs; so they made an assault upon the soldiers...and stoned the greatest part of them [soldiers]...and when they had thus done, they returned to the sacrifices which were already in their hands. (Ant. 17.216)

Here we have the first physical confrontation between the followers of Matthias and Judas and the soldiers of Archelaus. It seems as though the initial strategy of direct frontal warfare was not a well thought out program but rather one designed by the emotion of revenge. Also, note that those that stoned the soldiers at once returned to their sacrifices. This shows that the death of the soldiers was viewed as a victory for God, and that all such clashes would be the good of God versus the evil of Herod and Rome.

As they sacrificed at the Passover, another army of Archelaus came to the Temple and killed three thousand pilgrims in response to the earlier confrontation.(War 2.13) This stopped the Jews momentarily, but they regrouped at Pentecost (50 days after Passover) and organized a much larger army at Jerusalem.(The Acts 2 version had three thousand baptized on Pentecost.) It was at this time that the Romans became directly involved. In Jerusalem, great numbers opposed the Romans while the same occurred in the countryside. Judas at Sepphoris in Galilee (Judas the Galilean), "collected a considerable force, broke into the royal armoury, equipped his followers, and attacked the other seekers after power."(War 2:56) So a full scale war was under way, the forces of the innovators (those aligned against the foreign domination of Rome and their vassals—the Herodians) versus the power of Rome.

Within a short period of time, the outcome was secured in favor of Rome. Gaius captured the city of Sepphoris and burnt it, enslaving the inhabitants.(War 2.68)

Then Varus marched on to Jerusalem, where at the first sight of him and his forces the Jewish armies melted away, the fugitives disappearing into the countryside....Varus sent portions of his army about the countryside in pursuit of those responsible for the upheaval, and great numbers were brought in...[and] the ringleaders were crucified— about two-thousand. (War 2.72-75)

So it would seem that the uprising was finished or at least temporarily halted. For the fanatical Jews, or the "robbers" as Josephus called them, "those foreigners [Romans], who came to reduce the seditious to sobriety, did, on the contrary, set them more in aflame, because of the injuries they offered them, and the avericious management of their affairs."(Ant. 17.277) The brute force of Rome helped consolidate the Jewish forces who were opposed to foreign intervention. The more the Romans mingled in their affairs, increasingly the Jews' hatred for Rome grew, as a fire grows with more fuel. This presence of Rome united the innovators with a tie stronger than life itself.

But one lesson was learned by Judas the Galilean as he watched the city of Sepphoris being destroyed: Rome could not be defeated by a poorly equipped Jewish army. From that time on, the opposition led by Judas the Galilean would rely upon the power of God. Only God could destroy such a powerful foe as Rome. And according to the Scriptures, God had delivered Israel from Egypt, the Assyrians and the Babylonians. God could and would deliver His people once more. So Judas the Galilean set about to mold his followers in the ways of God. As in the past, he reasoned, God would respond favorably to those who followed his Laws.

The Fourth Philosophy was a reawakening. Judas centered his opposition forces in the caves and in all areas where Rome could not easily attack. (Thus, it should be no surprise that the coin data from Qumran is primarily from 4 BC-68 AD). The message was this: Israel must gain independence from their oppressors, both Rome and the Herodian hirelings. And to do this, his disciples must zealously follow God and His Law with all their hearts, minds, souls and strength.

In this. Judas was following the words of Mattathias, father of Judas Maccabee:

"If," said he, "anyone be zealous for the laws of his country, and for the worship of God, let him follow me," and when he said this, he made haste into the desert with his sons, and left all his substance in the village. (Ant. 12.271)

PHASE 2—THE KINGDOM OF HEAVEN

To the disciples of Judas/Jesus, the eradication of Roman influence and the accompanying taxation would have been a move towards the Kingdom of Heaven, where the Jewish nation would be free to follow God and His Law. This is consistent with the Maccabean principle set down by Mattathias to his sons: "recover your ancient form of government." (Ant. 12.280) But as long as Rome and their Herodian puppets ruled, this expression of freedom could not be realized. The chief priests were appointed by the Herodians, from Herod the Great to Agrippa junior. And these priests were often more concerned with politics and wealth than with the ministry of the Temple.

To combat Rome with its influence and military power, Judas understood that weapons alone could not succeed. He had witnessed the slaughters of Jerusalem and Sepphoris, noting the military superiority of Roman forces. The only way to fight Rome was through the power of God; had not Moses led Israel from the clutches of Egypt, and surely it was not Joshua's hand which stopped the sun from setting. But to accomplish what had been done in the far distant past would not come without effort on their part. Judas and his disciples planned to prepare the peoples for the coming of the Lord.

As mentioned earlier, there were two distinct commandments to obey: to love God and to love thy neighbor as thyself. To love God involved following the Law to perfection. "Anyone who breaks one of the least of these commandments and teaches others to do the same will be called least in the kingdom of heaven, but whoever practices and teaches these commands will be called great in the kingdom of heaven."(Matt. 5:19) Here Jesus stressed the importance of each word of the Law and the necessity of following it. This included not only circumcision and food purity laws but the upkeep of the Temple as well. When Jesus cleansed the Temple, he quoted Scripture saying, "My house will be called a house of prayer, but you are making it a den of robbers."(Matt. 21:13) The cynical money-making machine of the Herodians was temporarily placed out of order by Jesus. To Jesus and his disciples, the purity of the Temple was absolutely necessary for the Kingdom of Heaven to be realized.

As for love of neighbor, the Essenes and the Fourth Philosophy (Jewish Christianity) practiced pure communism, where each looked out for everyone else's needs. This was a poor lot, and the idea of sharing would have been heavenly to these hard-pressed Jews. The more one accumulates, the harder it is to relinquish any wealth, as was noted in the story of the rich young ruler (Matt. 19:16-24). Thus, there was a very powerful social aspect to this impending Kingdom of God. That is why the taxation issue was so important.

Judas the Galilean was propelled to the national limelight by his stance against Rome and the high priest, Joazar, during the census of Cyrenius. Josephus said Judas "tried to stir the natives to revolt, saying that they would be cowards if they submitted to paying taxes to the Romans, and after serving God alone accepted human masters." (War 2.118) Note that this was not just a matter of money but religion as well. Judas plainly linked obeying Rome with obeying another master, and he had only one master, God. This is similar to the saying in Matt. 6:24, "No one can serve two masters. Either he will hate the one and love the other, or he will be devoted to the one and despise the other. You cannot serve both God and Money." In the same way, Judas would have said, "You cannot serve both God and Rome." (Note that Paul preached the exact opposite, per Rom. 13:1-7).

Judas preached this Kingdom of Heaven throughout Judea and Galilee and gained quite a following. The census of 6-7 AD may have accelerated his plans. In Chapter Eight, we followed the career of Jesus as told by the Gospel writers. Jesus was made king at the Transfiguration and he rode into Jerusalem as the Son of David, the Messiah. But by traditional reckonings, this took place in 27-33 AD, twenty to twenty-six years after the census of Cyrenius. There are two explanations for the time lapse between these important events.

The easiest one is that Judas remained at large for a number of years, a fugitive from the clutches of Rome and Herod Antipas (Herod the tetrarch). This is conceivable considering the United States is still searching for Osama Bin

Laden, and cannot find him despite having the most sophisticated hardware at its disposal. That Judas the Galilean escaped the Romans and Herodians up to the traditional dating of the governorship of Pontius Pilate is a possibility.

The second alternative is that Judas was captured and crucified some time after the census, anywhere from 7-19 AD. He may have still had an extended three year campaign around Judea, and his entrance into Jerusalem may have been on a donkey, but the traditional Pilate of 26-37 AD would not have been there. As strange as it may sound, Pilate may have been procurator from 18-37 AD, putting him in an earlier era, that of Judas the Galilean. Is there any evidence which supports this argument? I think there is.

For the time period in question (7-19 AD), Josephus either did not possess any knowledge of events or his history was expunged for obvious reasons. Thus, this gap in history cannot be easily bridged. However, Tacitus and Suetonius may provide clues as to the death of Judas the Galilean. Concerning the years 16-18 AD and the issue of taxation, they wrote:

The provinces too of Syria and Judaea, exhausted by their burdens, implored a reduction of tribute. Tacitus, Annals, II.42

He [Tiberius] answered some governors who had written to recommend an increase in the burden of provincial taxation with: "A good shepherd shears his flock; he does not flay them." Suetonius, The Twelve Caesars, Tiberius 32.

From these passages, it is obvious that the taxation issue in Judea was still a hot topic. Certainly, by this time, Judas and his followers would have brought their message to all Israel and perhaps beyond.

In 19 AD, something was amiss in Rome concerning the Jews.

There was a debate too about expelling the Egyptian and Jewish worship, and a resolution of the Senate was passed that four thousand of the freedman class who were infected with those superstitions and were of military age should be transported to the island of Sardinia, to quell the brigandage of the place, a cheap sacrifice should they die from the pestilential climate. The rest were to quit Italy, unless before a certain day they repudiated their impious rites. Tacitus, Annals, II.85.

He [Tiberius] abolished foreign cults at Rome, particularly the Egyptian and Jewish, forcing all citizens who had embraced these superstitious faiths to burn their religious vestments and other accessories. Jews of military age were removed to unhealthy regions, on the pretext of drafting them into the army; the others of the same race or of similar beliefs were expelled from the city and threatened with slavery if they defied the order. Suetonius, The Twelve Caesars, Tiberius 36.

    Something had happened which prompted the Senate and or Tiberius to expel the Jews from Rome. Note that the younger, stronger Jewish men were banished to unhealthy regions. If Judas/Jesus had been crucified shortly before this decree, then the Roman authorities would have had notice to suppress any spontaneous uprisings among the disciples at Rome. Note that only those who did not repudiate their faith were to be banished. This fits precisely with Josephus' description of the Fourth Philosophy; they would rather die than compromise their faith.

    The above conclusion is reinforced by similar accounts in history reported by Tacitus and Josephus. Tacitus described a tale of Temple prostitution which preceeded the expulsion of Jews from Rome in 19 AD. It just so happens that this same event was related by Josephus after the introduction of Pilate and the crucifixion of Jesus. That the Josephus passages should have been in 19 AD is supported by the context of the prostitution passage which occurred in the Temple of Isis, the religion of Egypt. (Ant. 18.65-80) According to Tacitus and Suetonius, the worshippers of Egyptian religion were also expelled from Rome in 19 AD. Thus, the orthodox replacement passage of Jesus may have originally been a passage about the death of Judas the Galilean in 19 AD. In addition, Josephus also related a story of four Jews who defrauded an influential woman who embraced the Jewish religion. Because of this, Josephus claimed that the Jews were expelled from Rome. (Ant. 18.81-84) With this scandal in Rome and the crucifixion of Judas/Jesus in Jerusalem, it is easy to see why the Jews were expelled. This explanation solves a great mystery: Josephus described not only the life of Judas the Galilean in great detail but also his death. Likewise, Josephus never mentioned the life or death of Jesus.

    This sentiment is supported by a Christian apologist, Paul Johnson.

Josephus undoubtedly wrote about Jesus, but presumably in an unfavourable sense for all copies of his manuscript went through Christian control at some stage, Josephus's actual words were censored and an audultory passage was inserted. (3)

    I agree with this assessment except that the text of Josephus would have concerned Judas the Galilean, not the Jesus of the Gospels. It could not have been about the Gospel Jesus because his age would have ranged from twelve to twenty-three (born in 6 BC or 6 AD).

    The only question to the dating of Judas/Jesus' crucifixion in 19 AD concerns Pontius Pilate. The adulterated passage (Ant. 18.63-84) may have originally come after the description of Germanicus' death (Ant. 18.54) and before the first mention of Pilate (Ant. 18.55). But why would the pious editors move information concerning the temple prostitution? I believe that the editors simply changed the Judas crucifixion story into the Jesus crucifixion. In doing this, they introduced Jesus into Josephus' narrative but this by itself did not move the governorship of Pilate from 18-37 to 26-37 AD. To move Pilate from 18-37 to 26-37 AD, two other passages telling of terms of service needed to be changed. In Ant. 18.35, Josephus said that the procurator Gratus served for eleven years (15-26 AD) while in Ant. 18.89, the term of Pilate's tenure was set at ten years (26-37 AD). In context of Josephus' narrative, Gratus probably served three years, consistent with the three earlier procurators. If this were the case, then the introduction of Pilate at this time (18 AD) would make sense. As it stands, Pilate is mentioned as procurator at 26 AD while the narrative returns to 18-19 AD. If the editors of Josephus changed the tenure of Gratus from three to eleven years, then the overall reign of Pilate had to be changed as well, from eighteen to ten years. The reason for this sleight-of-hand was to remove Jesus from 19 AD and from the associated history of Judas the Galilean. Considering all the other changes to Josephus' history, this would certainly be possible. The second century Gospel writers simply used this different era as a way to distance Judas/Jesus from his true history. Thus, historians have focused upon 33 AD instead of the earlier date of 19 AD. These fourteen years have helped hide the true Judas/Jesus for two thousand years.

According to Josephus, the first action of Pilate as governor was to place standards (images of Caesar) in Jerusalem. This enraged the city and those towns dotting the countryside. Jews massed and went to Caesarea, begging Pilate to remove the abhorrent standards. He refused and had his soldiers surround the Jews with swords drawn. The Jews fell to the ground and bared their necks "shouting that they were ready to be killed rather than transgress the Law. Amazed at the intensity of their religious fervour, Pilate ordered the standards to be removed from Jerusalem forthwith." (War 2.169-174; also Ant. 18.55-59) Which groups would bare their necks for the Law? The Essenes and the Fourth Philosophy were known for this type of behavior. So the response to Rome was one of petition yet fierce opposition. The response to God was total submission; like the Golden Eagle Temple Cleansing, the Jews were willing to give their lives for the Law.

Not long after this, Pilate took the Temple money (sacred treasure) and used it for an aqueduct, a prudent act to any Roman. But this angered the people, so that when Pilate came to Jerusalem, they shouted him down. Pilate ordered his troops to mix with the crowd wearing civilian clothes and to use clubs to attack the protestors who were unarmed. (War 2.175-177 and Ant.

18.60-62) Note again that the people were protesting with words, not weapons. (It is very possible that the Fourth Philosophy remembered the Roman style of attack. Later, in the 50's and 60's, the Sicarii would use the same tactics to carry out their assassinations.)

These two moves by Pilate against the Temple and the people of Jerusalem must have goaded Judas/Jesus into his fateful decision to enter Jerusalem as Messiah. It is here that we would expect to see Josephus' description of Judas' second temple cleansing and his eventual crucifixion at the hands of Pilate. But instead, the history of Josephus was altered to include an other worldly teacher, the Gospel Jesus. (For a detailed analysis of Pilate, see Appendix 7).

In Ant. 18.63,64, a passage in Josephus described Jesus for the first and only time.

Now, there was about this time Jesus, a wise man, if it be lawful to call him a man, for he was a doer of wonderful works—a teacher of such men as receive the truth with pleasure. He drew over to him both many of the Jews, and many of the Gentiles. He was [the] Christ; and when Pilate, at the suggestion of the principal men amongst us, had condemned him to the cross, those that loved him at the first did not forsake him, for he appeared to them alive again the third day, as the divine prophets had foretold these and ten thousand other wonderful things concerning him; and the tribe of Christains, so named from him, are not extinct at this day.

Not only is this passage out of character for Josephus (he despised the miracle workers, calling them frauds and deceivers), but it seems that Josephus was a believer. This passage claims that Jesus was more than just a man; he was a teacher of truth and the Christ. In addition, Josephus supposedly endorsed the resurrection! However, in reality, we know that Josephus applied the Star Prophecy to Vespasian and not Jesus. This is confirmed by Suetonius who stated that:

...an ancient superstition was current in the East, that out of Judaea at this time would come the rulers of the world. This prediction, as the events later proved, referred to a Roman Emperor, but the rebellious Jews...read it as referring to themselves....Also, a distinguished Jewish prisoner of Vespasian's, Josephus by name, insisted that he would soon be released by the very man who had now put him in fetters [Vespasian], and who would then be Emperor. Suetonius, The Twelve Caesars, Vespasian 4,5.

The following comment from Origen around 230 AD should clear up the matter concerning Josephus and the passage about Jesus.

...that Flavius Josephus, when, in his twentieth book of the Jewish Antiquities, he had a mind to set down what was the cause, why the people suffered such miseries, till the very holy house was demolished, he said, that these things befell them by the anger of God, on account of what they had dared to do to James, the brother of Jesus, who was called Christ, and wonderful it is, that while <u>he did not receive Jesus for Christ</u>, he did nevertheless bear witness that James was so righteous a man. He said farther, that the people thought they had suffered these things for the sake of James.(4)

By the early third century, our current version of Josephus was not in circulation. Note that Origen said that Josephus did not receive Jesus as Christ, a complete contradiction of the supposed passage on Jesus. By the early fourth century, the passage on Jesus had been inserted into Josephus as told by Eusebius.(5) So if the passage in Josephus is a forgery and the tenure of Pilate has been altered, then there is no evidence outside the Gospels which points to the traditional date of the crucifixion.

But this goes even farther. Throughout this book, I have tied many of the events in the life of Jesus to the life of Judas the Galilean, from 5 BC to 7 AD. In fact, it seems as though the Gospel story has been lifted in part from the pages of Josephus. Now, the first Gospel written was Mark, after the year 70 AD or post Temple. I would move this date back at least thirty-five years, as the <u>War</u> was not translated until 75 AD and <u>Antiquities</u> 93 AD.(6) (This will be detailed in Appendix 4). Note that the <u>War</u> does not include any of the Roman procurators in the intervening time span from Coponius (6-9 AD) to Pilate (26-37 AD) and <u>Antiquities</u> only mentions the three procurators in passing. Since Josephus' writings were so important to Mark's composition, and Mark was totally ignorant of Jewish affairs in this time period, it is my conjecture that Mark used the later years of Pilate's governorship as the time when Jesus was crucified. After all, Josephus did spend considerable time detailing the events in Pilate's career, and it is quite probable that the Jewish Christian traditions about Judas/Jesus also included Pilate. Once these later years of Pilate were set down in stone, the later Gospels simply used the same time frame. The inserted passage of Jesus in Josephus was always in the time of Pilate, but in the early years (18-19 AD). The term of Pilate was eventually altered in Josephus for consistency with other falsifications.

The key to this may be John the Baptist. Remember that John was mentioned indirectly in Paul's epistles when discussing Apollos and the divisions in the Corinthian Church.

What, after all, is Apollos? And what is Paul? Only servants, through whom you came to believe—as the Lord has assigned to each his task. I [Paul] planted the seed, Apollos *watered* it, but God made it grow.(1 Cor. 3:5,6)

Certainly, Paul and the later church viewed the water baptism of John as inferior to Paul's baptism of the Holy Spirit. In Acts 18:18-28, it was alleged that Apollos knew only the baptism of John, and that he was taught more adequately by Paul's disciples, Priscilla and Aquila. This difference of baptisms must have been so well known that later Gospel writers felt it necessary to place John's teachings beneath Paul's. And since the Gospel writers had consistently made Jesus' teachings similar to Paul's, then it followed that John must also be subservient to Jesus.

In <u>Antiquities</u> 18.116-119, Josephus squarely placed John the Baptist in the governorship of Pilate, late in his tenure, approximately 34-37 AD. This is later than even the latest of the dates for the ministry of Jesus, that being 33 AD (and much later than the 19 AD date calculated in this book). Using this later date for the crucifixion, the beginnings of Jesus' ministry then was 30 AD. We are led to believe that John became a follower of Jesus at the baptism of Jesus, yet history tells us that the Baptist was doing his own thing many years later. So the baptism of Jesus by John is pure fiction as is the placing of Jesus in this time period.

Also, the main charge against Jesus in the Gospels is his insistence that the masses not pay taxes to Rome. This particular charge fits in quite nicely with the census of Cyrenius (post 6-7 AD). Judas the Galilean led the rebels against Rome at this time and if he were caught, then only one punishment would be meted out: crucifixion. It is my contention that Judas/Jesus was captured sometime after the tax revolt and was then crucified by Rome. This fits with the history as presented by Josephus and the types of disturbances that were going on. The Gospel story simply moved Jesus into the later Pilate era for synchronization with John as dated by their only source, Josephus.

So Judas/Jesus was either crucified sometime under the Procurators (Ambivulas 9-12 AD, Rufus 12-15 and Gratus 15-18) or under Pilate (19 AD). Either way, the movement hit a brick wall; the Messiah was dead. And if the Messiah were dead, so too the Kingdom of God and the Fourth Philosophy. How did the disciples overcome this crushing blow? How did they make their Messiah into a Messiah for generations to come?

PHASE 3—THE IMMINENT RETURN OF JESUS

As Judas/Jesus hung dying on the cross, it is probable that Cephas and James already knew of the resurrection. They had it planned all along, undoubtedly with the blessing of Judas/Jesus. Without the resurrection, the movement was finished. Would you follow a leader who led you straight to the cross or would you follow one who not only could conquer death but return as a super-human Messiah? The answer was obvious: Judas/Jesus must be resurrected and then return in the near future to lead the Jews against Rome.

It was important to find a scapegoat for Judas/Jesus' failure. The answer was simple enough: the Jews were not ready for salvation. A period of repentance and soul searching was necessary to allow Judas/Jesus to return. In the Garden of Gethsemane, the Pillar Apostles let Jesus and the Jewish nation down by falling asleep, certainly an act which did not merit any rewards from God. So it was very important to convey this message to all Jews: "Repent and be baptized, every one of you, in the name of Jesus Christ [Messiah] so that your sins may be forgiven."(Acts 2:38) Many believed and three thousand were added to their number that day.(Acts 2:41) Thus, the new recruiting tool was Jesus, the Messiah whose time had not yet come. When the numbers were complete, Jesus would return in glory and all disciples would partake in the victory.

How did this waiting affect the movement? Remember, the Fourth Philosophy started as an opposition movement to Rome and continued under the leadership of Judas the Galilean. Now, the Fourth Philosophy would react instead of act. Under Judas/Jesus, they marched into Jerusalem on a mission and expected victory in a few short days. After Jesus, the leaders could only react to events, hoping that Jesus would return as world conqueror. They themselves could not lead armed revolts, because they preached a message of prayer and repentance. Only Jesus could lead them to victory.

In the analysis of Josephus from 19 AD (probable date of Judas/Jesus' crucifixion) to 62 AD (the death of James), one would expect to see little violence but great attention to the Law and the Temple. From 19-37 AD, there is little recorded by Josephus. These would have been the early years of the movement without Judas/Jesus. According to the Book of Acts, the Apostles preached the resurrection and repentance. There is no need to doubt this, but the "Church" would have begun in 19 AD, not 33 AD as claimed by orthodox tradition. It is possible that this was an era of quiet, in that Josephus passed it over. After all, Tacitus stated that in Judea under Tiberius, all was quiet.(7) However, Tacitus' definition of all quiet included the provocative actions by Pilate and the crucifixion of Judas/Jesus. In a much more likely scenario, information about the early church may have been expunged from his record. Either way, from the death of Judas/Jesus (19 AD) to the mention of John the Baptist (34-37 AD), nothing else was reported.

John the Baptist emerged on the scene preaching repentance, a message in-line with the other disciples and consistent with the Book of Acts which stated, "Repent and be baptized for the forgiveness of sins." (Acts 2:38)

Now, some of the Jews thought that the destruction of Herod's army came from God, and that very justly, as a punishment of what he did against John, that was called the Baptist; for Herod slew him, who was a good man, and commanded the Jews to exercise virtue, both as to righteousness towards one another, and piety towards God....[John baptized not for the forgiveness of sins] but for the purification of the body; supposing still that the soul was thoroughly purified beforehand by righteousness. (Ant. 18.116-119)

John's religion was the same as that of Jesus and the Fourth Philosophy: love God and love thy neighbor. He was murdered by Herod Antipas because he had great influence over the people, and this threatened Herod. Again, the Jews did not revolt violently against Herod, but they did see God's power in the destruction of Herod's army. This was a prelude to Jesus' return, where God would lead them all in battle. In addition, John taught that baptism was for the purification of the body, not for the forgiveness of sins, as reported by Acts 2:38. He believed that the soul was purified by righteousness. This teaching was fifteen to eighteen years after the crucifixion, and such beliefs were surely held by other members of the movement. Note that the insistence on righteousness is at odds with Paul's gospel of grace.

The next disturbance came from Rome in the mad wishes of the Emperor Gaius (Caligula), around the years 40-41 AD. Caligula ordered a statue of himself to be erected in the Temple. On hearing this, the Jews "threw themselves down upon their faces, and stretched out their throats, and said they were ready to be slain...rather than to see the dedication of the statue...[they] were ready to die with pleasure, rather than suffer their laws to be transgressed."(Ant. 18.271-274) Again, the response of the most zealous of the Jews was peaceful protest, even to their own death. They were not yet taking up arms against Rome but were showing their devotion to God. In their minds, Jesus would return if they only stood up for God's Law.

If Caligula had lived and his orders followed, there would have been an insurrection in Jerusalem, verging on war. This statue would have been torn down just as Matthias and Judas had brought down the Golden Eagle of Herod the Great. Tacitus recorded the attitudes of the Jews during this period.

Under Tiberius all was quiet. But when the Jews were ordered by Caligula to set up his statue in the temple, they preferred the alternative of war. The death of the Emperor put an end to the disturbance. Tacitus, The Histories, v.9.

This passage from Tacitus has several important points. First, he said that under Tiberius (14-37 AD), all had been quiet in Judea. The only conflict recorded by Tacitus was in 19 AD, and that in Rome. If Judas the Galiean had been crucified for his bloodless rebellion (two swords on the Mount of Olives), then it is likely that such an action would not seem worthy of notice by the Roman historian. This quiet of Tiberius follows Josephus' account of the Jews reactions to events. This is consistent with the repentance phase of the Fourth Philosophy. Secondly, Tacitus stated that the death of Caligula (41 AD) put an end to the disturbance. Certainly, the Jews saw God's power in this. They had offered their lives for God and the Law, and He had answered their prayers. No statue to a divine Caesar would ever pollute their Temple. However, many Jews kept a keen eye upon Rome. Tacitus wrote:

It is true that the Jews had shown symptoms of commotion in a seditious outbreak, and when they heard of the assassination of Caius [Caligula in 41 AD], there was no hearty submission, as a fear lingered that any of the emperors might impose the same orders [setting up statues in the Temple]. Tacitus, Annals, vii.54.

In 43-44 AD, a certain Simon, who "appeared to be very accurate in the knowledge of the Law...[accused Agrippa as] not living holily, and he might justly be excluded out of the temple, since it belonged only to native Jews."(Ant. 19.332) Agrippa was not pleased by this development and had Simon brought to Caesarea for questioning. Like Jesus, Simon was silent before Agrippa, and because he raised no army or made threats, Agrippa decided to let him go. (Note that the Gospel writers copied this behavior in their treatment of Jesus before Pilate, and used this story as a template for Acts 10, where Peter met Cornelius in Caesarea). Once again, the zealous followers of the Law were more concerned with perfectly obeying the Law than with any armed revolts.

Concerning the kingdom of Adiabene, Josephus wrote this very telling story about Quenn Helena and her son Izates. Izates was brought over to the Jewish religion by a Jewish merchant named Ananias, who had convinced the king's women (wives and concubines) to worship God according to the Jewish religion. At the same time, Helena was being instructed by another Jew. This Jew, along with Ananias, convinced Helena to persuade Izates to forgo circumcision.

[Ananias said that Izates] might worship God without being circumcised, even though he did resolve to follow the Jewish law entirely; which worship of God was of a <u>superior nature to circumcision</u>….[however] a certain other Jew that <u>came out of Galilee</u>, whose name was Eleazar, and who was esteemed very skillful in the learning of his country, persuaded him [Izates] to do the thing [circumcision]. <u>Ant</u>. 20.34-43

The timing of this event preceeded the famine, which occurred from 44-48 AD. The broad gist of the story centers around conversion to Judaism. Note that two sets of Jewish teachers instructed Izates in his interpretation of the Law. Ananias told him that circumcision was unnecessary while the Jew from Galilee insisted upon circumcision. Izates submitted to the will of the Galilean and underwent circumcision. It should not be missed that this struggle for the soul of Izates corresponds perfectly with the argument recorded in Galatians, where Cephas and James turned their backs upon Paul for teaching against circumcision and the Law. This being the case, the dating of Paul's letters (Galatians, Corinthians and Romans) may be closer to 42-44 AD, not 55-57 AD as traditionally believed.

After the conversion to full Judaism, Izates and his mother, Helena, sent food and money to Jerusalem to help those starving in face of a serious famine. Josephus wrote that the famine stretched out during the terms of Fadus and Tiberius Alexander (44-48 AD). (<u>Ant</u>. 20.101) Note that in Paul's letters, he was asking the Galatians and Corinthians to send money to the poor in Jerusalem. Such a request rings true with the famine. In addition, the Book of Acts records four trips by Paul to Jerusalem. The first was after his conversion (35 AD) (Acts 9); the second during the famine (44 AD) (Acts 11); the third at the Council of Jerusalem (52 AD) (Acts 15); and the fourth in 58 AD, where he was arrested and imprisoned (Acts 21-28). In the letter to the Galatians, Paul stated that he was in Jerusalem twice, once three years after his conversion and the second, fourteen years later. The last trip can be accounted for, as Paul could not have known about his arrest and imprisonment. But what about the trip concerning the famine?

It is my contention that the trip to Jerusalem with the money from the churches was in connection with the famine. Therefore, Paul could not have written about it for it had not yet happened. This would place the last years of Paul's association with the Fourth Philosophy in the early 40's. The Jews from Galilee were now following Paul and his disciples everywhere, preaching the necessity of circumcision. There is no doubt that Paul was on the outside of the Jewish Christian movement, having been excommunicated. His only hope in retaining disciples came in trashing the apostles. This strategy was employed throughout Galatians, Corinthians and Romans.

The story of Queen Helena and Izates has also been used heavily in the creation of the "Church" mythology. In Appendix 6, the conversion stories of Acts and Galatians were compared, and it was determined that the Acts picture of the Damascus conversion was bogus. There was never an Ananias who led Paul into the city. However, in the story of Izates, Ananias does relate his Pauline version of the law to the king. This Ananias was simply incorporated into the mythology of Acts. In addition, Acts 8:26-40 relates the story of Philip and the Ethiopian Eunuch. This Eunuch relates to Ananias who "got among the women that belonged to the king." (Ant. 20.34) In addition, the Eunuch read Scripture which was then interpreted by Philip. After this, the Eunuch was baptized. In Josephus, Izates was reading Scripture in front of the Jew from Galilee, and he was convinced by this Jew to be circumcised. (Ant. 20.44-45) These coincidences, along with the many other coincidences, must give pause even to the most ardent supporter of the traditionalists.

About this time, things became more interesting. First, Agrippa died around 44 AD.(Ant. 19.350) Since his son Agrippa Jr. was too young to assume control, Rome sent a new procurator, Fadus (44-46 AD). This must have seemed like a step backwards to the Fourth Philosophy. Since the death of Judas/Jesus, those zealous for the Law had waited patiently for the return of Jesus, resisting affronts to their God with prayer and repentance. Surely, it was time for Jesus to return. A generation had passed since the death of Judas/Jesus, and many of the younger followers may have been losing their patience with inaction. Perhaps, they argued, they should follow in Judas/Jesus' footsteps. Just as Jesus strode confidently to the Mount of Olives with two swords, awaiting the power of God, so too they would act.

A certain magician, whose name was Theudas, persuaded a great part of the people to take their effects with him, and follow him to the river Jordan; for he told them he was a prophet, and that he would, by his own command, divide the river, and afford them an easy passage over it; and many were *deluded* by his words....[The Romans] took Theudas alive, and cut off his head, and carried it off to Jerusalem. (Ant. 20.97,98)

Three important points should be noted. First, Josephus shows his utter contempt for Theudas by calling him a magician and saying that he deluded the people. This, of course, was Josephus' attitude. This merely cements the argument that Josephus did not write the famous passage about Jesus, because Jesus was also a magician (healer) who had led a band of rebels in a hopeless cause against Rome (Mount of Olives). Secondly, Theudas was trying to recreate the miracles of Moses, by dividing the river Jordan, and of Joshua, by leading the people across the river. This was a mad attempt to gain God's attention. Maybe it was time for Jesus to return, and such an action would prove the faith of the masses. Unfortunately, Jesus did not return and Theudas forfeited his life. The third point concerns the name, Theudas. This Theudas may have been the son of Judas the Galilean. In the Gospel lists there is a Judas, a Thaddeus and a Thomas. Now Thomas is a nickname for twin. This Judas may have been known as Judas Thomas.(8) In addition, both Judas and his brother Joseph were surnamed Barsabbas in Acts, clearly showing a close relationship between the two. In any event, this Theudas was undoubtedly a member of the Fourth Philosophy.

The Fourth Philosophy (Jewish Christianity) was still practicing the restraint taught by Judas the Galilean, in that any attempt to resist Rome came from the hope in Godly miracles. This was soon to change under the administration of Tiberius Alexander (46-48 AD). At the time of the famine,

the sons of Judas the Galilean were now slain; I mean of that Judas who caused the people to revolt, when Cyrenius came to take an account of the estates of the Jews....The names of those sons were James and Simon, whom Alexander commanded to be crucified. (Ant. 20.102)

This must have been a very stressful time for the inhabitants of Judea in that a famine had stretched across the land. Josephus mentioned the famine and the help which Queen Helen doled out to the people. It was also at this time that the Romans moved against the sons of Judas the Galilean. It is probable that Rome still remembered their father, Judas, and wanted to rid the land of such troublemakers. Josephus does not mention anything else, so we are left to our own imaginations as to why these two were crucified. One thing is certain: the situation in Judea was becoming tense.

As discussed earlier in the book, the Gospel passage where the two sons of Zebedee ask to sit at the right and left hand of Jesus in his glory, relate directly to the crucifixion of the sons of Judas. In the Gospel story, the two brothers were to drink the same cup as Jesus, namely crucifixion. This James and Simon were Judas' own sons and were crucified just like he was, some twenty-six years earlier (if Judas were crucified around 19 AD). It is possible that the time had come for them to mount an attack against Rome, with the same method as that of their father. And once again, Rome triumphed and the radical Jews were slaughtered. This may have been the genesis of a split amongst the Fourth Philosophy, as the leaders were being killed and Jesus still had not returned. The reason for the Gospel story is now clear: like the story of the Pillar

Apostles sleeping in the Garden of Gethsemane, where all blame was taken away from Jesus and placed squarely upon the shoulders of the unprepared, the deaths of James and Simon were not a failure on the part of Jesus but a prophecy come true. Thus, Jesus was vindicated, and the movement should go on as before. Some believed this excuse and others did not.

I believe that the Fourth Philosophy was being wrenched in half, one group following James and the other following those who wished to confront Rome with weapons. Both groups still had the same goal: the liberation of Israel. But the methods were clearly different. James and Cephas still recruited amongst the Jews, but as every year passed their arguments grew weaker. Where was Jesus when Theudas called upon God? Why did Jesus ignore the pleas of his two sons, James and Simon? How long would it be until he returned in glory to fight Rome? Time and circumstances were working against the Jamesian branch of the movement. Those calling for direct confrontation could point to the failures of the miracle workers as proof that a better way must be found. And their way could also trigger the return of Jesus. Remember that Jesus said that two swords were enough. It is possible that the more extreme elements were calling for hundreds of swords.

However, during the reign of the next procurator, Cumanus (48-52 AD), the Jamesian wing still prevailed. Two events clearly show that the Jews were still waiting for deliverance. In the Temple, a Roman soldier lifted "his garment and bent over indecently, turning his backside towards the Jews and making a noise as indecent as his attitude. This infuriated the whole crowd, who noisily appealed to Cumanus to punish the soldier."(War 2.224,225)(See also Ant. 20.105-112) Shortly after this episode another event had the Jews howling. "In one village a soldier found a copy of the sacred Law, tore it in two and threw it into the fire. The Jews, as if their whole country was in flames, assembled in frantic haste, religious fervour drawing them together irresistibly, and on a single summons ran in their thousands from all directions to Caesarea" to petition Cumanus to punish the soldier.(War 2.229,230)(See also Ant. 20.115-117) Although the populace had not taken up arms, it appears as if tensions were growing and that a conflict was on the horizon.

The split in the Fourth Philosophy became more pronounced during the 50's and 60's, under the procurators Cumanus (48-52 AD), Felix (52-60 AD) and Festus (60-62 AD). In the latter years of Cumanus (51 or 52 AD), to avenge a Galilean murder, "the bandit and revolutionary element among them was led by one Eleazar, son of Dinaeus, and Alexander." This element took to arms instead of petitioning the governor.(War 2.234,235)(Ant. 20.118-124) This break in the method of revolt is significant in that it shows that the old guard (James, Cephas and John) was losing its grip of the movement. Under Felix,

Eleazar and his followers were captured and crucified. This Felix was a favorite of Claudius(9), who "indulging in every kind of barbarity and lust, exercised the power of a king in the spirit of a slave."(10)

At this time in Rome (51-52 AD), "because the Jews at Rome caused continuous disturbances at the <u>instigation of Chrestus</u>, he [Claudius] expelled them from the city."(11) The Jewish Christians at Rome must have received word that the two sons of Judas the Galilean had been crucified along with the many reports of Roman affronts to the Jewish nation. It is extremely revealing that Suetonius associated the rebellious Jews with Chrestus or Christ. In fact, the continuous disturbances were at the instigation of Christ. This ties in perfectly with the reaction of the Fourth Philosophy in Judea. (The traditional view of this passage contends that the Jews and Christian teachers were quarreling among themselves. This view does not make sense in the context of world events at that time, although it is necessary to prop up second century Gentile Christian propaganda.)

A short while later a new subgroup was introduced by Josephus.

When the countryside had been cleared of them [robbers], another type of bandit sprang up in Jerusalem, known as 'Sicarii'. These men committed numerous murders in broad daylight and in the middle of the City. Their favorite trick was to mingle with festival crowds, concealing under their garments small daggers with which they stabbed their opponents. (<u>War</u> 2.254,255)

The Sicarii are the assassins who used the element of surprise to their advantage, like Pilate had done some twenty years earlier. They may also have patterned themselves after the ten men who conspired to kill Herod the Great by concealing daggers in their garments. These ten considered this "a holy and pious action" for Herod had introduced practices contrary to the Jewish laws and customs. (<u>Ant</u>. 15.267-289)

Josephus clearly paints an unfavorable picture of these men, saying they murdered others for money and political power, even unknowingly aligning themselves with Rome if it were profitable.

Felix persuaded one of Jonathan's most faithful friends...to bring the robbers upon Jonathan [high priest] in order to kill him [for money]....Certain of these robbers went up to the city, as if they were going to worship God, while they had daggers under their garments; and by thus mingling among the multitude, they slew Jonathan. (<u>Ant</u>. 20.162-164)

The religious aspect of the Sicarii should not be missed. Their target was an unpopular high priest and the money gained could be used for recruitment against Rome—a win-win situation.

The Gospel writers also mentioned the Sicarii under the name Judas Iscariot. Continuing where Josephus left off, they made Judas into the ultimate picture of evil. It was Judas who betrayed Jesus as the Sicarii betrayed Israel. Judas Iscariot was a thief just as the above passage depicts the Sicarii. That the Sicarii were a later group (mid 50's—60's) did not deter the Gospel writers from using them in the 20's.

By this time, James, the brother of the Lord, was an old man. Although well respected by the masses, circumstances had complicated matters. Not only had a separtist wing deserted his campaign for Jesus (wait and see approach), but other more friendly elements were out of control.

In addition to these [the Sicarii] there was formed another group of scoundrels, in act less criminal but in intention more evil, who did as much damage as the murderers to the well-being of the City. Cheats and deceivers claiming inspiration, they schemed to bring about revolutionary changes by inducing the mob to act as if possessed, and by leading them out into the desert on the pretence that there God would show them signs of approaching freedom. (War 2.258-260)

Using the same methods as Jesus, who claimed inspiration and led his followers to the Mount of Olives, only to be captured, these "impostors" followed in his footsteps. Like Jesus, they too were captured and punished. This flurry of activity must have been extremely damning to James and his disciples. With all the attempts to contact God and Jesus, not one had proved successful. This may explain the forward looking prophecy put into the mouth of Jesus in Matt. chapter 24.

Watch out that no one deceives you. For many will come in my name, claiming, "I am the Christ," and will deceive many....Then you will be handed over to be persecuted and put to death, and you will be hated by all nations because of me....So if anyone tells you, "there he is, out in the desert," do not go out...For as the lightening comes from the east and flashes to the west, so will be the coming of the Son of Man.

Once again, the failures of those emulating Jesus were explained away by prophecy.

One other "impostor" must be mentioned. Out of Egypt was one who called himself a prophet. He led "the multitude of the common people" to the Mount of Olives and said by his command, the walls would fall down.(Ant.

20.169-172) The Egyptian, as he was called in Acts 21:38, was again trying to conjure up the same power that allowed Joshua to crumble the walls of Jericho. Like Jesus, he believed fully in the Scriptures. It may be from this episode that we get the infancy story where Jesus came back from Egypt and the quote, "Out of Egypt, I call my Son."(Hosea 11:1) Philo of Alexandria (20 BC-45 AD) claimed that a large following of the Therapuetae was located in Alexandria and throughout all areas where the Jewish Diaspora was strong. According to Alvar Ellegard, this Therapuetae was a branch of the Essenes and closely resembled the Jewish Christian movement.(13) That a "Jewish Christian" traveled from Egypt to Jerusalem to stage a miracle should not surprise us, for followers of the Jesus movement were throughout the Empire. This may show, however, how powerful the movement had become and how worrisome it was to the Romans.

By the beginnings of the 60's, the rifts among the Fourth Philosophy factions were becoming wider. There was a wild debate within the movement: to take up arms or to wait patiently for the return of Jesus. James, the venerated old holy man, still held considerable influence upon the masses, yet an uneasiness was felt around him. Would Jesus return soon or would there be war: Jewish arms against the power of Rome? Surely, James and his followers knew that open revolt was nothing more than suicide. Had they not witnessed the deaths of Judas the Galilean (Jesus), his two sons (James and Simon) and the many miracle workers who called upon God for salvation. And hadn't every armed revolt ended in mass crucifixions. The only solution for James was the return of Jesus. There was no other way out.

PHASE 4 DISINTEGRATION

Before Albinus (62-64 AD) arrived to assume control of Judea, the Sadducean high priest, Ananus, illegally assembled the sanhedrin and accused James, the brother of Jesus, as being a breaker of the law and had him stoned.(Ant. 20.200) This should remind us of the trial of Jesus where an illegal trial was also held. In fact, the trial of James was used as a basis for the trial of Jesus, as the actual trial of Jesus was not recorded by Josephus. In any event, the murder of James was the last straw. No one could stand against those who insisted upon armed rebellion. Only James the Just could have persuaded the masses from going wild, from committing suicide as a nation.

This sentiment is echoed in a deleted passage from Josephus. In the early third century, Origen paraphrased Josephus concerning James:

This James was of so shining a character among the people, on account of his righteousness, that Flavius Josephus, when, in his twentieth book of the Jewish Antiquities, he had a mind to set down what was the cause, why the people suffered such miseries, till the very holy house was demolished, he said, that these things befell them by the anger of God, on account of what they had dared to do to James, the brother of Jesus, who was called Christ; and wonderful it is, that while he did not receive Jesus for Christ, he did nevertheless bear witness that James was so righteous a man. He says further, that the people thought they had suffered these things for the sake of James.(14)

The above passage contains three important points. First, as already mentioned, Josephus did not consider Jesus as the Messiah. Thus, the passage in Antiquities concerning Jesus is a fourth century forgery. Secondly, Josephus considered James a righteous man and that the downfall of Jerusalem was due to his death, not the death of Jesus. This is why the passage was deleted by later Christians. The thought that Jesus was not the direct cause of the Jewish downfall was unthinkable. Thirdly, the attribution by the people that James was the reason why God had forsaken them, rings true when the people also believed Agrippa's army was destroyed because he had John the Baptist killed.

Although the split among the Fourth Philosophy had begun in the early 50's, the final blow was the murder of James. If James were simply a leader of an other worldly pacifist movement and not a member of the Fourth Philosophy, then his death would have had little impact upon Jerusalem and its eventual destruction. However, if James controlled the "Jesus wing" of the Fourth Philosophy movement, then his death would have been the cause of the increased hostilities. Though thoroughly anti-Roman, the Jesus wing held that the overthrow of Rome would occur upon the return of the Messiah. They had nothing against fighting, but their leader had to be Jesus. However, with each passing year and each failure, the Jesus wing was losing its grip upon the masses. This murder of James would have given the Zealots and Sicarii ample ammunition to recruit among the thousands disillusioned by this particular gory chain of events. In fact, James, at the grizzled age of ninety-six, may have been the last surviving member of the original movement started by Matthias and Judas the Galilean in 5 BC. Without James to direct the masses, the ensuing chaos was inevitable.

It is at this time that the Sicarii and Zealots (another war party) occupy all of Josephus' accounts. Under the procurator Albinus and with his express approval, the high priest Ananus profited by stealing tithes from the lower priests.(Ant. 20.204-207) Thus, the class struggle was accelerating.

Now too the revolutionary party in Jerusalem cast off all restraint, and its leaders bribed Albinus to shut his eyes to their subversive activities....Every scoundrel, surrounded by his own gang, stood out from his followers like a bandit chief or dictator and used his henchmen to rob respectible citizens. (War 2.274,275)

In other words, the gangs were robbing the rich and giving to the poor. Josephus viewed these bandits as selfish brutes who kept all gain to themselves. Undoubtedly, interspersed amongst the "honest" robbers were those who selfishly kept the booty to themselves.

In this time frame (64 AD), the great fire of Rome destroyed five-sevenths of the City, that capital called the harlot in the Book of Revelation (Rev. 17 and 18). In Chapter One, Tacitus reported that Nero used the Christians as a scapegoat to deflect criticism from himself. Some historians now see a more sinister past concerning these "Christians." These "Christians" were really members of the radical Jewish sect called the Fourth Philosophy by Josephus. Could it be that without James at the helm, members were taking this war directly to Rome, with swords or even fire? It is possible that the fire was propagated by these Jewish Christians. Such an action would have been consistent with the Jews' growing hatred in Judea and other parts of the Empire. So what was Nero's motive for persecuting the Jews: was he just a good administrator who punished the guilty or were the Christians simply scapegoated for his own actions? This will never be answered without doubt. But at least we should consider that the "Christians" were behind this fire.

Tacitus described the torture of Christians at the hands of Nero, but he never positively assigned the blame for the fire on Nero. "A disaster followed [fire], whether accidental or treacherously contrived by the emperor, is uncertain, as authors have given both accounts."(15) The following passage may further cloud the picture as to responsibility.

And no one dared to stop the mischief, because of incessant menaces from a number of persons who forbade the extinguishing of the flames, because again others openly hurled brands, and kept shouting that there was one who gave them authority, either seeking to plunder more freely, or obeying orders. Tacitus, Annals, xv.38.

Considering the fact that James had been murdered in 62 AD and Saul was once again persecuting the Fourth Philosophy (Ant. 20.214), the anger of Jews throughout the Empire must have been at fever pitch. The above passage seems to be describing actions of the most radical wing of the Fourth Philosophy, not paid henchmen of Nero. Why would a henchman risk the ire of Nero by proclaiming his boss was responsible for the fire? On the other hand, would not the Jewish Christians proudly proclaim the "one" who gave them authority to burn the harlot, Rome!

In any event, Nero blamed the Christians for the fire. By now, the reader should be aware that the Christians were not pacifist Gentiles but members of the Fourth Philosophy. In Josephus' description of the Fourth Philosophy, he stated that they would undergo any type of torture and fear rather than submit to Caesar as Lord. (Ant. 18.23-25) According to Tacitus, those who confessed to being Christian were convicted and put to death. "They were clad in the hides of beasts and torn to death by dogs; others were crucified, others set on fire to serve to illuminate the night when daylight failed."(16) Suetonius' assessment of the situation was much muted: "Punishments were also inflicted on the Christians, a sect professing a new and mischievous religious belief."(17) The new belief was undoubtedly the resurrection of Christ.

Next (approximately 66 AD), Eleazar, son of Ananias the high priest, persuaded the Temple ministers to accept "no gift or offering from a foreigner. This is what made war with Rome inevitable for they abolished the sacrifices offered for Rome and Caesar himself....Their numbers made them supremely confident, backed as they were by the toughest of the revolutionaries..."(War 2. 409,410) Note that even members of other parties were now being caught up in the war fervor. The revolutionary party was now being led by Zealots and Sicarii, while the Jamesian wing was all but discredited.

[Soon after this], their opponents [Eleazar and the Sicarii] rushed in and burnt down the house of Ananias the high priest and the palace of Agrippa and Berenice; then they took their fire to the Record Office, eager to destroy the money-lenders bonds and so make impossible the recovery of debts, in order to secure the support of an army of debtors and enable the poor to rise with impunity against the rich. (War 2.426,427)

This was the ultimate in class warfare. Remember those passages in the New Testament were Jesus and James supported the poor against the rich. Now the movement had taken these words to a new height. To burn and to pillage was not the founder's method but effective nonetheless. This also harkens back to the fire at Rome in 64 AD.

Meanwhile one Menahem, son of Judas the Galilean [probably grandson as his sons were killed twenty years earlier], the very clever rabbi who in the time of Quirinius [Cyrenius] had once reproached the Jews for submitting to the Romans after serving God alone, took his friends with him and went off to Masada, where he broke open King Herod's armoury and distributed weapons to his fellow-townsmen and other bandits. With these as bodyguard he returned like a king to Jerusalem, put himself at the head of the insurgents and took charge of the siege. (War 2:433,434)

Once again we encounter the name Judas the Galilean. Not only had Josephus called him a wise man but now a very clever rabbi as well. It is noteworthy that Judas' grandson used the same strategy as his grandfather had used seventy years earlier. Surely, the stories of Judas' exploits had been told and retold, especially by family members. Like Judas, Menahem broke into Herod's armory and distributed weapons to his followers (see Chapter Three)(War 2.56). After that, he marched to Jerusalem and set himself up as king, similar to Judas/Jesus (see Chapter Eight). However, this Menahem was killed by a rival party led by Eleazar.(War 2.445-447) The remnant of Menahem's party retreated to Masada and committed suicide there in 73 AD as one last act of resistance against Rome. The leader of those at Masada was also named Eleazar, and he too was a grandson of Judas the Galilean. (War 7.253) How fitting that the last members of the Fourth Philosophy were led by a descendent of its original author. It should not be missed that Judas Iscariot also committed suicide in the Gospel accounts.

A few other passages from Josephus must be quoted to further cement the argument tying Judas to Jesus. The first passage regards religious practice: the Jews attacked the Romans near Jerusalem "utterly disregarding the seventh day's rest, although this was the Sabbath, which they usually observed most carefully." (War 2.517) These men, zealous for the law, broke the Sabbath rest. However, a reading of the New Testament reveals that Jesus' attitude of the Sabbath was the same. He definitely kept the Sabbath unless there was a need to break it, such as in healing or in helping someone or in his flight from Herod. To attack the Romans on the Sabbath was in keeping with this philosophy and with a Maccabean precedent. Mattathias "taught them to fight even on the Sabbath day…and this rule continues among us to this day, that if there be a necessity, we may fight on Sabbath days." (Ant. 12.276-277)(see also Ant. 13.12-13)

Several other passages show that the movement that once valued experience and wisdom now placed its future in the hands of the reckless youth. "[In Jerusalem and in the countryside], factions reigned everywhere, the revolutionaries and jingoes with the boldness of youth silencing the old and sensible."(War. 4.133) And a little later, "[Ananus the high priest] roused the populous against the Zealots, though well aware that they would be most difficult to suppress now, numerous, young, and intrepid as they were…"(War 4.186)

And finally one last word about the Zealots. "The dregs, the scum of the whole country, they have squandered their own property and practiced their lunacy upon the towns and villages around, and finally have poured in a stealthy stream into the Holy City..."(War 4.241) In his hatred for the Zealots, Josephus does tie them to the earlier form in that they did not value private property. One must remember that Josephus represented those who highly valued property, and this revolt against Rome was no different than that of Spartacus, one hundred and fifty years earlier. And the results would be the same: as Spartacus and his followers were crucified along the Appian Way, so too would all Judea suffer because of the ideals of one group, the Way of Righteousness or the Fourth Philosophy.

CONCLUSION

Josephus goes into great detail describing the eventual slaughter of the Jews. It is not necessary to go farther in our search because the pattern has already been exposed. The Fourth Philosophy movement mirrored that of Karl Marx's communism, as each began as a way to liberate and each became a system to destroy.

Judas the Galilean, that wise man and clever rabbi, preached the kingdom of heaven and the eventual overthrow of Rome. His followers placed their trust in God, believing that righteousness could bring about a new era, one where God reigned on earth. However, each defeat brought doubt: first, Judas/Jesus was crucified, then his sons and finally James his brother was slain.

The Roman historians Tacitus and Suetonius wrote sparingly of the Jews, but their input only supports the picture left by Josephus. Their three accounts of Jews being expelled or persecuted in Rome occurred in 19, 52 and 64 AD, paralleling the deaths of Judas the Galilean/Jesus, the sons of Judas the Galilean, and James, the brother of Jesus. With the three historians, we are left with a coherent picture of the Fourth Philosophy and its connection with Christianity.

Over the course of forty-three years, from 19 AD to 62 AD, James the Just and Cephas guided the movement against Rome. But time was not on their side; every year the memory of Judas/Jesus dimmed. Those impatient youths not familiar with the early movement were not willing to wait for the return of Jesus. They wanted freedom whatever the cost; and the cost was dear.

The Zealots and Sicarii were completely destroyed by the Roman army. However, tradition tells us that the Jewish Christians escaped the city and the destruction. Considering what we have learned, it seems probable that the most ardent supporters of Jesus would not have fought without him. By the year 70 AD, this Jewish Christian movement was very insignificant. All its original leaders were dead and most of the youth were killed by the Romans. They became outcasts to their own people and were not accepted by the Gentile Christians either. In the early second century, Irenaeus described these Jewish followers, these Ebionites, so named for their poverty.

Those who are called Ebionites...use only the Gospel according to Matthew; they reject the Apostle Paul, calling him an apostate from the law. The prophetic writings they strive to expound with especial exactness; they are circumcised, and persevere in the customs according to the Law, and in the Jewish mode of life, even to the extent of worshipping Jerusalem, as if it were the abode of God.(18)

By the fifth century, the Ebionites were lost from recorded history.

For the past two thousand years, the truth concerning the Fourth Philosophy has been hidden behind false assumptions. No one has searched the New Testament writings and Josephus trying to find this Fourth Philosophy. But it is there. Jesus the Messiah was none other than Judas the Galilean and the Jewish Christians were simply members of the Fourth Philosophy. Everything fits, unlike most other hypotheses about Jesus. We have looked at all the relevant documents concerning the times, trying to tie together Judas with Jesus. If this is true, and I believe it is, then there must be serious ramifications. These will be examined in Chapter Eleven.

THE FOURTH PHILOSOPHY

(The Kingdom of Heaven)

Herod assass. attempt (1)	Golden Eagle Temple Cleansing (2)	Judas hailed as King (5)	Census of Cyrenius (6) Annas High Priest (7)		Caiaphas High Priest (7)		Judas/ Jesus crucified (7)
|---------|---------|-----|-----------|---------------|-----------|-----------------|							
25 BC	5	1	1 AD	7	15	18	19
Herod- Greek influence (1)	Herod the Great dies (3)	Archelaus and Barabbas (4)	Judas opposes census tax (6)		Gratus procurator (7)	Pilate procurator (7)	Jew swindles converted Jewess in Rome (8)

1. Herod the Great was a successful king in that he rebuilt the Temple and accomplished other fine works. He admired the Greek culture, and he desired to pull Judea into that world. To many, this was progress towards a better life. But to a growing number, this accommodation to the Greek world was a step backwards. Ten of these fanatics attempted an assassination, using a technique later employed by the Sicarii (hiding small swords under their garments). The attempt failed, and the ten were put to death.

2. Twenty years after the failed assassination attempt, Matthias and Judas persuaded their young students to pull down the Golden Eagle from the Temple. This cleansing of the Temple was a direct affront to Herod, who had adorned the Temple with this "gift". Herod had the young men arrested, along with Matthias and Judas. Matthias and a number of their young followers were burnt to death while Judas sat in prison awaiting his fate at the hands of Herod.

3. Shortly after the Temple Cleansing, Herod dies (4 BC).

4. Archelaus, the son of Herod, assumed power after his father's death. Sensing his weakness, the mob insisted that he lower taxes and release prisoners to them. Archelaus agreed to their wishes and released Herod's prisoners (4 BC). Some, like Judas, had been imprisoned by Herod for their part in the Golden Eagle Temple Cleansing (insurrection in the city).

5. After escaping the death penalty, Judas and his followers headed to Sepphoris in Galilee. In dire need of weapons, they bravely stormed the armory at Sepphoris and equipped themselves for the fight against Archelaus. What came against them was the power of Rome; the city of Sepphoris was destroyed. Judas learned his lesson; all fights against Rome and the Herodian hirelings must be attempted only through the power of God. Judas instituted his Kingdom of God, and was hailed as King or Messiah.

6. In 6-7 AD, Coponius became procurator of Judea and helped institute the census of Cyrenius. The High Priest, Joazar, helped convince the masses to accept this odious taxation. In opposition to Rome and the census tax stood Judas the Galilean. Judas had spent the previous ten years building his power base in Galilee. The census tax issue brought him nationwide attention, not only from the masses but from the Romans as well.

7. From 7-15 AD, Annas presided as High Priest, a tool of the Roman procurator. Judas the Galilean was a thorn in his flesh, opposing the tax and Rome at every turn. In 15 AD, Gratus became procurator and replaced Annas with annually appointed High Priests. His last appointment was Caiaphas, the son-in-law of Annas. In 18 AD, Pontius Pilate replaced Gratus as procurator. His first acts were especially heinous to the followers of Judas: he brought Roman standards into the city, and he used the Temple money for a building project. This disregard for the Jewish sensibilities brought Judas the Galilean to Jerusalem. His entry into Jerusalem must have caused quite a stir. The Romans had him cornered; he was arrested, brought before his old nemesis Annas and was finally crucified.

8. While the drama played out in Jerusalem, another event occurred in Rome which may have introduced the world to Saul, the eventual apostle to the Gentiles. The unnamed Jew swindled a converted Roman Jewess; he convinced her to send funds to the Temple in Jerusalem and absconded with said money. The unnamed Jew had the same modus operandi as Paul: he claimed to be a learned teacher of the Jewish people; he worked with others in the scam; his victims were naive converts to Judaism; and he promised them the grace of God if they only help those in Jerusalem, the seat of God's holy Temple. This scam provided ammunition for Tiberius and the Senate to expell the Jews from Rome.

THE FOURTH PHILOSOPHY

(The Imminent Return of Jesus)

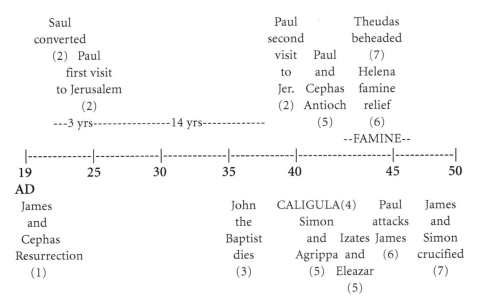

1. The resurrection of Judas/Jesus was the idea of Cephas and James who first reported the event to the disciples (1 Cor. 15:3-8). This may have been the brainchild of Judas/Jesus as a fall back position if the fight with Rome did not succeed on the Mount of Olives. Either way, the belief in the resurrection and immediate return of Jesus helped keep the movement strong and vibrant. As the years rolled along, this position was increasingly attacked by those in the movement who desired action instead of waiting.

2. A few years after the crucifixion of Judas/Jesus, Saul "converted" to the Fourth Philosophy. In Galatians, Paul stated that he went to Jerusalem three years after his conversion experience. Then fourteen years later, he returned to Jerusalem to privately discuss his work among the Gentiles with Cephas, James and John, the Pillars of the Church. Paul's concept of grace and his anti-Law attitude may have developed before his conversion to the Way of Righteousness. The unnamed Jew who started the uproar in Rome (19 AD) also claimed to know God's will, but had earlier been forced to leave Judea for teaching against the Law.

3. In 37 AD, John the Baptist was killed by the Herodians for criticizing their behavior—niece marriage (incest). John championed the cause of repentance.

Only repentance and the practice of righteousness would prepare the way for the Lord. In this sense, John was preparing the way for Jesus. But this was for the return of the conquering Jesus, not the introduction of the earthly Jesus.

4. Caligula was Emperor from 37-41 AD. He planned to have a statue of himself placed in the Temple, to be worshipped as a God. This would have started the Jewish war with Rome in the 40's. Luckily, Caligula was assassinated and no statue was placed in the Temple. This event caused the Fourth Philosophy to examine its policy towards outsiders. After this, the movement became even more exclusionary.

5. Three recorded events illustrate this exclusionary mentality. First, Simon preached that only native Jews should worship at the Temple. This enraged Agrippa, who sent for Simon to appear before him in Caesarea. Second, King Izates was schooled in Judaism by a "Pauline Jew" (Ananias) who preached that circumcision was not necessary. Later, a Jew named Eleazar, sent from Galilee, persuaded Izates to accept full Judaism and be circumcised. Third, the argument between Paul and Cephas was of the same order. Messengers from James told Cephas to withhold fellowship from the Pauline converts as they were not full Jews (circumcised). It is at this point that the Fourth Philosophy turned its back upon Paul. This excommunication enraged the apostle to the Gentiles, and his anger is evident in his letters to the Romans, Corinthians and Galatians.

6. According to Josephus, the great famine raged in Judea from 44-48 AD. Queen Helena and King Izates sent money and food to lessen the suffering in Jerusalem. This same fund-collecting activity was also occurring within the communities of Paul. Paul had started raising money for famine relief before his excommunication by Cephas. The letters to the Romans, Corinthians and Galatians are defenses against the charges brought against him. In the center of this defense was his desire to continue the collection for God's elect in Jerusalem. There is no doubt that Paul brought money to Jerusalem (see Acts 11:27-30), but the money did not go to the Fourth Philosophy but rather to the Herodians (Paul's family). This mismanagement of funds may have caused the fight between Paul and James, where James was seriously injured.

7. Shortly after Paul gained revenge against James, other prominent members of the Fourth Philosophy became targets of Rome. Theudas, basing his revolt on the miracle working methodology of Judas/Jesus, led a band into the desert and was eventually seized and beheaded. This Theudas may have been the son of Judas the Galilean. He may have also been represented in the Gospels as Judas Thomas or Thaddaeus. The second significant arrest of Fourth Philosophy leaders concerned Judas' two sons James and Simon. These two may have been known as the Sons of

Thunder, per the Gospels. These two drank of the same cup as Judas/Jesus; they were crucified.

THE FOURTH PHILOSOPHY

(Disintegration)

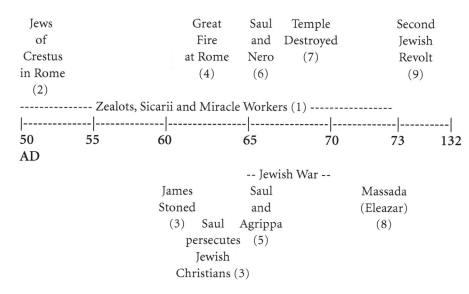

1. A clear sign of disintegration within the Fourth Philosophy was the creation of splinter groups which were now taking control of the movement. Josephus mentions these three groups (Zealots, Sicarii and Miracle Workers) as the main parties now causing trouble. The "Jamesian Wing" of the Fourth Philosophy weakened with every passing year and with each death of its original leadership.

2. Suetonius claimed that the Jews in Rome who followed Chrestus were continually causing disturbances. These disturbances may have been the result of Rome's effort to kill off the Jewish Christian leadership in Jerusalem. Note that the sons of Judas the Galilean had been crucified only a few years before.

3. In 62 AD, the last original leader of the Judas/Jesus movement was stoned to death. James, the brother of Jesus, was allegedly 96 years old at his murder. His stoning is very much like the stoning of Stephen in the Book of Acts. Like the Stephen episode, Saul was nearby when James died.

4. The Great Fire of Rome occurred during the reign of Nero, in 64 AD. Jewish Christians were blamed for the fire, either because they had set it or to deflect criticism away from Nero. Regardless, Nero used these Christians as a scapegoat. His tortures included being torn apart by wild animals, crucifixions and being set

ablaze to illuminate the night sky. Consistent with the Fourth Philosophy, these Christians willingly underwent these horrific tortures rather than deny God.

5. In the beginnings of the Jewish war, Saul was part of the "Peace Party" which desired reconciliation between the Jews and Rome. This desire stood against every faction of the Fourth Philosophy. In 66 AD, Saul escaped with his life from Jerusalem and went to see Agrippa. He petitioned Agrippa for an army to put down the insurgents.

6. After the war broke out, Saul willingly went to meet with Nero in order to excuse himself from the failures in Jerusalem. This was done in 66 AD, two years <u>after</u> Nero had mercilessly slaughtered members of the Jewish Christian movement in Rome. This desire on Saul's part to deal with the devil shows his utter contempt for the Jewish Christian religion of Judas/Jesus, Cephas and James.

7. In 70 AD, Titus led the Roman army into Jerusalem where the Temple was destroyed. The only remaining vestige of the Temple still stands today: the Wailing Wall.

8. When all appeared lost in Jerusalem, a Sicarii band escaped to the fortress at Masada. At first, this must have seemed a prudent move. The Romans encircled the fortress and began a seige which lasted three years. In 73 AD, the Romans broke through the defenses and were about to go on a killing spree. What met the Romans was beyond bizarre. Every last man, woman and child had already been killed, a mass suicide pact. This Sicarii group was led by Eleazar, the grandson of Judas the Galilean. How fitting that the last act by the Fourth Philosophy was led by a descendant of Judas/Jesus.

9. A second failed revolt against Rome was led by Bar Kochba in 132 AD. Remnants of the Fourth Philosophy were still fighting a lost cause. Note that no elements were still clinging to the hope in Jesus' return. If Jesus could not return in 70 AD, then he would never return.

CHAPTER TEN

GOSPEL TRUTH OR GREAT DECEPTION?

For two thousand years men and women have gladly followed the words of the New Testament, believing the message to have been delivered by God to man. And this was not believed by inference; the Gospels and letters of Paul directly invoked the authorship of God, so that we either believe or question the authority of God. It has always been and always will be the nature of man to follow the safest path. Thus, it is much easier to adhere to Orthodox teachings than to question the very words of God. Unfortunately, this has been the position of most scholars and historians. The fear of retribution, from God or from fellow Christians, has silenced the inquiring mind. However, over the past two hundred years, some scholars have attempted to find the real Jesus of history. Their greatest error has been their source documents. Many believed the Gospels and Acts to be filled with truth, with other truths buried just beneath the surface. But as you will soon see, such a path of inquiry is doomed to failure. And this is because the New Testament contains an interesting mix of falsehoods and truth. As the saying goes: garbage in, garbage out.

The Gospel writers took advantage of ignorance and superstition to successfully transmit their ideas by combining Jewish and Gentile teachings with various historical events, culminating in a sorrowful passion play. This powerful concoction of truth, falsehoods and myth created Jesus Christ and his Church. But why would grown men, probably serious and religious, fashion a story which neither relates the actual times and people nor the fundamental teachings of said individuals? Why would they lie?

After the Jewish War, the appeal of Jesus' message to the Jews was for all practical purposes dead. If Jesus did not return to protect his people against the Romans then he would never return, the Jews reasoned. Thus, the decline of the "Jesus Wing" of the Fourth Philosophy began with the death of James and ended when the last throat was slit at Masada. Yet, there remained a small

Gentile Christian movement which had had some contact with the main Jewish Way of Righteousness. These small pockets of Gentiles had been disciples of Paul, who had taught his disciples to follow him as he followed Christ. We know from Paul's own writings that he specialized in deceit; he acted the part of the Jew to win the Jews.(1 Cor. 9:20-22) And when found out, Paul and his disciples were expelled from fellowship by the Jewish Apostles.(Gal. 2) So although these Gentile churches had dealings with the Jewish Apostles, their mission and beliefs were totally different. As Paul wrote: "If anybody is preaching to you a gospel other than what you accepted, let him be eternally condemned....I want you to know, brothers, that the gospel I preached is not something that man made up. I did not receive it from any man, nor was I taught it; rather, I received it by revelation from Jesus Christ." (Gal. 1:10-12)

With the extinction of the Jewish Gospel or the true teachings of Jesus, the churches of Paul had to set out their own Gospel. This was easy enough if it just concerned spreading the message of grace and the cross. But the real problem centered upon the attachment of these sometimes anti-Jewish teachings to Jesus. Thus, the serious scholars of the late first and early second century had to build a framework in which Jesus could be hidden from history and where he could espouse Paul's ideas. Thus, Paul's concept of grace was placed back in history. The stumbling, bumbling Jewish Apostles were needed to show how the Jews misunderstood the teachings of Jesus. It was only when Peter met Cornelius in Acts 10 that the Jewish Apostles were enlighted to Paul's theology (and the supposed theology of Jesus). This whole history seems laughable since it is so unlikely to have happened this way, but it has miraculously survived the times.

The persecution of Christians also weighed heavily on the decision to distance Jesus from his Jewish heritage. Even after the Jewish war of 70 AD, the Fourth Philosophy survived, although the Jesus wing had been discredited. This Fourth Philosophy continued to agitate the people against Rome and finally brought about a second and final Jewish war; this time spearheaded by Bar Kochba in 132 AD. Thus, from 70-132 AD, Gentile Christians were easily confused with the Fourth Philosophy which had once taught about Judas/Jesus, the Messiah. This confusion among the Roman persecutors is best illustrated by a letter from Pliny to Trajan in 112 AD. In it, Pliny wrote that many of those who were charged with being Christian recanted and worshipped the image of Caesar and "cursed Christ, a thing...genuine Christians cannot be induced to do."(1) Surely, the legend of the Jewish Christians or Fourth Philosophy was still alive at this time. But the behavior of these "Christians" who recanted was totally inconsistent with the Jewish Christians or members of the Fourth Philosophy who even after the defeat of 70 AD were described by Josephus as steadfast.

Subjected to every form of torture and bodily suffering that could be thought of, for the one purpose of making them acknowledge Caesar as lord, not a man gave in or came near to saying it.... (War 7.418)

The Gospels were written in this era of persecution (100-132 AD). The Gentile Christians had to weather the storm of hatred brought upon them by the memory of the Jewish Christian movement. Unlike the Jewish Christians, the Gentile followers of Paul did not exhibit, as a whole, the utter devotion to God. Instead, most recanted rather than risk their own lives. In fact, this may have been a Gentile Christian strategy of survival, just as the Gospels were used to deflect criticism away from the Gentiles onto the Jews.

In this chapter, I will explore the different strands that are woven throughout the Gospels and Acts. These are as follows:

1. the actual Jewish teachings of Jesus,
2. the teachings of Paul which are attributed to Jesus,
3. the Jewish excuses of why Jesus failed,
4. the fulfillment of Old Testament Scriptures,
5. the framework of Josephus used to develop Jesus,
6. the framework of Paul's letters which were used to develop Church history,
7. and the use of second century events and culture.

When all these disparate elements are brought together, we find Jesus Christ as described in the Gospels. The only authentic pieces of information were the Jewish teachings, the history of Josephus (describing Judas the Galilean) and the Jewish excuses of Jesus' failures. All else was included to throw us and the Roman persecutors off the scent.

THE TEACHINGS OF JESUS

It is not an easy thing to distinguish the actual teachings of Jesus from those placed into his mouth by second century writers. Some passages appear authentic until given away by a theology different from the early first century Jews. The real Jesus had the following attributes: he followed the Law; he credited God with miracles; and he concentrated his message on sharing and purity. Any other teachings must be treated with the greatest suspicion.

The most obvious passage concerning the Law is found in Matthew 5:17-19.

Do not think that I have come to abolish the Law or the Prophets; I have not come to abolish them but to fulfill them. I tell you the truth, until heaven and earth disappear, not the smallest letter, not the least stroke of a pen, will by any means disappear from the Law until everything is accomplished. Anyone who breaks one of the least of these commandments and teaches others to do the same will be called least in the kingdom of heaven, but whoever practices and teaches these commands will be called great in the kingdom of heaven.

This passage has long been pushed under the carpet by Christian commentators. They argue that the resurrection was the completion of the Law. If this were the case, then following the Law was unnecessary. But was that what Jesus believed? It is interesting that the Jewish disciples of Jesus still worshipped at the Temple and followed the Jewish Law. And these acts of Jewish piety were recorded in the Book of Acts. If Jesus taught that the Law was no longer necessary, then why were his disciples so scrupulous in following it. In fact, by the year 50 AD, the pillar Apostles (Cephas, James and John) were still attached to the Law; their very teachings the object which Paul condemned as "another Gospel". (Gal. 1)

Note that the above passage says to perfectly follow the Law until heaven and earth disappear. Now, since heaven and earth have not disappeared, it seems logical that true followers of Jesus would still adhere to the Law. And that is exactly the position of the Fourth Philosophy, espoused by Judas the Galilean. The traditional interpretation of this passage is dependent on Paul's theology (rejected by the pillar Apostles) and the subsequent second century spin.

Other passages also concentrate upon the importance of the Law. An interesting passage to consider is Mark 7:1-23—Clean and Unclean foods. In this passage, Jesus denounced those who were substituting the traditions of man for the commands of God. Jesus said that it was wrong to withhold money (or help) from your parents because said money was promised to the Temple. Note that one of the Ten Commandments was "Honor your Father and Mother." To withhold help to them would break the commandment. Jesus then complained that the ritual washings were not always necessary, citing the above example of Law over tradition. But did Jesus ever declare all foods clean? The interpretation given in Mark 7:19 contends that his argument favored the abolition of the Old Testament purity laws. But that is absolutely false! Note that Jesus would not have upheld the Law concerning parents and then turn around and say the laws of God concerning foods were null and void. No teacher worth his own salt could possibly be that incoherent. The confusion was undoubtedly sown by the Gospel writers who plainly followed Pauline theology.

One other set of passages relate to the issue of the Law. These sayings concern the Sabbath. Now remember that Jesus upheld all of God's commandments, with the Sabbath being central to Jewish life. Therefore, any interpretation of the Sabbath passages must be made within these parameters. The passage in Mark 3:1-6 deals with a healing on the Sabbath which was opposed by the Pharisees and Herodians. Here the New Testament pits Jesus against other Jewish sects. But before accepting the opponents as reported, let us examine each sect separately. First, the Herodians were not a sect as reported by Josephus but rather a ruling elite, descended from Herod the Great. These individuals would have been against Jesus every step of the way because of his stance on taxes. (Judas the Galilean/Jesus championed the little man against the power of Roman taxation and their hirelings, the Herodians.) To include the Herodians in any argument over the interpretation of the Law was simply placed into the story to muddy the waters. They would have hated Jesus, but not because of his views of the Sabbath.

In the earlier passage concerning the commands of God versus the traditions of man, Jesus weighed in on God's side. The same is true in his understanding of the Sabbath. When Jesus healed on the Sabbath, he was doing good to his fellow Jew, thus fulfilling the command to love thy neighbor. And in his opinion, he was not breaking the Sabbath law. The Maccabees had also made it a point that battle was allowable on the Sabbath if it were in self defense. They argued that God did not want his people to be slaughtered because of the Sabbath. Thus, Jesus was simply following in the footsteps of Judas Maccabee in his Sabbath interpretation. But by questioning the established traditions, Jesus may have insulted many Pharisees. It is most probable that a number (not all) of Pharisees would have been outraged. But these Pharisees would have been outside the Way of Righteousness. From Chapter Four, we must remember that Judas/Jesus' second-in-command was a Pharisee. So the opposition by the Pharisees consisted of a segment of that particular sect.

This thinking is further illustrated in Matthew 12:1-14. Here Jesus and his disciples were picking heads of grain on the Sabbath because they were hungry. Some Pharisees rebuked Jesus, but his answer to their charges put the whole episode into focus. Jesus would not have purposely broken the Sabbath, and his reason for picking grain was based upon an event that occurred in the life of David. While being chased and in danger of losing his life, David gave permission for his followers to eat consecrated bread. This was done out of necessity. In the same way, Jesus and his disciples may have been under extreme stress, in that the authorities were pursuing them. Thus, the picking of grain was wholly justified.

Matthew puts his spin on the Sabbath events with the following: "But the Pharisees went out and plotted how they might kill Jesus." This sinister plot by the Pharisees again places them firmly against Jesus. But another passage in Luke 13:31 may shed some light on the confusion. "At that time some Pharisees came to Jesus and said to him, 'Leave this place and go somewhere else. Herod wants to kill you.'" It appears as if there were actually some good Pharisees wishing to help preserve Jesus' life. In actuality, it was the Herodians who wanted to silence Jesus and they may have been assisted by some unscrupulous and well paid Pharisees. But to blame the majority of Pharisees cannot by supported from the New Testament and certainly not from the pages of Josephus.

The second test of authenticity revolves around miracles. But even here there is a problem. Some miracles were no doubt Jewish stories about Jesus while others were second century Gentile stories intertwined with the earlier traditions. Miracles would have been accepted by both Jews and Gentiles, so the exclusion of these events (a la Thomas Jefferson) may have helped explain what really happened but does not help to identify the source. You see, the Jews' history was steeped with miracles, from the Exodus to the miracles of Elisha. Even the letter of James referred to the supernatural.

Elijah was a man just like us. He prayed earnestly that it would not rain, and it did not rain on the land for three and a half years. Again he prayed, and the heavens gave rain, and the earth produced its crops. (James 5:17,18)

One overriding point must be made. James credited God and not Elijah for providing this miracle. Elijah prayed, but it was God who delivered. James also said in verse 16: "The prayer of a righteous man is powerful and effective." To James, the power of prayer was limitless as God's power was limitless. But to access that power one had to pray and be righteous. Jesus would have had unlimited access to the power of God by this definition.

So the events in Mark 4:35-41 where Jesus calmed the storm and in Mark 6:45-56 where Jesus walked on the water are consistent with the Jewish pattern of a holy man. Whether they really happened or not is not the question at hand. Were they early Jewish traditions about Jesus is what needs to be answered. From the passage in James, there is nothing here which is outside Jewish thought. However, there are some miracle passages which are not consistent with the above definition. Those will be explained in the section detailing the Pauline influences on the Gospels.

The third group of passages which can be directly assigned to Jesus concern his teachings on sharing, doing (works) and sincerity (honesty). The most famous parable expressing these Jewish ideals is the Parable of the Sower, found in Mark 4:1-20.

Listen! A farmer went out to sow his seed. As he was scattering the seed, some fell along the path, and the birds came and ate it up. Some fell on rocky places, where it did not have much soil. It sprang up quickly, because the soil was shallow. But when the sun came up, the plants were scorched, and they withered because they had no root. Other seed fell among thorns, which grew up and choked the plants, so that they did not bear grain. Still other seed fell on good soil. It came up, grew and produced a crop, multiplying thirty, sixty, or even a hundred times....Don't you understand this parable? How then will you understand any parable? The farmer sows the word. Some people are like seed along the path, where the word is sown. As soon as they hear it, Satan comes and takes away the word that was sown in them. Others, like seed sown on rocky places, hear the word and at once receive it with joy. But since they have no root, they last only a short time. When trouble or persecution comes because of the word, they quickly fall away. Still others, like seed sown among thorns, hear the word; but the worries of this life, the deceitfulness of wealth and the desires for other things come in and choke the word, making it unfruitful. Others, like seed sown on good soil, hear the word, accept it, and produce a crop—thirty, sixty or even a hundred times what was sown.

Unlike the Pauline notion of salvation by faith, Jesus set out a difficult lifelong struggle for the disciple. He mentioned that those without a strong root or dedication would fall away from the movement during persecutions. We know from Josephus' writings that the Fourth Philosophy endured torture and death because of their firm commitment to the cause. Also, the worries of this life and the allure of wealth inhibited people from producing good works (fruit). These individuals would rather live like the rest of the world than to follow the demands of Jesus. Only a lifelong commitment to sharing and following God's word could possibly be rewarded. (See also James 1:9-12) Note how much different this thinking is compared to the Pauline theology taught in the churches today. If people really followed the teachings of Jesus, only the first few pews in church would be filled.

Another passage which has been zapped of its original power is the feeding of the five thousand (Mark 6:30-44 and Mark 8:1-13—four thousand). Throughout the years, this miracle has been a hocus-pocus routine where

Jesus created loaves and fish out of thin air. This interpretation of the five thousand cannot be correct for matter cannot be created out of thin air. However, an even greater miracle did occur; that being the power of sharing. When Jesus broke the loaves in front of the masses and shared with his disciples, those in the crowd followed his example. That is why there was so much food left over. No one hoarded the food but shared instead. This may help explain the passage following the feeding of the four thousand (Mk. 8:14-21) when Jesus warned his disciples to beware of the yeast (teachings) of the Pharisees and Herod. These individuals did not believe in sharing. Their whole structure depended on hoarding wealth and prestige for themselves.

One other passage which fits into this pattern is found in Mk. 9:33-37, where Jesus taught the disciples the true definition of greatness. The greatest among them was not the richest or the most powerful but rather the one who served others for the glory of God. The key to this greatness was working for the glory of God. Jesus did criticize those Pharisees who acted religiously in order to bring attention to themselves and not to God. This selfish attitude was justly denounced by Jesus. So you see, the quality of one's life was paramount to Jesus. As James said, "even the demons believe".(James 2:19) To the Fourth Philosophy of Judas/Jesus and James, works were a sign of one's devotion to God. This was so unlike Paul's faith theology which downplayed works.

THE TEACHINGS OF PAUL

Within the New Testament are letters assigned to Paul, the Apostle to the Gentiles. For our purposes, we will use only the letters to the Romans, 1 and 2 Corinthians and Galatians. Some of the other letters have a Pauline tilt but may have been written later by people trying to emulate Paul's style. However, these four authentic letters have within them Paul's complete gospel. These teachings of Paul can be whittled down to the following: the necessity of faith in the crucified and resurrected Christ; the superiority of the baptism in the Holy Spirit over works or water baptism; the importance of obeying the ruling authorities and paying taxes; the belief that the Law had been abolished or superceded by the death and resurrection of Christ; and the denigration of Cephas, James and John, the Jewish Pillar Apostles.

In the previous section, we argued that many of the miracles of Jesus were part of the Jewish record. In these miracles, Jesus gave thanks to God or accessed God through prayer. In the miracles patterned after the Pauline model, people unknown to Jesus access the power of God through faith in Jesus. So regardless of that person's lifestyle, faith in Jesus was all that was needed to obtain the miracle. A good example of the Pauline version is found in Mark 5:21-43. Here a sick woman heard about Jesus and was determined that just a touch of Jesus' clothes would heal her. When she touched Jesus' clothes in passing, Jesus sensed that power had gone out from him. He found the woman, and she explained her reasoning to Jesus. He replied, "Daughter, your faith has healed you. Go in peace and be freed from your suffering." Note that her faith was in Jesus, not God, and that the type of lifestyle she lived was not even questioned. The Parable of the Sower emphasized the importance of a lifelong commitment to God. In the above passage, faith was all that was necessary. This definitely described the teachings of Paul but not Jesus.

A second core teaching of Paul was that of the Holy Spirit. To Paul, the believer received the Holy Spirit upon accepting the resurrected Christ through faith. Thus, this baptism in the Holy Spirit was much more important than physical circumcision or water baptism as practiced by the Fourth Philosophy preacher, John the Baptist. In 1 Cor 3:1-23, Paul tried to put himself on an equal footing with other preachers of the day. Some of his followers were influenced by Cephas and his insistence on the Law while others were swayed by Apollos, a minister who preached repentance a la John the Baptist. Later in Corinthians and certainly in Galatians, Paul reiterated that his message was the true message of God. And Paul's Gospel included the baptism of the Holy Spirit.

It is fascinating that the Gospels have John the Baptist playing second fiddle to Jesus, considering the fact that John appeared on the scene after Jesus, even by traditional dating. (John died somewhere between 34-37 AD while the traditional range of Jesus' death was between 27-33 AD). In Mark 1:7-8, John was recorded as saying, "After me will come one more powerful than I, the thongs of whose sandals I am not worthy to stoop down and untie. I baptize you with water, but he will baptize you with the Holy Spirit." This subjugation of John to Jesus is similar to that of Apollos to Paul. In fact, the Book of Acts even has Apollos receiving proper training from Paul's disciples because he knew only the baptism of John. (Acts 18:24-26)

A strange Gospel passage concerning the Holy Spirit has troubled commentators throughout the ages. Jesus said, "I tell you the truth, all the sins and blasphemies of men will be forgiven them. But whoever blasphemes against the Holy Spirit will never be forgiven; he is guilty of an eternal sin." (Mark 3:28,29) How one blasphemes specifically against the Holy Spirit has never been adequately explained. However, there may be one passage in Galatians which may shed some light upon this subject. In defending his Gospel of faith and power of the Holy Spirit, Paul wrote, "But even if we or an angel from heaven should preach a gospel other than the one we preached to you, let him be eternally condemned." (Gal. 1:8) It should be noted that this venomous remark was directed at Cephas and James.

Now it should strike home that if Cephas and James did not preach the gospel of Paul, that gospel of faith in Jesus and the gift of the Holy Spirit, then Jesus did not teach it either. So it was imperative for the Gospel writers to attach the Pauline doctrine of the Holy Spirit to Jesus. At the same time, they had to figure out a way to move the Apostles (Cephas and James) to the Pauline position. This was done in two steps. First, the Apostles were made out to be dim-witted fools. Certainly, they were unable to discern Jesus' true teachings. Thus, even after the death, burial and resurrection of Jesus, these Apostles did not grasp the truth. It was not until Acts 10, where Cephas (Peter) met Cornelius, that the true nature of Jesus' teachings were understood by the Jews. This meeting moved Cephas towards the Pauline teachings. As noted elsewhere in this book, a meeting between a Simon and Agrippa occurred in the pages of Josephus. However, in this story, Simon opposed letting a half Jew worship at the Temple. So, in reality, Cephas never met with Cornelius and never moved towards Paul's teachings. That is why Paul was removed from the movement. (Gal. 2)

A third message of Paul which has been attached to Jesus concerns Paul's desire to please the governing authorities and to support the payment of taxes. (See Romans 13:1-7 for a full description of Paul's subservient views regarding the governing authorities.) The Gospels successfully mask the political struggles which were ongoing in Judea at the time. We get only a glimpse of Roman power and are misdirected concerning Roman taxation. For instance, when asked whether Jews should pay taxes to Rome, Jesus replied, "Give to Caesar what is Caesar's, and to God what is God's." (Matt. 22:21) After knowing Paul's view of taxes, it is easy to interpret Jesus' reply as an affirmation to the question. But when we consider that Jesus was put to death because he taught against the payment of taxes, the above explanation to Jesus' answer needs revision. (Note also that Judas the Galilean led a tax revolt against the Romans.) It is most probable that Jesus' reply meant this: This money belongs to Caesar and this land belongs to the Jews. Take your money and leave our land! Such talk as this was a death sentence for Jesus.

Along with the taxation issue, Paul's teachings concerning the occupying nation (Rome) were diametrically opposed to that of the Fourth Philosophy. Josephus plainly stated that the followers of Judas the Galilean would rather die than submit to an earthly master (Rome). This zealotry is missing in the Gospels. Replacing these sentiments are passages which show the Roman admiration of Jesus. For example, Pilate knew that Jesus was innocent, but the Jews <u>forced</u> him to crucify Jesus. And at the death of Jesus, the Roman soldiers said, "Surely he was the Son of God." (Matt. 27:54) Is it any wonder that the truth has been hidden for so many years?

A fourth core teaching of Paul was the transitory nature of the Law. To Paul, this was not an everlasting covenant but a passing phase of God's plan of salvation. This contempt for the Law is most obvious in the following passage.

Now if the ministry that brought death, which was engraved in letters on stone, came with glory, so that the Israelites could not look steadily at the face of Moses because of its glory, though fading it was, will not the ministry of the Spirit be even more glorious? If the ministry that condemns men is glorious, how much more glorious is the ministry that brings righteousness! For what was glorious has no glory now in comparison with the surpassing glory. And if what was fading away came with glory, how much greater is the glory of that which lasts! (2 Cor. 3:7-11)

To Paul, the Law was fading away, and his gospel of the Spirit was everlasting. To the Jews, God gave Moses an everlasting covenant. Is there any wonder why these two groups could never have coexisted peacefully. It should be fully understood that as soon as Cephas, James and John realized what Paul was teaching, they excommunicated him from their group. That is the simple fact of the matter!

Now there are several Gospel passages which take this teaching—the fading of the Law—and apply its origin to Jesus, not Paul. We have already quoted the passage from Mark 7:1-23, where Jesus supposedly overturned the Jewish dietary laws. This not only goes against the grain of the overall passage, where Jesus was upholding the Law against traditions, but it ignores the actions of the Jewish Apostles long after the death of Jesus. In Galatians, Paul denigrated Cephas because he would not eat with his Gentile followers. However, Cephas would have eaten with them if they were merely God-fearers (Gentiles who followed most Jewish Laws except circumcision). But when Paul's teachings were fully understood, Cephas could not lawfully eat with individuals who had no concern for whether a food had been sacrificed to an idol or not.

This same concern over the dietary laws is found in Acts Chapter 10 where Cephas (Peter) supposedly met with Cornelius. We know that this event was much different in that Simon met with Agrippa over the exclusion of Herodians from the Temple. In reality, the Fourth Philosophy was exclusionary. In a 180 degree turn from truth, the Book of Acts made Peter appear to throw out the dietary laws and circumcision. This was not the behavior of a good Jewish Christian but rather the acts of a mythical character written by a second century Gentile Christian, following the teachings of Paul.

In fact, the whole Book of Acts was designed to turn the Jewish Apostles away from the Law to Paul's vision of grace. The first major attack on the Law was Acts 10. The second and final assault came in Acts 15 where the Pillar Apostles ruled in Paul's favor. However, like Acts 10, Acts 15 was totally fictional and this from Paul's own account. (See an analysis of the Jerusalem Council in Appendix 6). The subtleties of the removal of the Law per the New Testament must be admired. As we read the Gospels and Acts we feel the actual move from Law to grace, from Judaism to Christianity. That is why the deception has worked so wonderfully throughout the centuries. And the cleverest of the New Testament scholars can even explain why the Apostles followed the Law many years after Jesus' death. According to them, the Apostles relapsed into Judaism after knowing the saving power of grace. This is poor history and an unwillingness to test their own hypothesis. After all, if the Jewish Apostles were strictly following the Law in 50 AD, would it not follow that Jesus practiced the Law during his lifetime? The New Testament has obviously placed Paul's contempt of the Law on other characters, such as Jesus and Cephas, who would never have taught such things.

The fifth aspect of Paul's teachings which the Gospel writers incorporated into the story of Jesus was his distain for Cephas and James. In Galatians, Paul belittled Cephas, James and John by saying he spoke to "those who <u>seemed</u> to be leaders" and once again referring to these three as "those <u>reputed</u> to be pillars". It is not surprising that the Gospels are filled with anti-brother and anti-family statements.

Mark introduced Jesus' family in a very negative way. In Mark 3:20-35, the Gospel writer "quoted" the family members as saying, "He [Jesus] is out of his mind." And later in that same passage, Jesus ignored his own family and pointed to his disciples saying, "Here are my mother and my brothers! Whoever does God's will is my brother and sister and mother." And later, Jesus said, "Only in his home town, among his relatives and in his own house is a prophet without honor." (Mark 6:4) Thus, from the Gospel account, there was an antogonistic relationship between Jesus and his brothers. But this picture does not jibe with Paul's letters or with what we know of the Fourth Philosophy and the history of the Church.

Paul acknowledged the power of James and John in the early Church. In fact, Paul's pillars were Cephas, James and John. His James and John were the brothers of Jesus. In the Gospels, the James and John were the sons of Zebedee, no relation to Jesus. As explained earlier, this switch was made to de-emphasize the role which the family of Jesus played in the early Church. Also, it has been noted that the entire Fourth Philosophy or Jewish Christian movement was patterned after the Maccabees, where family ties were paramount in importance. Also,

Church history states that James, the brother of Jesus, was the chief apostle in Jerusalem until 62 AD. So you see, the antagonism between Jesus and his brothers was invented to remove the family members from the story of Jesus. And the only possible reason for this would be the letters of Paul. The hatred and jealousy was not between Jesus and his brothers but was central in Paul's relationship with James and John, the brothers of Jesus.

The belittling of Jesus' family occurred throughout the Synoptic Gospels but was raised to even greater heights in the Gospel of John. In John, the brothers were wicked enough to advise Jesus to march upon Jerusalem, where he faced a certain death. These brothers were no better than the brothers who sold Joseph into slavery.

So when we encounter Jesus in the Gospels, we often see a dim reflection of Paul, the man who denigrated such notables as John the Baptist, Cephas (Peter), James and John. Without these anti-family and anti-Law sentiments, the Jesus of the Gospels would be much closer to Judas the Galilean. And considering that Jesus was put to death by the Romans and the Herodian hirelings, the only picture which makes sense is that of Judas the Galilean.

JEWISH EXCUSES FOR FAILURE

There are several passages in the Gospels which were attributed to Jesus and had but one purpose: to explain away obvious failures. If Jesus were King or Messiah, it would not do to simply accept his defeat at the hands of Rome. The death of Jesus and his disciples had to be made part of a greater plan by God. Thus, the deaths could be viewed as examples of martyrdom, and this martyrdom would be rewarded by God.

In Jesus' march to Jerusalem, the Gospels declared that Jesus uttered the following prophecy:

"We are going up to Jerusalem," he said, "and the Son of Man will be betrayed to the chief priests and teachers of the law. They will condemn him to death and will hand him over to the Gentiles, who will mock him and spit on him, flog him and kill him. Three days later he will rise." (Mark 10:33,34)

This passage may contain some later additions such as the treatment by the Gentiles as well as the three days, but the overall gist is as follows: Jesus will be betrayed, captured, killed and resurrected. This would all fit in the early stages of the Jesus movement (Fourth Philosophy). This cannot be attributed to Paul. Paul preached the betrayal, crucifixion and resurrection, but he did not invent these stories. Paul's new gospel was simply a different interpretation of the established facts in the case, which were from an earlier Jewish source. However, to attribute these mystical prophecies to Jesus is beyond belief. The entry into Jerusalem on a donkey, fulfilling the prophecy of Zechariah, must lead us to the obvious conclusion that Jesus expected to fulfill the victory on the Mount of Olives as prophesied by Zechariah. When Jesus was captured, an excuse for the failure was necessary for the movement to continue.

As an alternative position, Jesus instructed the inner circle of disciples (Cephas, James and John) to portray him as the Suffering Servant, if in fact he were captured and killed by the Romans. Although Jesus would have expected victory, the memory of the earlier defeat at the Golden Eagle Temple Cleansing would have prepared him for the worst. If he were captured and killed like his old partner, Matthias, then he too would become a powerful martyr figure. The Suffering Servant of Isaiah 53 would have been the perfect model for this failure. "Yet it was the Lord's will to crush him and cause him to suffer." (Isaiah 53:10) So either in Judas/Jesus' victory or defeat, the Fourth Philosophy was positioned to exploit the situation.

In connection with this Suffering Servant excuse is the story of Jesus' main companions (the Pillar Apostles—Cephas, James and John) falling asleep throughout the most important night of their lives. This lack of righteousness and unpreparedness were factors contributing to the failure of Jesus. After the death of Jesus, the Jewish Apostles stressed repentance as a way to usher in the return of Jesus. John the Baptist's message of repentance fits nicely into this model.

When the two sons of Judas the Galilean (Jesus) were crucified, the Jewish Church had to come up with a rationalization of why God would allow such a thing. The only solution was to cryptically place this crucifixion into the words of Jesus.

Then the mother of Zebedee's sons came to Jesus with her sons and, kneeling down, asked a favor of him. "What is it you want?" he asked. She said, "Grant that one of these two sons of mine may sit at your right and the other at your left in your kingdom." "You don't know what you are asking," Jesus said to them. "Can you drink the cup I am going to drink?" "We can," they answered. Jesus said to them, "You will indeed drink from my cup, but to sit at my right or left is not for me to grant. Those places belong to those for whom they have been prepared by my Father." (Matt. 20:20-23) (See also <u>Ant</u>. 20.102 for the crucifixion of Simon and James, the two sons of Judas the Galilean.)

In the above passage, Jesus told the two sons of Zebedee that they would drink of his cup. From the context and from other parts of the Gospel, we know that this drink was crucifixion at the hands of Roman justice. Since neither

James nor John were crucified, the mythical sons of Zebedee could not have been the true subjects of this passage. The only disciples who were crucified were James and Simon, the sons of Judas the Galilean. And this makes sense in the context of the above passage. Would a mother of two unrelated disciples plead their case before Jesus? Isn't it more likely that his own wife and the mother of his two sons, James and Simon, would be the one who asked for such an extraordinary favor. The sons of Judas the Galilean were the only disciples who perfectly fit the conditions of this "prophecy".

In another twist, the author of Acts incorporated the crucifixion of James and Simon into his own perverted history of the times. In Acts 12:1-19, Peter and James were imprisoned with James being beheaded and Peter escaping. This occurred at the same time as the true capture of Simon and James, the sons of Judas the Galilean. The author of Acts simply changed the story in order to rid his narrative of the mythical James, just in time to introduce another James, the brother of Jesus. (See Chapter Eight).

The last excuse concerns the failure of the miracle workers as reported by Josephus. Many of these miracle workers, such as the Egyptian, were patterned after Jesus himself. When they were defeated by Rome, it must have been a terrible public relations disaster for James in Jerusalem. In order to combat this obvious failure, another prophecy was attributed to Jesus. In Matthew Chapter 24, Jesus supposedly said:

At that time if anyone says to you, "Look, here is the Christ!" or "There he is!" do not believe it. For false Christs and false prophets will appear and perform great signs and miracles to deceive even the elect—if that were possible. See I have told you ahead of time. (Matt. 24:23-25)

According to Josephus, these false prophets had large followings, mostly from the ranks of the Fourth Philosophy. Members of the movement were growing tired of waiting for the return of Jesus. The false prophets promised miracles such as performed by Joshua and Moses, in order to hasten the day of the Lord. They believed that their actions might bring Jesus back. After all, inaction had not worked!

In the above incidents, the failures of Jesus and his movement were excused by either placing words in Jesus' mouth (prophecy) or by showing that the disciples were not quite ready for God's deliverance. This helped keep the Jesus movement relevant for half a century. After all, if Judas/Jesus died in 19 AD and James kept the hope alive until 62 AD, some stretching of the truth may have been necessary.

FULFILLMENT OF OLD TESTAMENT SCRIPTURE

The New Testament refers back to the Old Testament time and time again. But before we dissect the Gospels, we must see how the Scriptures were used in the writings of Paul and James. It has been said that any argument can be supported by the Bible, or rather the Old Testament. The reason is clear: the Old Testament contains an incredible wealth of information. Rarely though is a single passage used for diametrically opposed viewpoints. This happened amazingly in the New Testament letters of Romans and James.

Paul wrote the letter to the Romans, and his agenda has already been covered. In short, Paul preached a gospel of grace, contingent on faith. On the other hand, James preached the Jewish Law which was built upon obedience to God and works. Both used the example of Abraham to support their particular belief system.

To support his argument, Paul quoted a passage from Genesis 15:6. "Abraham believed God, and it was credited to him as righteousness." To Paul, righteousness could only be given by God through faith or belief. After all, isn't that what the passage said?

James, however, had a completely different take on this passage.

You foolish man, do you want evidence that faith without deeds is useless? Was not our ancestor Abraham considered righteous for what he did when he offered his son Isaac on the altar? You see that his faith and his actions were working together, and his faith was made complete by what he did. And the scripture was fulfilled that says, "<u>Abraham believed God, and it was credited to him as righteousness</u>," and he was called God's friend. You see that a person is justified by what he does and not by faith alone. (James 2:20-24)

In context, James claimed that the passage supported works, or what a person does. If Abraham did not obey God then his faith would be meaningless. In fact, faith without works was not an option to James.

This disagreement on interpretation is an example of how the Old Testament Scriptures could be used to support an argument. As mentioned in the above section, the early Jewish Church excused the defeat of Jesus by claiming that he predicted his own death. This claim was then bolstered by the Old Testament ideal of the Suffering Servant as described by Isaiah Chapter 52:13-15 and 53. This famous passage helped shape our present understanding of Jesus, regardless of whether Jesus would have approved or not. We see Jesus as a "lamb led to the slaughter" and one who was "pierced for our transgressions."

We do not envision Jesus as the conqueror of Rome as Judas/Jesus clearly saw himself. And this cleverly exploited passage helped usher in the repentance stage of the Fourth Philosophy.

One other Old Testament Scripture must be mentioned. In Isaiah 7:14, the prophet wrote: "The virgin will be with child and will give birth to a son, and will call him Immanuel." This Scripture was used to certify the truth of Jesus' virgin birth. (Matt. 1:18-25) The Hebrew and Greek versions of the Old Testament use different terms to describe the virgin. In the Hebrew, the sense of the passage would be as follows: "The young woman will be with child." The Greek translates young woman into virgin. Thus, a completely different meaning comes forth depending on which translation one uses. The second century Gentiles used the Greek version and thus produced a Greek God like Heracles.

Knowing that the Old Testament Scriptures have been twisted or purposely misinterpreted to create the Gospel story should give us pause. In the three examples listed, the first was interpreted in two different ways. The second passage was used to support an excuse for failure. And the third Scripture was based on a faulty translation from Hebrew to Greek. Each additional Old Testament Scripture used in the New Testament should be studied carefully to ascertain the purpose of its use.

JOSEPHUS—A FRAMEWORK FOR JESUS

The sayings of Jesus were comprised of a curious mixture of Jewish and Pauline teachings. The life story, however, followed the history of Josephus. It was Josephus who chronicled the life of Judas the Galilean. And Judas the Galilean was the primary framework for the life of Jesus. Even if Jesus were some much earlier figure as the Mythicists claim, his story was shaped after the Judas of Josephus' writings.

This Judas the Galilean participated in two Temple Cleansings, one at the beginning of his career and one at the end. The Gospel of John placed the Temple Cleansing at the start of Jesus' ministry while the Synoptics had Jesus clearing the Temple shorty before his death. Consider the odds against this similarity.

Judas the Galilean was crowned Messiah in Galilee, near his home base of Sepphoris. He was constantly on the move to evade the clutches of Archelaus. His message was a mixture of nationalism, the Law and sharing (pure communism). To him and his disciples, this gospel was the Kingdom of Heaven. His second-in-command was named Sadduc, and from these two teachers sprang forth a powerful movement—the Fourth Philosophy. Jesus of Nazareth also preached in Galilee and was coronated Messiah by his disciples. In the Gospels, he was always on the move. We are not privy to why he went from town to town, but surely it was safer to be on the move than to be a sitting target. His Kingdom of Heaven also centered on loving God and loving your neighbor as yourself. This message was exactly the same as the core of Judas' teachings. And Jesus also had a lieutenant to help him administer his Kingdom, and his name was Cephas. This name means rock, and it may have been a nickname just as Sadduc (Holy Man) was not the given name for Judas' lieutenant.

The trial of Jesus contained many elements found in the story of Judas. The most spectacular example is that of Barabbas, that thief who had raised an insurrection in Jerusalem. This story line came directly from Josephus, where Judas the Galilean and others were released at the mob's request in the year 4 BC. This historical event occurred after an insurrection in the city and was timed with the Passover. However, the most convincing piece of information concerns the reasons for Jesus' conviction. In the Gospels, Jesus was crucified for two reasons: he urged his disciples to revolt against the payment of taxes to Rome and he was proclaimed a King, or Messiah. Judas the Galilean headed the opposition to the census of Cyrenius in 6-7 AD. Thus, he too would have been crucified for his stand on taxes and for claiming to be Messiah.

Other similarities in the trial of Jesus to Josephus are as follows:

1. Pilate washed his hands of responsibilty for the death of Jesus because of his wife's dream. In the Golden Eagle affair (5 BC), the High Priest stepped down from his duties for one day because of a dream he had concerning his wife.

2. Jesus was mocked by the guard. They dressed him in purple, wove a crown of thorns and beat him with a staff. Upon his death, Herod the Great (4 BC) was adorned in a purple robe, a crown of gold and a scepter in his hand. Even so, many mocked him. (Ant. 17.177;197)

3. Jesus was silent before Pilate. In the story of Simon and Agrippa, Simon was silent during his interrogation. This may have been the case for all loyal rebels. Both Jesus and Simon kept their movements safe by their refusal to talk. In the U.S. war on terrorism, captured opponents are offered sweet deals if they squeal on their former compatriots.

4. Both Jesus and Judas would have been crucified. Although Judas' career spanned twenty-four years, the later years were during the governships of Coponius through Pilate. The standard method of punishing a political prisoner under Roman administration was death by crucifixion.

In addition to these events being used in constructing a framework for Jesus' life, other passages from Josephus helped build our current understanding of the early Church. The story of Simon and Agrippa was turned upside down in order to make Cephas (Peter) into a Pauline supporter. This occupies Acts 10, 11 and 15. The crucifixion of Judas the Galilean's two sons, James and Simon, is the basis for the imprisonment of James and Peter in Acts 12. And the three passages about Saul (see Appendix 6) are incorporated into Acts 8 and 23:23-26:32. Without these historical nuggets from Josephus, the New Testament story would be devoid of cohesion, just a mangle of sayings and theology. Unwittingly, Josephus gave life to Jesus and his Church.

If this does not fully convince the reader that the Gospels and Acts were dependent on Josephus, then Appendix 4 should be closely studied. In this Appendix, I have listed the Bible passages in comparison to the appropriate sections in Josephus. And as stated elsewhere, if the Gospels and Acts were using material from Josephus, then the composition of these documents must have been post-Josephus. This means that the story of Jesus (Judas the Galilean) was not written by contemporaries but by Gentile followers of Paul, nearly a century after the crucifixion.

PAUL AND HIS IMPACT ON ACTS

Clearly the Gospels and Acts used materials from Josephus in constructing the mythical Jesus and his idealized Church. But the history of Josephus was not the only literature used to compose the story. Paul's own letters were instrumental in filling out the story line of Acts. Some may see this relationship as proof that the Book of Acts is authentic. However, in many cases, the story according to Paul was very different than the story of Acts. It is my contention that Acts was necessary to sanitize the true situation in the early Church; that Paul and the Pillar Apostles were teaching different gospels and that the Jewish Apostles had excommunicated Paul.

The first mention of Paul is in Acts 8:1-3, where he gave approval to the murder of Stephen and then went on a rampage against the disciples of Jesus. Paul's only mention of his life before Christ gave no details of any events relating to this particular incident.

For you have heard of my previous way of life in Judaism, how intensely I persecuted the church of God and tried to destroy it. I was advancing in Judaism beyond many Jews of my own age and was extremely zealous for the traditions of my fathers. But when God, who set me apart from birth and called me by his grace, was pleased to reveal his Son in me so that I might preach him among the Gentiles, I did not consult any man, nor did I go up to Jerusalem to see those who were apostles before I was, but I went immediately into Arabia and later returned to Damascus. (Gal. 1:13-17)

Paul only said that he persecuted the Church. He went on to say that after his conversion he "went immediately into Arabia and later returned to Damascus."

The writer of Acts took this material and invented a story included in Acts Chapters 7-9, 22 and 26. The murder of Stephen may have been the murder of James as found in <u>Ant</u>. 20.200. It just so happens that Saul was mentioned shortly thereafter persecuting those weaker than himself. This fits in precisely with the vision of Paul in Acts 8:1-3. However, the murder of James occurred in 62 AD and the persecutions of Saul were therefore post 62 AD. Acts simply transported the story of Saul back in time to agree with Paul's own statement about formerly persecuting the Church. (Note that the post 62 AD persecution of the Jewish Church came after he had been excommunicated from the group, per the account in Galatians).

Acts' story of Paul's conversion on the road to Damascus bears no resemblance to Paul's own version of events as quoted above. The only similarity concerns Damascus. In Acts, Paul was led by the hand into Damascus, while Paul stated that he first travelled into Arabia and then entered Damascus. And the reason for leaving Damascus was also changed by the author of Acts. Paul escaped Damascus from a window in the wall because agents from King Aretas were trying to capture him. (2 Cor. 11:32,33) In Acts 9:23-25, it was the Jews who were trying to kill him. These are not trivial differences in that they convey different meanings than what actually happened. It just goes to show that the meager information of Paul was transformed into lengthy stories with Paul as the hero and the Jews as the villains.

The Council of Jerusalem was invented by the author of Acts as a way to move the Jewish Apostles towards the teachings of Paul. Note that Paul's version of events differ wildly from the version of Acts. Paul said he revealed his gospel <u>privately</u> to "those who seemed to be leaders." In Acts, Paul proudly explained his new gospel to the approval of all the Jews. (See Gal. 2:1-5 and Acts 15). In reality, Paul probably omitted many of the finer points of his gospel from the leaders. For instance, he could not have told them about his distain for the Covenant with God, the Law and the seal of the Covenant, that being circumcision. Paul's double game came to an end when the Church leaders unearthed his true teachings. But in order to keep peace, the author of Acts brought everything out in the open. And with the help of Peter's new understanding, given him through the Cornelius episode (a twisting of Simon and Agrippa), Paul won the day.

Chapters 16-21 of Acts cannot be trusted any more than the rest of Acts. An example of this is the story of Apollos. In 1 Cor. 3:1-23, Paul argued against divisions in his churches. Other teachers were treading on his soil, and his disciples were being splintered away; some followed Cephas while others favored Apollos. In this passage, Paul wrote, "I planted the seed, Apollos watered it, but God made it grow." From this, the Book of Acts said that Apollos knew only the Baptism of John, and that he was taught more adequately by Paul's disciples, Priscilla and Aquila. (Acts 18:24-26) The purpose of the Acts interpretation was to subordinate Apollos to Paul, even though Paul had not expressly done this in his letter to the Corinthians. It also smoothed out any divisions in the early Church, making it one big happy family.

One other section of Paul's writings which was used extensively by the writer of Acts is 2 Cor. 11:22-33, where Paul defended his ministry by telling of his many hardships. This list of hardships included the following: floggings, imprisonment, being beaten by rods and stoned, and being shipwrecked. Yet Paul did not elaborate on any of these events. In Acts 16:16-23, Paul and Silas were flogged and then imprisoned. Another passage which was drawn from Paul's list is Acts 27:13-44, where Paul was shipwrecked on Malta. This whole section is blatantly false as Josephus had Saul in Jerusalem at this time.

To further explore the background and exploits of Paul, see Appendix 6. This will help the reader to fully understand the man and his impact on Gentile Christianity.

GENTILE CULTURE

The Gospel writers could not resist using Greek mythology as well as Roman attempts to also capitalize upon the Gods. In Chapter Two, the birth of Jesus was examined. This birth was a classic case of borrowing from the Gods. Jesus was born to a human mother just as Heracles, but both were fathered by a God. This same pattern was used by Suetonius in describing the birth of the greatest Roman Emperor, Augustus. Such legends were current in the early second century and may have had a wide array of followers. In the attempt to make Jesus relevant to the Gentile audience, Jesus was made to be a Greek God or even better, a rival to the Emperor. Certainly, this was much more attractive than the plain truth: that Judas/Jesus was just a man like everyone else.

The Book of John used the wedding at Cana to ascribe to Jesus the same powers as Dionysis. This hocus-pocus Jesus would have been popular to the Gentile masses just as he is to the uneducated in our own time. In reality, the wedding at Cana was probably an event in the life of Judas the Galilean: the vows between Judas and his wife, Mary.

The Gospels also contain some statements of faith which were being questioned by some in the early second century. For example, John wrote: "The

Word became flesh and lived for a while among us." (John 1:14) This was included to combat the heresy known as Docetism, where Jesus was not believed to be flesh and blood but rather an apparition.

In the process of separating Judas/Jesus from his Jewish roots, the Gospel writers used Greek Gods, Roman Emperors and hocus-pocus to make Jesus more acceptable to the Gentile population. To those who went too far in creating new concepts of Jesus (Docetists), the Gospels set in stone that mythical Jesus which has held sway for two thousand years. The Gospel Jesus was not the authentic Judas/Jesus, but his mutation into even stranger forms was effectively stopped by the second century efforts of those named Matthew, Mark, Luke and John.

CONCLUSION

The Gospels and Acts were written by second century Gentile authors with the intent of making Jesus' life and teachings consistent with the theology of Paul. In doing this, they cleverly twisted different elements into their story. Jewish and Pauline teachings were placed side by side, and even the interpretation of the Jewish passages were tainted by the exposure to Paul's theology. In addition, the actual events in this great saga were either lifted from the pages of Josephus or were wholly invented from ideas left behind by Paul's letters.

This effort was nothing short of brilliant. If it were written today, however, it would not pass the smell test. But at the time, ignorance of the true events was universal. And as the centuries passed and the power of the Church grew, anyone with a questioning mind was silenced. This same mentality grips most Christians to this very day. That is why reading and studying something so different is a challenge.

DATING THE NEW TESTAMENT

Traditional Dating

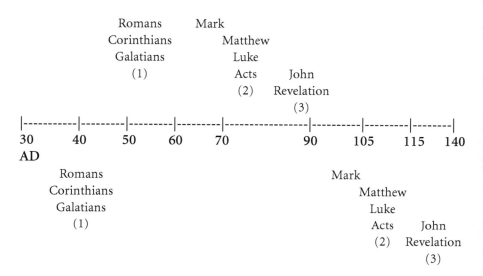

My Dating

1. The traditonal dating for Paul's main epistles approximates 57 AD or a year before the time of the Egyptian, per Josephus. This dating is wholly dependent on Paul's own account of his ministry, which covered around twenty years (conversion, trip to Jerusalem after three years, another trip to Jerusalem fourteen years later, the split from James and Cephas, and the eventual third trip to Jerusalem.) If Jesus died in 33 AD and Paul converted a few years later, then the earliest he could have been in Jerusalem the third time would have been 55 AD. This is near the above dating of 57 AD.

   My dating for the writing of these letters is fourteen years earlier or around 40-44 AD. Working backwards, Paul must have undergone conversion between 20-24 AD. Besides the obvious connection with the earlier crucifixion of Judas/Jesus (19 AD vs. 33 AD), there are three events in these letters which point to the early 40's, not the late 50's. First, in Corinthians, Paul mentioned a Jewish Christian by the name of Apollos who "watered" his converts. Most scholars believe this refers to John the Baptist (Acts admits this—Acts 18:24-26). If this is the case, then it is much more likely that a follower of John the Baptist would be preaching his baptism soon after the Baptist's death, not twenty years afterwards. Second, the disagreement between Paul and Cephas over circumcision and the Law was no different than two other events recorded by Josephus and dated in the early 40's. These two stories concerned Simon and Agrippa at Caesarea, where Simon tried to bar non-Jews from worshipping at the Temple, and King Izates, Ananias and Eleazar, where Ananias had taught King Izates to forego circumcision but was rebutted by Eleazar, sent from Galilee, who insisted upon circumcision for the King. Third, in his letters, Paul was in the process of collecting money for the poor in Jerusalem. This coincides with the famine and the relief effort done by Queen Helena and King Izates. The famine covered Judea from 44-48 AD. This famine relief trip was not mentioned by Paul in his letters because it had not yet happened. It is, however, cited by Luke in Acts 11:27-30.

2. Most scholars place the Gospel of Mark at 70 AD and Luke and Matthew a few years later. Certain predictions in the Gospels about the destruction of Jerusalem certainly point to a post 70 AD time frame. Also, Luke and Matthew have material in common which is not found in Mark. This source is referred to as the Q material (source). Since Acts was written by Luke, then it must also have been written in this time frame (70-90 AD).

    I believe this dating of the Gospels is much too early as the Gospel framework is heavily dependent upon Josephus. The War was written in 75 AD and Antiquities in 93 AD. As such, the Gospels could not have been written before 93 AD. (See Appendix 4 for further review). Since dissemination of information was not as speedy as today, I would ballpark the Gospel of Mark to 105 AD and Luke and Matthew to around 120 AD.

3. Christian scholars believe that John, the son of Zebedee, wrote the Gospel of John and Revelation on the island of Patmos around 90-95 AD. I have already debunked the Zebedee myth, where John was really the brother of Judas/Jesus. The age of John in 95 AD would have been 128 years if he were one year younger than James (James was 96 in 62 AD). Thus, any tie to John is mere nonsense. The Gospel of John is much different than the other Gospels. The hatred of Jews is much more pronounced in John, and the fight against other heresies is also evident. The "Word became flesh" was meant to dissuade Christians from the Docetist viewpoint, where Jesus never appeared in the flesh but was just spirit. In short, the Gospel of John was written after the other three Gospels and has nothing to do with John the Apostle. As for Revelation, the core of this book may be very early as Rome is the harlot and Jesus is seen as the Messiah returning in power. Such a message as this would have been popular in the 40's, 50's and 60's. This core message was then adulterated by Gentile Christians in the second century. The first three chapters refer to synagogues of Satan. Such language could only have come from a much later source.

CHAPTER ELEVEN

RAMIFICATIONS

As already noted, the New Testament teachings on Christianity are not as straightforward as many would like you to believe. There was not one unified church in the earliest years of Christianity, but two separate and conflicting movements, one including Jewish disciples zealous for the law and the other comprised of Gentile believers who exalted grace over works of the law. Paul stated that he was the apostle to the Gentiles while Cephas was the apostle to the Jews (Gal. 2:7). Unbeknownst to most Christians today, the two messages or gospels were completely different, enough so that Paul called the Jewish apostles followers of Satan (2 Cor. 11:13-15) and teachers of a false gospel (Gal.1:6-9). The Jewish Christians hounded Paul, questioning his credentials and his motives for personal gain (2 Cor. 12:14). (His collections from the Corinthian and Galatian churches may have ended up in his own pockets.) That the two teachings became one may be the only real miracle of the New Testament.

Jewish Christianity is in itself a misnomer. The earliest followers of Jesus in Judea were not called Christians but Nazirites, followers of the Way (Way of Righteousness) and later as Zealots and Sicarii. (They may have been derisively called Christians by the pagans in Rome.) These disciples of the Way differed from other Jews in the following: they were fiercely nationalistic, and that meant removing the Romans in one way or another; their devotion to the Law was matched only by the Essenes (James' followers were called "zealous for the Law" in Acts 21:20-21); and their peculiar belief in the resurrection of Jesus (started by James and Cephas as a way to keep the movement going) would have been bitterly opposed by less nationalistic Jews, such as the Herodians, Sadducess and most Pharisees. With their strict adherence to the Law, the earliest followers of Jesus had nothing in common with Paul, except for the resurrection. And even this was interpreted differently. To the Jews, Jesus would return to lead them against Rome, an earthly king in the order of David. This belief faded after the Jewish War and the disaster which befell the Jews. You see, Jesus never returned. Thus, the end of true "Christianity" occurred in the first century, around 70 AD. In a later revolt against Rome (132 AD), Bar Kochba led the rebels as Messiah, the movement of Jesus amongst the Jews long since discredited.

But the beginnings of a counterfeit "Christianity" took root in the mid-first century. Paul's version differed from Jesus in the following ways: Paul preached that one was saved by grace (Rom. 4) although this is argued against by James (James 2); Paul's resurrection was an other-worldly event, not physical but spiritual (1 Cor. 15: 35-58); Paul's source of his gospel was personal revelations (Gal. 1:11), not contact with the earthly Jesus; Paul preached friendship to the Roman Empire, the very Empire which murdered John the Baptist and Jesus (Rom. 13:1-7); and while the Jews of the Way taught a primitive form of communism, Paul accepted rich and poor alike, freeman and slave. The Way proudly forced compliance into its social arrangement (Acts 4:32-5:11), while Paul accepted everybody as they were.

Is it any wonder why so much confusion reigns concerning Christianity today? Fundamentalists, as well as most traditional main-line churches, claim the teachings of Paul and the history of Jesus, even though the two are in utter conflict. In large cities, small towns and rural communities, churches are formed primarily upon social status, where the rich attend in one area and the poor in another. The pure communism of the Way never made it out of the first century, except in monasteries and nunneries. The concept of grace also is a mainstay of modern Christianity, even though it is morally bankrupt. Any teaching which conveys a loosening of personal responsibility cannot be good. Paul's own converts lived immoral lives while living in the "Spirit". (1 Cor. 5:1-6:20) He even tried to teach them some of his own version of law after hearing of their way of life. And in the same way, we see religious people living the most immoral lives. Things have not really changed, have they!

Throughout the ages, different religious movements have gone against the grain of traditional Christianity. The monastic orders were throwbacks to the communism of Jesus. Not long ago, Liberation Theology was the rage. This Christian interpretation used strains from the New Testament which supported equality and freedom. In many ways, this brand was much closer to Jesus and his Jewish disciples. However, such a movement can only be popular among the poor and downtrodden, having little or no appeal in our comfortable churches. And anyone who would support such a religion would be in danger of losing his life, as Martin Luther King did. The social upheaval proposed by Jesus and by men like Dr. King always end the same, in the death of the reformer.

So, how will this new look at Jesus affect the way business is performed in our churches? After all, if the myth is destroyed, then shouldn't the priesthood and ministries of deception be destroyed as well? In some cases, that is exactly what will happen. Open-minded individuals may find my hypothesis on Judas the Galilean refreshing and may decide to support charities other than the church. However, the majority will not change. The same people who believe in the actual resurrection, the virgin birth, the Creation myths, and in every literal word of the Bible will not give my hypothesis another thought. There is much to be lost here. Too many people rely upon the mythical Jesus for employment and for peace of mind.

CHRISTIAN DOCTRINES

Several major church doctrines will be challenged by my Judas the Galilean hypothesis. First and foremost, the mythological Jesus will melt away, leaving behind only the earthly Jesus, a human being like all other human beings. Thus, the man-god savior religion of today (and of the first-century Roman Empire) will give way to a more rational religion. Christianity is the only major religion which places a man on equal footing with God. In Judaism and Islam, such teachings are heretical, an affront to the power of God. To remove Jesus from the intermediary status may actually move people closer to God. Certainly, the people who wrote the Dead Sea Scrolls understood that God alone forgives sins and that God's mercy is free to those who are in a right relationship with Him. Put another way: God loves those who love Him and who love their neighbors. In fact, this is the holy commandment quoted by Jesus. The idea of a godly savior sacrifice is not necessary today as it was not two thousand years ago. God never needed such a device in order to forgive sins. God has always been greater than that.

This loss of the man-god also affects the theological groundwork of Paul's religion, grace. As noted above, the Jews already believed in the grace of God, but it was not through the sacrifice of a man-god. Grace, as Paul believed (his beliefs came through personal revelations), was utterly dependent on the disciples accepting Jesus as a personal savior. Thus, this intermediary was necessary for man to have a relationship with God. This led to massive abuses, from sexual immorality to all sorts of perversions. (1 Cor. 5&6) And this is the case today in Christian churches. Since our sins are forgiven through the sacrifice of Jesus Christ, a moral lifestyle is not mandatory (although preferred). You see, a Christian is "saved" regardless of the quality of his/her life. The same abuses recorded two thousand years ago are alive and well today. Contrasting this salvation by faith, James wrote that works are important and the fundamental way that man exhibits his love for God.

What good is it, my brothers, if a man claims to have faith but has no deeds? Can such faith save him?...Show me your faith without deeds, and I will show you my faith by what I do. You believe that there is one God. Good! Even the demons believe that—and shudder. (James 2:14-19)

Jesus, like James, taught people to live in the Way of Righteousness. There was no short cut to God for Jesus, just a way of life.

Along with the loss of the man-god, Mary and the saints lose all of their spiritual allure. In the preceding chapters, we learned that the birth narratives were patently false, and that Mary, the mother of Jesus, was really Mary, the wife of Jesus. Consider the impact that this would have upon the Catholic Church and European tourism. In that institution and geographical area, Mary is as important as Jesus, and to many parishioners, even more so. The fertility goddess who Mary replaced in many locales might fade away into the past. And it is possible that the veneration of Mary, the mother of Jesus, would simply disappear. There is no evidence to support such a woman. If this would happen, then I suppose the church would worship Mary, the wife of Jesus, the ever-loving wife instead of the ever-virgin mother.

These losses would be miniscule next to the inevitable conclusion which must accompany your decision concerning my hypothesis. If Jesus and Judas were one, then the whole moral authority of the New Testament comes into question. After all, how can a book filled with half-truths and lies tell us how to live our lives? The perfect Word of God would become the imperfect—the infallible, fallible. Such an admission would destroy Christianity as it stands today. Fundamentalists would shriek and howl and cover their eyes and ears. Catholics would not only lose the Bible but the Papacy as well: two institutions in one blow! Nothing in church doctrine would ever be the same, nothing could ever be trusted again.

As for those who believe in the rapture and the imminent return of Christ, the picture is pretty bleak. Christians have been eagerly awaiting Jesus for two thousand years; what's another few thousand years among friends. Catholics and most Protestant groups would most likely take this in stride as most are not committed to Jesus returning in their lifetimes. However, the Fundamentalists would not accept any change to their beliefs concerning the rapture. These "Christians" preach that all believers will be raptured into heaven before the great tribulation. This doctrine is based upon Matthew 24:36-41.

No one knows about that day or hour, not even the angels in heaven, nor the Son, but only the Father. As it was in the days of Noah, so it will be at the coming of the Son of

Man. For in the days before the flood, people were eating and drinking, marrying and giving in marriage, up to the day Noah entered the ark; and they knew nothing about what would happen until the flood came and took them all away. That is how it will be at the coming of the Son of Man. Two men will be in the field; one will be taken and the other left. Two women will be grinding with a hand mill; one will be taken and the other left.

Fundamentalists believe that true Christians will be taken into heaven and the heathens left on earth to face the wrath of God. But a closer reading of the passage reveals the exact opposite; it is the unfaithful and unaware people who will be taken away as in the days of Noah. People who cannot recognize this would not know truth if it struck them between the eyes.

In short, if my hypothesis is correct, then all honest Christians may have to question their belief systems. The basis of a good life will not change: to love God and to love thy neighbor as thyself. But the doctrines of an established church will most certainly topple down. No longer will Christians be able to hide behind Jesus, Mary and the Saints. In fact, according to the Scrolls, there is no need to hide from God, for He is gracious and forgiving. So life will go on for the majority. As for the Fundamentalists, they will never believe anything which contradicts their God—the Bible.

POLITICS

It may seem strange to discuss politics alongside religion, but in our society the two are intertwined. This is true even though we officially proclaim a separation of Church and State. Our founding fathers had a great fear of the Church's power as they experienced the control the Church of England exerted upon the English government. Churchmen should have control in the church but not in the statehouse, they reasoned. And for two hundred plus years we have unsuccessfully tried to limit the Church's influence upon our politicians.

But such songs as "God Bless America" and "God Bless the USA", along with the 9/11 mentality, have placed God on the political agenda with a vengeance. Even though the super-liberals try to take Jesus out of everything—even Christmas, the majority of Americans believe God is actively working for the United States. And this God sanctions only Christianity, so much that the U.S. is considered a "Christian Nation". This in itself is not dangerous; for if we all acted like good Christians then this world would be a better place. The problem occurs when we excuse our actions, whether good or evil, in the name of God. Thus, our stand in the Middle East is deemed correct since we are a

Christian Nation and our ideals are sanctioned by God. However, the Moslems feel the same way. Who is right? It depends upon whom you ask.

Looking back two thousand years, we can observe the religious society implemented by Judas the Galilean and his Fourth Philosophy. Their vision was that of a Jewish society based upon the Law and the Temple of God; thus, a truly Jewish nation. They believed God would protect them if they followed His will, thus the name Way of Righteousness. That is why they waged war upon Rome, suicide by any other reasoning. When Jesus awaited the Romans in the Garden of Gethsemane, he asked that his disciples bring only two swords, a minimal show of force (Luke 22:38). Like Gideon, Jesus and his poorly armed followers would defeat the Romans with the power of God. Not long after this meeting, Jesus was crucified. The lesson is this: God may be all-powerful, but we should not attempt to manipulate Him.

Anytime the U.S. plays the moral card of "Christian Nation", we as citizens should look past the simplistic slogans and should logically evaluate each action our country takes. If we blindly follow our leaders with the faith that our nation cannot fail, then we may find ourselves in the same position as the followers of Judas, in the fortress of Masada with our enemy waiting for the kill. So if there is anything to be learned from Judas and the Fourth Philosophy, it is humility. As a nation, we are no more protected by God than the Jews were. Only time will tell when our arrogance will destroy us.

This arrogance is best exhibited by the right wing Republican Party, particularly the "Christian Right". In the name of God, Fundamentalists have attacked a small segment of society, namely the homosexual community. In this, they are in step with the Fourth Philosophy. But this homophobia is hardly consistent with "We the People", where all men and women have the same rights of life, liberty and the pursuit of happiness. In their zeal, the right wing "Christians" scapegoat the homosexuals just as the early Jewish Christians (John the Baptist) attacked the immorality of the Herodians.

As noted above, the Fourth Philosophy of Judas had little sympathy for anyone different from themselves. Thus, the accepting, loving portrayal of early Christianity is a myth. If one did not do things according to the Way, then that person did not last long. (See Acts 5 and the exaggerated punishment of Ananias and Sapphira, which is consistent with the Community Rule). Paul talked a good game, but he was as intolerant as the Jewish Christians. On the one hand he wrote, "There is neither Jew nor Greek, slave nor free, male nor female, for you are all one in Christ Jesus." (Gal. 3:28) But earlier in the same letter he attacked those in disagreement with his revelations, "But even if we or an angel from heaven should preach a gospel other than the one we preached to you, let him be eternally condemned." (Gal. 1:18) So both Jewish and

Gentile Christianity were exclusionary, accepting only those who walked in the straight and narrow paths of the founders, whether they be Jesus or Paul. Unfortunately, this intolerance is practiced by most churches. In this, at least they are following the earliest teachers of the movement.

Secondly, the "Christian Right" supports Israel based upon a misinterpretation of the Gospel passage concerning the rapture (see above). This support of Israel would be fine, if the effort was aimed at solving the stalemate between Israel and the Palestinians. However, to the "Right", Israel is a necessity leading to the last days or the return of Jesus. Maybe a healthy dose of Judas the Galilean would put the "Right" on the right path. The support of Israel should be done with compassion for the other peoples in the area.

Finally, there is a widespread belief that Christianity and capitalism go hand-in-hand. There is nothing farther from the truth. The early church practiced primitive communism: "All the believers were together and had everything in common. Selling their possessions and goods, they gave to anyone as he had need." (Acts 2:44,45). However, the most striking condemnation of capitalism comes from James. (Remember that capitalism is simply the accumulation of capital or money in a few peoples' hands.)

Now listen, you rich people, weep and wail because of the misery that is coming upon you. Your wealth has rotted, and moths have eaten your clothes. Your gold and silver have corroded. Their corrosion will testify against you and eat your flesh like fire. You have hoarded wealth in the last days. Look! The wages you failed to pay the workers who mowed your fields are crying out against you. The cries of the harvesters have reached the ears of the Lord Almighty. You have lived on earth in luxury and self-indulgence. You have fattened yourselves in the day of slaughter. You have condemned and murdered innocent men, who were not opposing you. (James 5:1-6)

Note that the whole idea of communism was based upon the passage of "love thy neighbor as thyself." To the Way of Righteousness, the inequalities of wealth contradict this command of God. After all, do you really love your neighbor if he is hungry and you live in luxury?

In addition, the Fourth Philosophy and those of the Dead Sea Scrolls also practiced pure communism. In fact, when the Zealots gained control of the Temple during the Jewish War, "they took their fire to the Records Office, eager to destroy the money-lenders' bonds and so make impossible the recovery of debts, in order to secure the support of an army of debtors and enable the poor to rise with impunity against the rich." (War 2.427,428)

Our "Christian Nation" is really a "Consumer Nation". We measure success by our possessions, our job titles and our salaries. Those who try to practice primitive communism are derided as liberal nuts or as cultists. Even the so-called worship of God is surrounded by all the trappings which money can buy: a beautiful church building, a well-paid preacher and fine suits and dresses for the members. It is all a show, a show not for God but for ourselves. We like to impress people and our church attendance is no different. The extreme example of this Capitalist Christianity comes in the form of televangelism. Men such as Billy Graham, Jim Bakker, Jerry Falwell and Pat Robertson have made a nice living for themselves, asking others to give so that God may bless and that they themselves may live in fine houses.

How has Christianity fared over the past two thousand years? We have discarded the one feature which enriches the soul and that is <u>voluntary</u> communism. (I say voluntary because forced communism is a dreadful system, where the state sides with business against the people). This has been replaced by an overriding desire to accumulate wealth for ourselves. And the most negative aspect of early Christianty that we have kept is our feelings for outsiders, whether they be Black, Oriental or Gay. So how can my hypothesis on Judas the Galilean hurt the spiritual growth of this country? If anything, it will help. Maybe people will look at their lives a little differently, no longer believing that God condones selfishness.

THE JEWS AND MOSLEMS

So how does this hypothesis affect the Jews? After all, Jesus was a law-loving Jew and a Messiah figure to a great many people. Eisenman details how the Jewish survivors of the Jewish War denounced the politics of Jesus and became sympathetic to the Roman cause. Like Josephus, Rabbi Yohanan, a Pharisee, applied the Star Prophecy to Vespasian. Rome rewarded him with the academy of Yavneh where the foundations of Rabbinic Judaism were laid. These accommodating Pharisees removed the First and Second Books of Maccabees from their Bible because these writings encouraged revolt against the ruling powers.(1) (These books are also absent from Protestant Bibles).

So the Jews of today come from a different strain than those of Jesus' day. Today's Jews are comfortable with their version of Judaism, just as Christians are with their corrupted religion. A flight to the equality of Jesus' movement can only occur amongst the poor, and this is more likely to happen with the Palestinians than with the Jews. However, the flight to the nationalism of Judas the Galilean has already taken root in modern Israel. The nation of Israel, which fights for its very existence, is consistent with the Jesus movement. The only difference is this: today, the United States and Israel can be compared to Rome, the very state which hung Jesus on the cross.

As noted in an earlier chapter, the followers of Judas the Galilean were willing to give their lives for their religion. Note that they were also promised rewards in heaven for their deeds. Does this remind you of any terrorist groups the U.S. has encountered recently? You see, Judas the Galilean was a terrorist in the eyes of Rome, just as Osama Bin Laden is a murderous terrorist in our eyes. And likewise, Bin Laden is as much of a freedom fighter to his followers as Judas was to his disciples. And just as Judas the Galilean, his sons and his followers were crushed by Rome, so too will this happen to Bin Laden and his cronies. For religion can be powerful, but the superpower of the day often absorps religion or merely crushes it.

In an ironic twist, Jerry Falwell recently stated on national television that Mohammed was a terrorist and did not represent good peace-loving Moslems.(2) If Falwell were capable of understanding that the Jesus movement was none other than the Fourth Philosophy of Judas the Galilean, then his focus on terrorists would have been directed at Jesus' later disciples (Zealots and Sicarii), not Mohammed. As it stands, Falwell's ignorance has left many speechless and has angered the Moslem community the world over.

CHAPTER TWELVE

CONCLUSION

In traditional Christian teachings, the life of Jesus began amidst the stench of a stable in Bethlehem, circa 4 BC, and ended upon the cross, that instrument of torture perfected by the Romans and used primarily as a punishment for political crimes. The crimes of Jesus were not committed against the Pax Romana (Peace of Rome), but rather, against the harsh rules of the Pharisees and teachers of the Law. Pontius Pilate, the Roman procurator from 26-37 AD, was nothing more than a puppet in the hands of the Jews, who insisted that Jesus be crucified, accepting the responsibility of his blood on their hands for all eternity. Thus, the blame for Jesus' death was squarely upon the Jews, for Pilate saw the good in Jesus and washed his hands of the whole sad affair. This Roman esteem for Jesus even extended to the crucifixion where the Roman soldier worshipped Jesus, saying, "Surely he was the Son of God." (Matt. 27:54) As opposed to the Roman admiration of Jesus, the Jews appeared bloodthirsty, crying for his crucifixion for no other reason than that he challenged their law. The resulting picture of Jesus is one of an other-worldly redeemer, sent to the Jews, rejected by those same Jews, and finally accepted by the Gentiles through the Gospel of St. Paul. Hundreds of millions have accepted this version of the Jesus story over the past two thousand years.

Hopefully, the first eleven chapters challenged the traditional picture of Jesus in the minds of the readers. First, Jesus was not named Jesus from birth, but rather Judas. This Judas came from Galilee or across the River Jordan in Golon. The nickname, Judas the Galilean, did not refer to his place of birth but to his ultimate sphere of influence. In his early career, Judas taught young men at the Temple in Jerusalem (6-4 BC). At this time, Herod the Great introduced an idol into the Temple—the Golden Eagle. Judas' foiled attempt at cleansing the temple cost many lives as well as his co-teacher, Matthias. This brush with death at the hands of Herod the Great radicalized Judas, and he began his career as a freedom fighter (a terrorist in the eyes of Roman authorities.) After being released by Archelaus in the Barabbas episode, Judas went to Sepphoris in Galilee where he stormed the armory and equipped his followers. For years thereafter, Judas preached in Galilee, all the while increasing his influence throughout the countryside.

In 6 AD, Judas led a national revolt against the new Roman taxation, and his ever-growing movement was penned by Josephus as the Fourth Philosophy. It was this Fourth Philosophy which concerned Josephus throughout the <u>War</u> and <u>Antiquities</u>. While Josephus described Judas' movement in detail, information concerning the Gospel Jesus was nonexistent, leading one to believe that either Jesus was unimportant, or was in fact, the leader of the Fourth Philosophy.

Judas appointed Sadduc, a Pharisee, to the position of second-in-command, replacing the slain Matthias. It was Cephas (Sadduc) who declared Judas, Messiah. At this point, Judas the Galilean became Jesus the Galilean or Jesus of Nazareth as the Gospels declare. Just as Hoshea became Joshua in the Old Testament (Nu. 13:8; 13:16), assuming a savior-like role amongst the early Jews, Judas retained the same name, a title pregnant with glory (Jesus and Joshua both mean savior). Thus, Judas the Galilean and Jesus the Galilean were the same person.

The death of Judas/Jesus occurred at the beginning of Pilate's term as governor (19 AD), not long after the initial tax revolt (6-7 AD). (Per Appendix 7, Pilate's administration began in 18 AD, not 26 AD as the traditionalists preach.) Roman procurators, Pilate included, were sent to govern and collect taxes. Whether intended or not, these governors often stirred the soup, arousing the ire of the fanatical Jews. Judas/Jesus could not resist the opportunity to fight the Roman evil. After Pilate placed standards in Jerusalem and robbed the Temple to build an aqueduct, Judas/Jesus entered Jerusalem and cleansed the temple, just as he and Matthias had done some years earlier. Unfortunately, Judas/Jesus could not escape the power of Rome any more than Matthias could Herod the Great. Like Matthias, Judas the Galilean was martyred for his cause, and forevermore, his name would be Jesus—Savior.

James, the brother of Judas, replaced the crucified leader and restored order amongst the movement, along with Cephas. Together, they would rule the movement until their deaths: James in 62 AD and Cephas (50-70 AD?). Their main adversary in the years following the death of Judas/Jesus was Paul, the Herodian who once persecuted the church but then converted. However, Paul's attack on the movement only changed from being a charlatan to a secret agent, now destroying the movement from within. A final showdown recorded by Paul in Galatians details the break. The Jewish Christians could not tolerate Paul's attitude about their Law. Once his teachings were understood, the Jewish Christians excommunicated the "Apostle to the Gentiles."

The Jewish war ultimately destroyed the Fourth Philosophy of Judas the Galilean. If Judas could not return for this monumental struggle, then he would never return, and a new Messiah must be found. However, to Paul's Gentile converts, the Jesus movement was just an adaptation of the earlier mystery religions. Thus, Jesus the Christ thrived as a pagan man-god, and it is this Jesus that is worshipped to this very day.

Going back to Chapter One, I mentioned three books that inspired this effort. <u>Revolution in Judaea</u>, by Hyam Maccoby, traced the life of a Jewish teacher, a champion of his day who was admired by the poor peasants. This is undoubtably true as Judas the Galilean amassed a veritable army of disciples during his life, and this following grew even after his death, continuing up to the war with Rome. Jesus was said to be a Pharisee, and his teachings no different than the past teachers of Judaism. In this, Josephus states that the Fourth Philosophy had much in common with the Pharisaic beliefs, the only difference being the Fourth Philosophy's desire for political independence. Maccoby painted Paul as a sympathizer with the Sadducees and Herodians, standing against the real Jesus and his close followers. A close reading of the New Testament gives many clues as to Paul's ties with the Herodians. (See Appendix 6) In addition, Maccoby was on the right path in his explanation concerning Barabbas. For Maccoby, Jesus Barabbas was a character created by the Gospel writers so that the Jews could choose between a good Jesus and a bad Jesus. Of course, the Jews chose the bad Jesus, the Barabbas of legend. So in all these things, Maccoby was right. However, Maccoby did not recognize the tie between Judas the Galilean and Jesus. Without this knowledge, he had no idea that a Barabbas episode actually occurred during the lifetime of Judas the Galilean (4 BC).

As for Eisenman's <u>James the Brother of Jesus</u>, Jesus was much like his brother James, who is portrayed as a very holy man, well-respected by all Jews until his murder at the hands of Roman collaborators in 62 AD. James is depicted more as an Essene than a Pharisee, and this may be correct based upon all that has been written about James. Like Maccoby, Eisenman counts the blood relationship between Jesus and his brothers paramount in importance. Like the Maccabean family, the family of Jesus would rid the land of the Roman infection. Eisenman also portrays Paul as a betrayer of the faith, calling him the "Liar" who is railed against in the Dead Sea Scrolls. It was Paul who changed the Jewish Messiah figure into an other-worldly redeemer for the Gentiles. However, without realizing the connection between Judas the Galilean and Jesus, his Dead Sea Scroll hypothesis (James as the Righteous Teacher and Paul as the Liar) is off by a generation. Thus, his hypothesis is dismissed by the orthodox because his main players are too late for all the external evidence.

The third book, Pagan Christs, by Robertson, is correct in stating that the Jesus revealed in the New Testament is a mythical character. The institution of pagan sacraments (eating the flesh and drinking the blood) in Christianity was no different than a number of other contemporaneous religions, an example being Mithraism. Also, the presentation of the Jesus story is in the form of a play, where the final scenes cover only a short time span. And within this play are items of incredible improbabilities: the release of Barabbas by the Roman procurator; the intentional blood sacrifice of Jesus; the shifting of blame from Pilate (Rome) to the Jewish mob and the betrayer's name of Judas which closely resembles the name Jew. With all these problems, it is easy to see why Robertson and the Mythicists believed Jesus to be ahistorical.

All three books dovetail nicely into my hypothesis of Jesus' true background. The only thing missing is Judas the Galilean. You see, Judas the Galilean was reality, or history. The Jesus of Paul and the Gospels was romanticized into a God, divorced from the issues of Judea—Roman taxation and occupation. Therefore, the discovery of the flesh and blood Jesus is impossible if he is viewed from only the New Testament account. That record is counterfeit, and that Jesus is pure myth. The real Messiah was named Judas the Galilean. He became the Messiah, the Savior, the Jesus. Any attempt to find the Jesus of history apart from Judas the Galilean has been and will always be doomed to failure.

APPENDIX 1

I have listed thirty-three similarities between Jesus of Nazareth and Judas the Galilean. Some are general in nature and others quite specific. Although any such listing does not prove a 100% foolproof case, the odds overwhelmingly favor my hypothesis that Jesus was simply the title for Judas the Galilean. Let's say that fifteen of the thirty-three similarities could be pure coincidence. As such, these fifteen will be removed, leaving eighteen which must be explained. Of these eighteen, let's assume that there is a one in two chance of each event happening to Jesus in the time of Pilate and Judas a generation earlier. The mathematical formula for this would be 2 to the eighteenth power, or put simply: there would be one chance in 262,000 that Jesus and Judas were separate individuals. Although my case is not 100% certain, this would come very close—99.9996%. And consider this: would the release of prisoners in 4 BC (the Barabbas event) be only one chance in two or would it be one chance in a thousand, or a million? Likewise, the release of prisoners on the Passover would not be one in two but one in six, in that six festivals were celebrated by the Jews each year. As you can see, the one chance in 262,000 of Jesus and Judas being separate people is a gross understatement of the odds favoring my hypothesis. To put it another way: would you risk your life savings on a lottery where you had only one chance to lose out of 262,000?

SIMILARITIES—JUDAS THE GALILEAN AND JESUS

1. Jesus was born in 6-4 BC (Matthew) and in 6 AD at the Census of Cyrenius (Luke). Judas was mentioned by Josephus in 5 BC (Temple Cleansing—Ant. 17.149-167) and in 6 AD, regarding the census of Cyrenius (Ant. 18.1-10).

2. Both Jesus and Judas cleansed the Temple in Jerusalem. (Matt. 21:12,13)(Ant. 17:149-167) Actually, Judas probably cleansed the Temple twice. The first cleansing was the Golden Eagle Temple Cleansing where Matthias and he were captured by Herod the Great. The second cleansing

can be deduced from inference. Judas the Galilean's grandson, Menahem, followed his grandfather's modus operandi and seized an armory before marching on Jerusalem. It is most probable that Judas the Galilean marched on Jerusalem in 6-7 AD (after the census) and cleansed the Temple as a Messianic act. It is interesting to note that the Gospel of John placed the Temple cleansing at the beginning of Jesus' career (John 2:12-25) while the Synoptics have it at the end of his ministry.

3. Jesus and Judas were both called the Galilean. Actually, Jesus was referred to as Jesus of Nazareth, which is a city in Galilee. It is possible that this is a corruption of Nazirite as there are no references to Nazareth in the Old Testament or in Josephus. Jesus' disciples were called Galileans (Mk. 14:70) and it may have been a sleight-of-hand which changed Jesus the Galilean to Jesus of Nazareth. Judas the Galilean is mentioned in several passages by Josephus (War 2.118; War 2.433 and Ant. 20.102). Josephus did state that this Judas was from Gamala, across the river Jordan (Ant. 18.4) but he was known as the Galilean, as attributed by the above references.

4. Judas opposed the Roman tax and Jesus was crucified for the charge of opposing the tax. (Luke 23:2)(Ant. 18.4) The era of Judas (6-19 AD) relates to the tax issue. Not only was there a census in 6-7 AD, but Tacitus stated that Judea was exhausted by its tax burden (16-18 AD). (Tacitus, Annals, II.42)

5. Judas was the founder of the Fourth Philosophy (Ant. 18.1-10). Jesus was credited with the founding of Christianity, a new religion.

6. Josephus detailed the life but not the death of Judas while mentioning the death but not the life of Jesus. Josephus invested much effort in recounting Judas' life, even touching upon the lives of his sons, Judas and Simon, and his grandsons, Menahem and Eleazar. (Ant. 20.102; War 2.433,434; War 7.253) It is possible that the death of Judas was removed by a Gentile Christian who believed the death of Judas by crucifixion might attract too much attention. We have already detailed in Chapter Nine our belief that the death of Jesus in Josephus was a late third or early fourth century addition.

7. Both Judas and Jesus had a second-in-command, Sadduc and Cephas respectively. Sadduc was a priestly title while Cephas was his name or nickname (Rock). (Ant. 18:4)

8. The followers of Jesus and Judas were zealous for the Law. (Acts 21:20)(Ant. 17.149-154) It is true that Paul taught his Gentile followers

that the law was unnecessary. However, the Jewish Christians clearly denounced that teaching and excommunicated Paul. (See Galatians)

9. Zealots and Sicarii arose from Judas' Fourth Philosophy. The names of two of Jesus' apostles were Simon the Zealot and Judas Iscariot (a garbling of Sicarios). Since the Zealots and Sicarii are not introduced until the late 50's and early 60's, titles of that sort would not have been used in Jesus' time (4 BC-10 AD or 27 AD). These names were placed on Apostles by Gentile Christians, nearly one hundred years after the facts.

10. Both Jesus and Judas were centered in Jerusalem and Galilee. (Ant. 17.149-167 describes the activity in Jerusalem and Ant. 18.1-10 details the movement in the countryside, in Galilee.)

11. Jesus taught at the Temple at the age of 12. Judas taught young men at the same Temple. (Luke 2:41-52)(Ant. 17.149)

12. Judas and Jesus were both called wise men by Josephus. (Ant. 17.152 and Ant. 18.63) As the Jesus passage was a late third or early fourth century addition, the use of wise man was pulled from the description of Judas and Matthias.

13. Disciples of both were willing to die for their cause. The Neronian persecution reported by Tacitus and the description of the Fourth Philosophy by Josephus show a willingness to die happily for God. Jesus said, "Blessed [are] the ones being persecuted because of righteousness, for theirs is the Kingdom of God." (Matt. 5:10) In the same way, Judas and Matthias stressed the rewards of righteousness if they were to be punished by Herod. (Ant. 17.149-167) The followers of Judas the Galilean gladly accepted death for the sake of righteousness. (Ant. 18.23-24)

14. Both teachers put a high value on the sharing of wealth or pure communism. (Matt. 6:19-27; Acts 2:42-45; Acts 4:32-37; James 5:1-6)(Ant. 18.7; War 2.427)(Essenes—War 2.122)

15. The sons of Judas and the "brothers" of Jesus were named James and Simon. (See Chapters Six and Eight).

16. The sons of Judas were put to death by crucifixion. The only other individual mentioned by name to be crucified was Jesus. Also, two apostles were to drink the same cup as Jesus, namely crucifixion. (Matt. 20:20-23)(Ant. 20.102)

17. The movements of Judas and Jesus expanded throughout the Roman Empire. The Fourth Philosophy of Judas was responsible for the war against Rome. Although centered in Jerusalem and Galilee, Judas'

followers were numbered throughout the Empire and suffered greatly during the Jewish war. We know that Paul's Gentile churches were scattered amongst the great cities, but the Jewish Christian movement must have been much greater. While Paul was the lone apostle to the Gentiles, the influence of Cephas and others must have reached a great multitude. In fact, the early church would have placed most of its resources in the "conversion" of the Jewish community to the Way of Righteousness.

Note also that Suetonius tied the rebellious, trouble-making Jews to Chrestus, or Christ. (Suetonius, The Twelve Caesars, Claudius 25) This passage definitively connected the Fourth Philosophy to Christ. While this particular disturbance was at Rome, it seems most probable that all large Jewish congregations of the Diaspora would have contained an element sympathetic to the nationalism of Judas the Galilean/Jesus.

18. The movements continued after the deaths of Judas and Jesus. It is interesting that Acts downplayed the movement of Judas the Galilean, saying that Judas was killed "and all his followers were scattered." (Acts 5:37) In reality, the Fourth Philosophy of Judas did not end with Judas' death but grew to a great degree according to Josephus. (Ant. 18.1-10) So the speech by Gamaliel in Acts was an attempt to alter history. The author of Acts did not want people to associate the Roman destruction of the Fourth Philosophy (70 AD) with the Gentile Christian movement of the second century. It is true, however, that when the story of Acts was written (early second century), the followers of Judas the Galilean had been smashed and scattered.

19. Both Judas and Jesus were considered fine teachers of the Law. (Matt.5:17-20; Mk. 12:28-34)(Ant. 17.149; War 1.648)

20. Herod the Great tried to kill Judas after the Temple Cleansing. Herod the Great tried to kill the baby Jesus. (Matt. 2)(Ant. 17.149-167)

21. In the trial of Matthias in the Temple Cleansing, the high priest was also named Matthias. This Matthias had once relinquished his office for a day, a day celebrated by a fast, because of a dream where he had sexual relations with his wife. Pilate washed his hands of responsibility on a single day because of his wife's dream concerning Jesus' innocence. (Matt. 27:19-24)(Ant. 17.166)

22. Herod the Great sent Matthias and the rebels to Jericho for questioning concerning the Temple Cleansing. Pilate sent Jesus to Herod for questioning. (Luke 23:6,7)(Ant. 17.160)

23. Under Herod the Great's son, Archelaus (4 BC), prisoners were released to appease the mob. One of these prisoners may have been Judas the Galilean. (War 2.4) This same story was repeated at the trial of Jesus. In that story, Pilate released Barabbas to the mob instead of Jesus. (Matt. 27:15-26) One point must be noted: the Romans did not release political prisoners; they crucified them. On the other hand, the release of prisoners by Archelaus rings true as he was dealing with the remnants of the Matthias and Judas following. It is here that the crowd would have wished for Barabbas, the son of the Father.

24. In the Gospel story, Barabbas led an insurrection in the city—Jerusalem. (Mark 15:7 and Luke 23:19) A year before the prisoner release of 4 BC, Matthias and Judas led the Golden Eagle Temple Cleansing—an insurrection in the city, where many of the rebels had been burnt alive while others, Judas included, were held for later punishment. (Ant. 17:149-167; 17.204-206)

25. The trial of Jesus and the release of Barabbas occurred at the Passover feast. (Mark 14:12) The release of prisoners in 4 BC also coincided with Passover. (Ant. 17.213) As there were six Jewish feasts (Passover, Pentecost, Trumpets, Tabernacles, Dedication and Purim), the odds of this "coincidence" is one in six.

26. King Herod died a week or so before the Passover feast. At his death, Herod was clothed in purple, with a crown of gold upon his head and a scepter in his right hand. (Ant. 17.197) Before his death, Jesus was mocked by the Roman soldiers who put a purple robe on him and wove a crown of thorns to be placed upon his head. A staff was used to beat him. (Mark 15:16-20)

27. Jesus was mocked by the Roman soldiers. (Mark 15:16-20) Herod the Great was afraid that the people would mourn his death in "sport and mockery" only. (Ant. 17.177)

28. In the Gospels, the crowd (Pharisees etc.) preferred Barabbas over king Jesus. (Mark 15:1-15) Josephus described the crowd as followers of Matthias and Judas, who preferred these teachers over king Herod. (Ant. 17.204-206)

29. In the infancy story, Jesus was born at the time of a star rising in the east. (Matt. 2:2) Scholars are not sure when and what this star was. In the story of the Golden Eagle Temple Cleansing, there was an eclipse of the moon (5 BC). This is the only mention of an eclipse of the sun or moon by Josephus. (Ant. 17:167) It is possible that the celestial event of Jesus' birth was merely this eclipse mentioned by Josephus.

30. Joseph returned to Israel after the death of Herod the Great but was afraid to settle in Judea because of Archelaus. Having been warned in a dream, Joseph moved his family to Nazareth, in Galilee. (Matt. 2:19-23) After being released by Archelaus, Judas went to Sepphoris in Galilee, where he led an uprising against the son of Herod. (War 2.56) Sepphoris was in the tetrarchy of Herod Antipas, not under the control of Archelaus. Both events occurred because Herod the Great had died and the country was in unrest.

31. Jesus was proclaimed Messiah or King, in Galilee, or close by. Before the Transfiguration, they were in Caesarea Philippi (Matt. 16:13) and afterwards they travelled to Capernaum. (Matt. 17:24) After Jesus was proclaimed King, he marched to Jerusalem.

    Judas was also proclaimed King in Galilee, around Sepphoris. This was done after he captured Herod's armory and equipped his followers. (Ant. 17.271-272; War 2:56) He also may have marched upon Jerusalem, but this would be deduced by examining the behavior of his grandson, Menahem, who proclaimed himself King after capturing Herod's armory at Masada. He then marched straight to Jerusalem. (War 2.433) Judas the Galilean's entrance to Jerusalem may have been in 19 AD, so his kingship may have actually lasted twenty-two years, from 4 BC to 19 AD. This is different than Jesus who went directly to Jerusalem. However, the Gospels may have telescoped the career of Jesus into a few short years just as Josephus compressed the sixty-five year movement created by Judas into a few paragraphs. (Ant. 18.1-10)

32. The Gospels do not mention the early life of Jesus, except for the one story in which he taught at the temple at the age of twelve. Otherwise, no information was given from 6 AD (Census) to 26 AD (Pilate). This lack of information reproduces Josephus' War where nothing is written from 6 AD (Census) to 26 AD (Pilate). (War 2.167-169) Josephus barely expanded on this paucity of information in Antiquities, where he listed the Roman procurators during this twenty year stretch but little else. (Ant. 18.26-35) It is possible that these missing years from Josephus could have been the result of "pious" editing. The actual crucifixion of Judas the Galilean may have been deleted. Note that Josephus detailed the deaths of Judas' two sons, James and Simon, and his grandsons, Menahem and Eleazar. With each of these occasions, Josephus referred back to Judas the Galilean. It is hard to believe that Josephus omitted the circumstances behind the death of Judas.

33. When Jesus was arrested, he was brought first to Annas, the father-in-law of Caiaphas and former high priest. This Annas was appointed high priest in 7 AD by Cyrenius and Coponius, in the days of the census. Opposing the census and Annas was none other than Judas the Galilean. It would seem that Annas would have been much more interested in the death of Judas the Galilean than the Gospel Jesus. (For further analysis, see Appendix 7.)

ASSUMED DISSIMILARITIES

1. Jesus was not married while Judas had at least two sons, James and Simon. However, it would have been consistent with Jewish practices if a wife and family were following Jesus, not a mother and brothers (See 1 Cor. 9:5). The wedding in Cana may have been the wedding feast of Jesus and Mary. Note that Jesus and Mary were concerned about the wine situation, a likely concern for those involved with the wedding.(John 2:1-10) In addition, Cana was halfway between Judas' power base (Sepphoris) and the birth place of his wife, Mary Magdalene (Magdala).

2. Jesus was a healer, a miracle worker. Josephus does not mention this trait concerning Judas. However, Judas must have been extremely charismatic to develop such a massive following. In addition, Josephus claimed that the most onerous innovators (rebels) were the miracle workers. Thus, Jesus would have fit in nicely next to Theudas or The Egyptian. (Ant. 20.98; Ant. 20.160; Ant. 20.167,168; Ant. 20.169-172 and Ant. 20.188)

3. Jesus started his ministry at the age of thirty (Luke 3:23) and preached for three years before his crucifixion. However, this age is not reliable. Per Luke's history, Jesus was born in 6 AD and died in 39 AD, two years after Pilate left Judea. Luke probably meant to use 6 BC and the thirty-three years would have placed Jesus at the hands of Pilate in 27 AD. The thirty years was just a number to get Jesus to the Pilate era.

   Judas would have been at least 40-45 years old at the census of Cyrenius. He was probably the junior member with Matthias, possibly a young man of thirty in 5 BC. If Judas was crucified in 19 AD, then his age would have been a respectable fifty-four. Even in his early career, Judas would have had great respect among the people because of his earlier affiliation with Matthias. In addition, Judas' little brother, James the Just, would have been fifty-three in 19 AD. (Legend has James being murdered in Jerusalem in 62 AD at the age of ninety-six.) Thus, there is no discrepancy concerning age. Judas the Galilean was probably a robust middle-aged man at his death. And the age of Jesus as reported by Luke probably described Judas/Jesus in the time of the Golden Eagle Temple Cleansing.

SIMILARITIES—JUDAS THE GALILEAN AND JUDAS

Many scholars do not believe that Judas the Galilean was the same Judas as was described in the Golden Eagle Temple Cleansing. In War 1.655, Josephus claimed that the rabbis were put to death, although not mentioning them by name. However, in Ant. 17.167, only Matthias died and it appears as if Judas was either imprisoned or on the run. If imprisoned, he was undoubtedly released by Archelaus in 4 BC (War 2.4). Either way, he was free until recaptured.

The following passages from Josephus and the Gospels will bring these two Judases together.

1. There are two Gospel references which may describe Jesus fleeing from Herod the Great rather than Herod Antipas. "At that time some Pharisees came to Jesus and said to him, 'Leave this place and go somewhere else. Herod wants to kill you.'" (Luke 13:31) And in Matt. 12:1-8, Jesus and his disciples picked heads of grain and ate them on the Sabbath, thus working on the Sabbath. As a defense, Jesus referred his critics to David, who ate consecrated bread while being chased by Saul. Jesus' argument seems to place him in the same position as David, fleeing from the authorities. These two passages may harken back to Judas escaping the death sentence imposed upon Matthias and forty others. (Ant. 17.149-167) In fact, Judas was probably imprisoned by Herod and then released by Archelaus in the Barabbas scenario noted earlier. (War 2.4)

    Since Herod Antipas was Tetrarch of Galilee from 4 BC-39 AD, the references to this Herod do not necessarily put Judas/Jesus in a later time frame. The above passages may also describe the efforts put forth by Herod Antipas to capture Judas after his escape from Jerusalem. After all, Judas did break into the armory at Sepphoris. Therefore, Herod Antipas would have been after Judas in 4 BC as well.

2. Josephus mentioned a bandit leader named Judas, who led a rebel group at Sepphoris in Galilee, around 4-3 BC. This Judas attacked the royal armory and equipped his followers.(Ant. 17.271; War 2.56) The Golden Eagle Judas was the son of Sepphoris, per the account in War 1.648. In one instance, Sepphoris is a city, in another, a name. Also note that Archelaus

released political prisoners to the populous, hoping to atone for his father, Herod the Great.(War 2.4) If Judas had been captured with Matthias, he might have been in prison and released. Shortly after this prison release, Josephus writes about Judas the bandit.

3. The teachings of Matthias and Judas were similar to those of Judas the Galilean. Both were obsessed with following the Law and keeping the Temple pure. They also would gladly die rather than worship idols or Caesars. (Ant. 17.151; Ant. 18.23) Note also that Matthias and Judas cleansed the Temple from an idol, the Golden Eagle, thereby confronting Herod the Great with sedition. In 41 AD, the Jewish fanatics were willing to go to war with Rome if Caligula placed a statue of himself in the Temple. (Tacitus, Histories, V.9) The followers of Hezekias, Judas the bandit's father or grandfather, also had a presence at the Temple. (Ant. 14.168)

4. The High Priest in 5 BC at the Temple Cleansing was Joazar (Ant. 17.164). Joazar persuaded the people to accept the Roman taxation of 6 AD which was opposed by Judas the Galilean. (Ant. 18.3)

5. Matthias and Judas worked as a team. Judas the Galilean also had a second-in-command, Sadduc. (Ant. 17.149; Ant. 18.4)

6. Matthias and Judas were referred to as wise men by Josephus, a high honor indeed.(Ant. 17.155) Judas the Galilean was called a clever rabbi by Josephus in War 2.433.

7. The grandson of Judas the Galilean broke into king Herod's armory in Masada (66 AD) just as Judas the bandit had done in Sepphoris (3 BC). (War 2.433; War 2.56) This definitely links the 3 BC Judas with the 6 AD Judas the Galilean. And this also shows that Judas the Galilean would have been active at the time of the Golden Eagle Temple Cleansing of 5 BC.

8. The father or grandfather of Judas the bandit was Hezekias (Ezekias). This Hezekias was put to death by Herod the Great. Hezekias' followers petitioned at the Temple for justice in regards to Herod's actions. These followers of Hezekias had a presence in Galilee and in Jerusalem, just as Matthias and Judas in 5 BC and Judas and Sadduc in 6 AD. In addition, King Hezekiah purified the Temple, so the name Hezekias may harken back to this as well.

9. Matthias and Judas resemble Mattathias and Judas Maccabee in that both cleansed the Temple and the names are similar. Judas the bandit and Judas Maccabee were both terrible to all men. (Ant. 12.314; Ant. 17.272) And

Judas the Galilean and Sadduc were also based upon the Maccabean precedent of a leader and a second-in-command.

10. After the death of Matthias and the imprisonment of Judas, their followers petitioned Archelaus for the release of Judas (Barabbas) and for tax relief. (Ant. 17.204-205) Judas the Galilean led his followers in opposing the Census tax of Cyrenius. (Ant. 18.1-10)

APPENDIX 2

TIME LINE

4-6 BC   Matthew—Birth of Jesus in Bethlehem, outside Jerusalem. Josephus (Ant. 17.149-167)—The first mention of Judas and Matthias, two teachers in Jerusalem. They are the central figures in the Temple Cleansing.

4 BC   Herod the Great dies.

4 BC   Archelaus releases political prisoners. One of the prisoners was probably Judas the Galilean, known as Barabbas or son of the Father.

4-3 BC   Judas organizes a resistance group in Sepphoris, where he breaks into Herod's armory and arms his followers.

6-7 AD   Luke—Birth of Jesus in Bethlehem at the time of the census of Cyrenius. Josephus (Ant. 18.1-10)—Judas the Galilean leads a revolt against the census tax imposed by Rome.

14 AD   Tiberius becomes the Roman Emperor.

15-18 AD   Gratus is appointed procurator by Tiberius. He ruled for three years and apponted four high priests, the last being Caiaphas.

18-37 AD   Pontius Pilate becomes the Roman procurator of Judea, per the analysis in Appendix 7.

19 AD   Judas the Galilean/Jesus is crucified. This dating correlates to a disturbance in Rome as reported by Tacitus (Tacitus, Annals, II.85) and by Josephus (Ant. 18.65-84). This expulsion of Jews occurred in 19 AD, after the introduction of Pilate and the spurious Jesus passage in Josephus. In addition,

Caiaphas was high priest in 19 AD and Annas was an active player in the political scene. Both men interrogated Jesus after his arrest.

26-37 AD   This is the traditional date when Pontius Pilate becomes the Roman procurator of Judea.

26 AD   Josephus (Ant. 18.63-64)—At the beginning of Pilate's term, Jesus is crucified. However, this is undoubtedly a fourth century forgery. Per the New Testament, Jesus is crucified at the hands of Pilate, but no concrete date is given, although most church historians place the event at 30-33 AD. (See Appendix 7).

26-33 AD   Acts 1—James becomes co-leader with Cephas. This is consistent with Paul's account of the pillars in Galatians 2:9. As this happened right after the crucifixion of Judas/Jesus, the date may have been as early as 19 AD.

29 AD   Luke 3:1-20—John the Baptist starts his ministry in the 15th year of Tiberius.

34-37 AD   Josephus (Ant. 18.109-119)—John the Baptist is killed by Antipas for opposing his marriage to Herodias. Luke 3:20—John is killed by Herod the Tetrarch (Antipas) for the same reason, although a date is not mentioned.

37 AD   Pilate is relieved of duty for his part in the Samaritan slaughter. This may be described in Acts 8:1-25.

41 AD   Caligula orders the Jews to place a statue of himself in the Temple (Emperor worship). This would have caused a war if the order had been carried out. Luckily for the Jews, Caligula was assassinated.

44 AD   Ant. 20.38-48—Eleazar from Galilee persuades King Izates to follow the whole law and be circumcised. Acts 8:26-39—Philip approaches an important government official of Candace, queen of Ethiopia, and convinces him to be baptized. (Note the Jewish story is given a Christian twist.)

44-46 AD   Fadus named procurator of Judea.

45 AD   Ant. 20.97-98—Theudas, a magician who leads the people in revolt at the River Jordan, is captured and his head is cut off.

46-48 AD   Tiberius Alexander becomes procurator of Judea.

47 AD   Ant. 20.102—James and Simon, the sons of Judas the Galilean, are crucified. Acts 12—James and Simon (Peter) are captured. James is killed and Simon escapes.

50-55 AD   Paul is officially excluded from the Jewish Christian movement.

52-60 AD   Felix, a favorite of Claudius, becomes procurator. According to Tacitus, he "indulged in every kind of barbarity and lust." (Tacitus, Histories, V.9)

58 AD   According to Acts, Paul is rescued at the Temple by the Romans after the Jewish Christians tried to kill him. This event was near the time of the Egyptian, a miracle worker described by Josephus.

58-60 AD   According to Acts, Paul is in prison under the Roman Procurator, Felix.

60-62 AD   According to Acts, Paul is still in prison under Felix's successor, Festus. This is where Paul meets with King Agrippa.

62 AD   According to Acts, Paul is sent to Rome where he spends at least two years. This is where the story of Acts ends.

62 AD   James is killed in Jerusalem. At this point, the rush to war seems inevitable. (Ant. 20.200)

62-64 AD   The whole set of events described by Acts for the years 58-62 is put into question by Josephus' chronology of Saul's actions. In 62-64 AD, Saul is seen persecuting those weaker than himself (The Way). (Ant. 20.214) Saul might have been a participant in the murder of James, just as Acts said he approved of the death of Stephen. (Acts 8:1)

64 AD   Rome is set ablaze by Nero or by the Jewish Christians.

66 AD   Saul is sent to Agrippa, where he asks the king to bring an army to Jerusalem to stop the insurrection. (War 2.418-419)

66 AD   Menahem, the grandson of Judas the Galilean, breaks into the armory at Masada and proclaims himself king. This recreates the story of his grandfather from 3 BC to 19 AD. (War 2.433-434. He is later killed by a rival. (War 2.445-447)

66 AD   Saul goes to see Nero in order to lay the blame for the insurrection on Florus. (War 2.556-558) Note that the interview with Nero was after Nero slaughtered the Jewish Christians for their part in the Great Fire of Rome in 64 AD.

66-73 AD   The Jewish War begins and ends. Jewish Christianity or the Way is crushed. After this, Christianity is for the Gentiles and for one lone Jewish group called the Ebionites. The Ebionites were not accepted by either Jews or Gentile Christians and eventually disappeared from history.

73 AD   Eleazar, another grandson of Judas the Galilean, convinces the Sicarii to commit mass suicide at Masada. (War 7.253-406)

APPENDIX 3

FAMILY TREE OF JESUS

In Chapter Two, we discovered that Joseph was not really the father of Jesus. If this is true, then can the genealogy be recreated? In Josephus, the father of Judas the Galilean is likewise in doubt. In the description of the Fourth Philosophy in Ant. 18.1-10, Josephus does not mention the family background of Judas, only that he came from Gamala. Therefore, we might suspect that Josephus had no idea of Judas' genealogy.

However, in the description of Matthias and Judas in War 1.648, the father of Judas was said to be Sepphoris. This was changed in Ant. 17.149 to Saripheus. Note that Sepphoris was a city where Judas broke into an armory to arm his followers. In War 2.56, this Judas was the son of Hezekias, a robber executed forty-five years earlier by Herod. (Ant. 14.159-160) In Ant. 17.271, this Hezekias was named Ezekias. And to top off this confusion, we must not forget that Judas may have been referred to as Barabbas or son of the Father.

First of all, we must discount Sepphoris as this clearly is a place name. The name Saripheus may just be a garbling of Sepphoris as it is unlikely that this obscure information would have been corrected by Josephus.

Hezekias and Ezekias may, however, give us some clues as to Judas' parentage. (Antiquities has used the Greek form of Hezekias, which is Ezekias). Hezekias was a robber who was opposed to Herod in the early years (48 BC). Thus, it may be that this strain of hatred for Herod was passed down to Judas. But upon further examination, Hezekias died forty-five years before the Judas of 3 BC. Thus, this Judas may have been anywhere from forty-five to sixty-five years old. This seems out of step with the traditions of Jesus being only thirty-three and is older than our hypothesis concerning Judas the Galilean in 3 BC. (Judas may have been forty-five in 10 AD but I believe him to be around thirty at the Temple Cleansing.)

Hezekias may harken back to the days of King Hezekiah who cleansed the Temple. The Golden Eagle Temple Cleansing may have drawn comparisons between Hezekiah and Judas. If this is the case, then Josephus simply attached an identified "robber" to Judas. In <u>Antiquities</u>, Josephus only mentions Hezekias by name as an important nemesis of Herod. There were no other robbers named. Thus, the combination of Hezekias to Judas would have been good reading but not necessarily good history.

There is one other possibility concerning Ezekias (Hezekias). In our study, Zebedee has been identified as a code name for the family of Jesus. James and John, the sons of Zebedee, were really the brothers of Judas/Jesus. So it is possible that the Gospel writers took the names Ezekias and Galilee and combined them to arrive at Zebedee. Note that the Gospel writers had used a similar treatment for Judas Iscariot, where the I and S of Sicarios were switched. In the case of Zebedee and Ezekias, the E and Z were switched. However, this does not prove that Ezekias was the father of Judas, but only that the Gospel writers used the name to invent the name Zebedee.

So are we back to ground zero? Are there any more clues? The most probable case concerns the name Barabbas, preserved in the Gospels but not directly mentioned in Josephus. Barabbas means son of the father. This may have two very different meanings. First, this may refer to Judas/Jesus' relationship to God. The Lord's Prayer calls God Father. But Judas' prayers would not have differed from those of Matthias. Both could have been referred to as Barabbas if this were the case. Secondly, the name Barabbas may simply be a reference to a father or a father figure. The only man who had great significance in the life of Judas was his co-teacher Matthias. Could it be that Matthias was the father and Judas the son. This would fit the Maccabean model, with Mattathias and Judas Maccabee.

When Matthias was martyred by Herod in 5 BC, the crowds mourned him and cried for the release of Judas. (Herod probably kept Judas alive as an insurance policy against the rebels). Judas would have remained in prison and eventually executed had not Herod died. But Herod's son, Archelaus, released Herod's prisoners to the mob. Certainly, the crowd cried for Barabbas, the son of the father. This name, Barabbas, takes on a different meaning if Matthias was the father of Judas.

In the genealogy of Jesus, Matthew records the father as Joseph, the grandfather as Jacob and the great-grandfather as Matthan. Luke has Joseph as father, Heli as grandfather and Matthat as great-grandfather. If we remove the nonhistorical Joseph from the lists, the grandfather would be Matthan or Matthat, not far from our Matthias. And the father figures could also be removed because the Gospels put Jesus a generation later than when he really lived. So it is possible that the Gospels point towards Matthias.

Of course, this is all conjecture, for the actual father of Judas/Jesus will never be known for sure. However, we do know that Jesus had two brothers,

James and John. And he had four sons: James, Simon, Judas and Joseph. His wife followed him on his journeys, and her name was Mary. From Josephus, we also know that Menahem and Eleazar were grandsons. I am sure that the brothers and sons of Judas/Jesus had children, but their names are truly lost to history.

FAMILY TREE OF JESUS

Matthias or
Hezekias?

			(Sadduc)
James	Judas the Galilean	John	Cephas
(brother of Jesus)	d. 19 AD	(brother of James)	
d. 62 AD		alive at 50 AD	

	Mary		Mary—wife of Clopas
Judas?		John Mark?	
Joseph?		Barnabas?	

Joseph Judas	Salome	James Simon	Simeon Bar
twin brothers	daughter	(Younger) (Zealot)	Cleophas
May have been		Executed by	James son
James' sons		Tiberius Alexander	of Alphaeus

Grandsons of Judas the Galilean

James?	Zoker?	Menahem	Eleazar
Questioned under		d. 66 AD	d. 73 AD
Domitian 81-96 AD*		Son?	

* Eusebius, <u>The History of the Church</u>, Book 3.20.

APPENDIX 4

THE NEW TESTAMENT AND JOSEPHUS

The purpose of this section is to identify and list the Gospels' and Acts' reliance upon the writings of Josephus. Note that the War was written in 75 AD and Antiquities in 93 AD. If we find that a Gospel section can be attributed to the War, or to the War and Antiquities, then the Gospel cannot have been written before 75 AD. If a section relates only to Antiquities, then it could not have been written before 93 AD. This is very important, as most scholars place the synoptic Gospels and Acts in the 70-90 AD range. A later range can pose problems for the traditional view, such as authorship. If Matthew was written in 95 AD then the author was definitely not the Apostle Matthew. The same can be said for Mark and Luke. Thus the link between the Gospels and Jesus is severed as no contemporaries of Jesus were involved in the Gospel composition.

For this appendix, I am going to list the New Testament passages and the corresponding references in the War and or Antiquities. Some Gospel passages will be omitted because critics may argue that a passage about Jesus has no counterpart in Josephus. Thus, the passages concerning the Temple Cleansing and the taxation issue will be set aside even though I believe they are related to Judas the Galilean as reported by Josephus. In addition, there are certain Gospel passages which may also be reported by Josephus but may come from an earlier written or oral tradition. These will be listed at the end of the appendix.

I. The Synoptic Gospels, Acts and Josephus

A. Matt. 3:1-12; Mk. 1:1-18; Lk. 3:1-20   Ant. 18.117

The Gospels claimed that John the Baptist preached a baptism of repentance for the forgiveness of sins. This interpretation is a twisting of Josephus' words. Josephus clearly stated that John's baptism was not for the forgiveness of sins "but for the purification of the body; supposing still that the soul was thoroughly purified beforehand by righteousness." Thus, we see why the Gospel writers altered Josephus' meaning. According to Paul's message (the one accepted by the Gentile Church), forgiveness came only through the blood of Jesus. John the Baptist said that forgiveness came through righteousness, a totally different teaching. This change to Josephus was definitely done at a late date, when all Jewish input was long since forgotten.

B. Matt. 14:1-12; Mk. 6:14-27; Lk. 3:20   <u>Ant</u>. 18.119

The Gospels all attest that John was arrested and placed in prison. They do differ on who desired to kill John. Matthew said that Herod wanted to kill John and this is consistent with Josephus. Mark gives us the idea that Herod was forced to kill John because of his wife, Herodias', hatred for John. In any event, the detail of the imprisonment is found only in <u>Antiquities</u>. Josephus said that John was taken prisoner and sent to the castle, Macherus, and there put to death.

C. Matt. 26:59; Mk. 14:53; Lk. 22:66-23:1   <u>Ant</u>. 20.200,201

The Gospels state that Jesus was illegally tried before the whole sanhedrin as a Law breaker. This same scenario was offered by Josephus in his passage concerning James, the brother of Jesus. Both may have been similarly handled but this seems too convenient an explanation. Surely the Gospel writers had much more information concerning James than Jesus. James died in 62 AD while the death of Jesus was at latest, 33 AD and at earliest, 10 AD.

D. Matt. 27:14; Mk. 15:5; Lk. 23:9   <u>Ant</u>. 19.334

The Gospels present Jesus as silent before Pilate. This serene approach helped win over Pilate. Only the mad desire of the Jews convinced Pilate to execute Jesus. In a passage concerning a certain Simon who was well versed in the Law, this Simon also was silent before Agrippa. And the result was the same. Agrippa did not punish Simon but let him go. These two events are too similar to be coincidence.

E. Matt. 27:15-26; Mk. 15:6-15; Lk. 23:18-25
War 2.4; Ant. 17.204,205

The Gospel passages are about a man named Barabbas, a revolutionary who was set free upon the demands of the Jewish crowd. This has troubled commentators as there is no other case in recorded history where a Roman governor (in this case, Pilate) released a prisoner as part of a celebration (such as Passover). In fact, the Romans were very efficient in how they handled political enemies, and the solution was not release but rather, crucifixion.

Josephus does give us a clue as to where the Barabbas story originated. Archelaus, the son of Herod the Great, released prisoners to appease the mob (4 BC). And this act was brought against him to Caesar, who would not have approved. Thus, the Gospel story reached back to 4 BC to come up with the Barabbas prototype. But this should not be surprising. Almost the whole story relates to this earlier time period.

As to the dating, the story is found in both the War and Antiquities. Therefore, we cannot be certain upon the 93 AD date as the War was published in 75 AD. However, it does show how the Gospels used Josephus to a great extent.

F. Matt. 27:45-48; Mk. 15:33; Lk. 23:44,45   War. 6:290,291

The Gospels claim that Jesus died at the ninth hour while Josephus said that at the ninth hour a light shone around the alter which was a sign of the impending disaster, culminating in the destruction of the Temple. This may just be a coincidence but the destruction of the Temple is at the heart of both stories, the earthly temple of Jesus and the physical Temple at Jerusalem.

G. Matt. 2:1   Ant. 17.155

The Wise Men of the infancy story may be borrowed from the description of Matthias and Judas in the Golden Eagle Temple Cleansing. Note that Josephus did not call many of his historical characters wise men. In the period in question (4 BC to 70 AD), only a couple of others were deemed wise men. In the late insertion concerning Jesus, Jesus was called a wise man. Josephus also called Cherea a wise and courageous man. This Cherea was responsible for the assassination of Caligula. Josephus said that Cherea had "virtue that is necessary for a wise man."(Ant. 19.210) And he said that the Jewish nation considered himself (Josephus) a "wise man who is fully acquainted with our laws..."(Ant. 20.264,265)

H. Matt. 2:15   War 2.261-263; Ant. 20.169-172

The passage in Matthew is "Out of Egypt, I call my son." This refers to the story where Jesus was taken to Egypt to avoid the persecutions of Herod the Great and later was returned as a young child. The references in Josephus concern the Egyptian, who led a large revolt around 60 AD. There is a good chance that this story from Josephus was conveniently placed here and later in Luke 21:38, where Paul was confused with the Egyptian.

I. Matt. 27.19   Ant. 17.166

In Matthew, Pilate's wife had a dream which led Pilate to wash his hands of the whole affair. This same thing occurred in the trial of Matthias, where the high priest resigned because of a dream concerning his wife.

J. Birth of Jesus—Matthew states 6 BC   War 1.648-665; Ant. 17.149-168
   Birth of Jesus—Luke states 6-7 AD   War 2.117-118; Ant. 18.1-10

Perhaps the clearest clue concerns the birth of Jesus. Matthew and Luke give two dates which are not even close to one another. But these dates perfectly fit with the mentions of Judas the Galilean in the writings of Josephus.

K. Luke 23:1-25   Ant. 17.160

Luke had Jesus sent to see Herod. In the trial of Matthias, Matthias was sent to Jericho where Herod (the Great) passed judgment.

L. Matt. 28:1-4   War 7.29-30

After the destruction of the Temple in 70 AD, a resistance leader named Simon thought he might escape by astonishing and deluding the Romans. He put on a white frock and appeared magically out of the ground where the Temple once stood. At first, those who saw him were astonished and stood still. But later, they approached Simon at ask who he was.
In the Gospels, an angel came down from heaven and rolled back the stone in front of the tomb. "His appearance was like lightening, and his clothes were white as snow. The guards were so afraid of him that they shook and became like dead men." This angel later spoke to Mary Magdalene and the other Mary.

M. Luke 24:20-21; Matt. 28:63   War 3.27-28

The Gospels state that Jesus would be raised from the dead on the third day. Now whether or not this was an original tradition can be questioned. Obviously, the followers of Jesus believed that Jesus was resurrected, but some details of that resurrection left behind by Paul's letters can be questioned. In 1 Cor. 15:4, Paul stated that Jesus was raised on the third day according to the Scriptures. It is possible that this creed was added by a later church leader as was the passage in 1 Cor. 15:6.

Josephus related a story about a Jewish commander named Niger. The Romans assumed they had killed him, but he managed to escape through a subterraneous cave. On the third day, he appeared to those who were searching for him. His followers were filled with joy, thinking that God had preserved Niger so that he could still be their commander.

N. Acts 10:1-48   Ant. 19.332-334

The Peter and Cornelius episode was clearly an adaptation of the Simon and Agrippa meeting. In both cases, a Simon was escorted to Caesarea.

O. Acts 12:1-19   Ant. 20.102

In Acts, Peter escaped and James was beheaded. In the true version, Simon and James, the sons of Judas the Galilean, were crucified.

P. Acts 12:19-23   Ant. 19:350

In Acts, Herod was eaten by worms and died. Josephus merely stated that Herod died of a stomach illness. The data for the more fanciful version came from Josephus and nowhere else.

Q. Acts 1:21-26   War 1:648-665; Ant. 17.149-168

Matthias, an otherwise unknown figure, was added to the Eleven Apostles as a replacement for Judas Iscariot. As we already know, the election was a replacement for Jesus, not for the mythical Judas Iscariot. The name Matthias simply comes from the source of many of the other "borrowings," the Golden Eagle Temple Cleansing.

R. Acts 21:17-38   Ant. 20.167-172; War 2.261-263

After digesting A-Q, it becomes clear that the author of Acts had a way of using Josephus' history line and characters in creating a unique historical framework for Jesus and Paul. In Acts 21, Paul was sent to the Temple by James in a purification rite. This is unbelievable since Paul had already been repudiated by James and Cephas (Galatians). So the whole affair concerning Paul was invented by the author of Acts and placed in the time frame of Felix. Note that Acts 21:38 has the Roman commander asking, "Aren't you the Egyptian who started a revolt and led four thousand terrorists out into the desert some time ago?" Only with information from Josephus could this conversation be created between Paul and the Roman commander. Ant. 20.172 says, "But the Egyptian escaped out of the fight, but did not appear anymore."

One could argue that the account in Josephus merely corroborates the version in Acts. However, several other passages by Josephus have a "Saul" in the thick of things from 62-66 AD. The above passage in Acts places Paul in prison in 58 AD, and he is later sent to Rome in 62 AD. Therefore, if the Acts version is correct, then Josephus' Saul must be another unrelated Saul. But we will soon see in S, T, U and V that the Saul of Josephus was the Paul of Acts.

S. Acts 8:1-3; Gal. 1:13   Ant. 20.214

The New Testament accounts of Paul persecuting the church can be ballparked to the mid to late thirties. Note that Paul's account simply stated that he persecuted the church because of his religious zeal. The account in Acts is very similar to that of Josephus, where Saul had assembled a group of "wicked wretches" to "plunder those that were weaker than themselves." This particular zeal was one of class warfare, because in Acts and in Josephus, Saul associated his cause with the High Priest against those weaker than himself (The Way). It is probable that the writer of Acts knew of Paul's persecution of the church from Paul's own version in Galatians, and fleshed it out by using the information from Josephus. One must note that the Josephus account occurred between 62-64 AD. Therefore, Paul was persecuting the church at the end of his career as well as in the beginning. And this later persecution may have had sinister results. The mention of Paul persecuting the church in Acts 8:1 came after the stoning of Stephen. Coincidentally, Josephus' account of Saul persecuting the church came after the stoning of James, the brother of Jesus. According to Robert Eisenman, Stephen was a stand-in for James. If this is true, then the plot thickens.

T. Acts 24:26-27   War 2.273

Acts portrayed Paul as languishing in prison while Felix was procurator. They often spoke as Felix hoped to receive a bribe from Paul in return for a pardon. This type of activity actually occurred during the governorship of Albinus (62-64 AD). "[Albinus] allowed those imprisoned for banditry…to be bought out by their relatives, and only the man who failed to pay was left in jail to serve his sentence." The author of Acts was simply beefing up his story and giving reason why Paul remained in prison. In fact, Paul was not in prison but was cavorting with his old Herodian friends.

U. Acts 25:26-32   War 2.418-419

Per the Acts rendering, the conversation with Agrippa occurred during the term of Festus (60-62 AD). And the discussion concerned religious matters relating to Paul's interpretation of the Christ. However, in Josephus, Saul and his kinsmen were sent to Agrippa to secure an army to suppress an insurrection in Jerusalem. This occurred in 66 AD. So again, the author of Acts took a meeting between Saul and Agrippa and gave it a new meaning. In the sanitized Acts version, the meeting was all religious while the meeting in War had to do with politics and war. Note that Paul was working against the Fourth Philosophy, according to Josephus.

V. Acts 26:32-27:1   War 2.556-558

In Acts, Paul was sent to Caesar (Nero) by his own request. Once there, he spent at least two years in prison, bringing the date to 62-64 AD. In the War, Saul requested to see Nero in order to lay the blame for the war upon Florus, the Roman procurator. This occurred in 66 AD.

This last "coincidence" should convince the reader that Saul and Paul were one in the same. The Acts' version simply twisted events in the life of Paul into an acceptable story. After all, Paul had to be the hero, not the villain.

W. Acts 8:26-40; 9:10-19; 11:27-30   Ant. 20.34-53

After realizing that Acts is merely a distorted image of Josephus, the above comparisons (W) will destroy any vestige of imagined truth as related by Luke. The passage from Josephus tells a story about Queen Helena and her son, Izates. Both were converted to a form of Judaism by Ananias and another Jew. These men taught that circumcision was unnecessary and even inferior to their version of Judaism. Later, another Jew from Galilee convinced Izates that he must be circumcised. This fight between the two versions of Judaism was the same as that fought by Paul and Cephas as relayed in the letter to the Galatians. The dating of the Izates version was around 44 AD. The account by Paul was not a copy of the Josephus story, but it is my contention that the date of Paul's letter to the Galatians was in the same time as Izates, approximately 44 AD. This compares to the traditional dating of Paul's letter of 57 AD.

Right after the story of the circumcision of Izates, Josephus tells of the assistance that Helena and Izates gave the Jews at Jerusalem during the great famine. It should not be missed that Paul was making a collection for the poor of Jerusalem, as noted in Galatians, Corinthians and Romans. This collection was due to the famine and the desperate needs of those in Jerusalem.

In Galatians, Paul detailed his two visits to Jerusalem, one three years after his conversion and the other fourteen years later. The Book of Acts had Paul in Jerusalem four times: first, after his conversion; second, at the famine (44 AD); third, at the Council of Jerusalem (53 AD); and Fourth, at his arrest and imprisonment (58 AD). The above accounts from Paul and Luke cannot be reconciled through traditional dating. Note that Paul never mentioned his trip concerning the famine. The reason for this is simple: it had not yet occurred! The conversion of Paul and the "Council" happened some ten to fourteen years earlier than traditionally assumed. This being the case, the letters asking for money were written in the early 40's AD, and the trip by Paul occurred after these were written. When Paul made this famine relief trip to Jerusalem, he had already been excommunicated by James and Cephas (see Galatians). It is at this time that the Pseudoclementine Recognitions state that Paul attacked James. This could only have happened under the Judas the Galilean hypothesis. The traditional dating answers no questions.

There are several parts of the Izates story which were borrowed by the author of Acts. The Jew who converted Izates was named Ananias. This name, Ananias, was also used in the conversion story of Saul (Acts 9). In Appendix 6, the story of Paul's "Road to Damascus" conversion has been debunked. It never happened! The sweet story of Saul being instructed by Ananias was nothing more than massaging the story of Izates and Ananias.

In Acts 8, Philip met a Eunuch on his king's business. This Eunuch was reading the Scriptures, and Philip interpreted them for him, telling him to be baptized. This correlates to Ananias and Izates, and later to Izates and the Jew from Galilee. Before Ananias preached his version of Judaism to Izates, he converted the women of Izates (wives and concubines). Thus, Ananias and the Eunuch had their professions in common. When the Jew from Galilee heard

Izates reading the Scriptures, he interpreted them, and Izates was soon circumcised.

This passage from Josephus helped build Acts 8, 9 and 11 as well as expose the timeline of Paul. It is perhaps the most blatant of all the "borrowings" by Luke. It also is contained only in <u>Antiquities</u>, meaning that Acts had to have been written after Josephus.

II. Acts, Josephus and the Fourth Philosophy

It is also interesting that Luke wrote about important Fourth Philosophy figures in the Book of Acts. They are as follows:

A. Acts 5:36 Luke mentioned Theudas in terms of 30 AD while he was placed by Josephus in 44-46 AD.(<u>Ant</u>. 20.97,98)

B. Acts 5:37 Luke incorrectly positioned Judas the Galilean after Theudas. According to Josephus, the sons of Judas the Galilean were crucified a few years after Theudas. However, in this passage it does mention Judas the Galilean and the census of Cyrenius. Luke must have confused the times and the individuals involved.(<u>Ant</u>. 20.102)

C. Acts 21:38 Luke had the Romans confusing Paul with the Egyptian.(<u>Ant</u>. 20.169-172)

If the Fourth Philosophy was not so vitally important, then why were its members mentioned so often. Perhaps Luke tried to distance the "Christian" movement from the Fourth Philosophy by emphasizing the failures of the Fourth Philosophy. Surely, the "Christian" movement could not be related to these "Losers".

III. Jewish Christian Excuses

There is one last grouping of passages which are included in Josephus but may have originated from an earlier Jewish Christian source. They are as follows:

A. Matt. 24:1-35 Jesus condemned the "miracle workers". This may have been placed in the mouth of Jesus by Jewish Christians as an explanation of why the miracle workers failed. Surely, opponents to the Jewish Christians would have pointed at these miracle workers as a reason to abandon the Jesus wing of the Fourth Philosophy.(See <u>Ant</u>. 2.258-260)

B. Matt. 20:20-28 Jesus predicted that two brothers would die the same death as he, namely crucifixion. This too was placed in the mouth of Jesus as a means to explain away the deaths of James and Simon, his two sons.(<u>Ant</u>. 20.102) However, since the Gospels were written many years after the Jewish war, the cover up had been started. The two sons of Jesus now became the sons of Zebedee, a mythical character.

C. Matt. 26:36-46 While Jesus was praying in the Garden of Gethsemane, his trusted friends slept. Therefore, the failure was due to the Apostles, not Jesus. Like the above cases, it was necessary to place blame elsewhere to keep Jesus above failure. This must have been a very early tradition amongst the Jewish Christians.

From the above, I think it is clear that the Gospels and Acts borrowed a great deal from Josephus. And many of these passages were from <u>Antiquities</u> which was not published until 93 AD. Therefore, the earliest date for the Gospels would be 95 AD. The latest date would be 115 AD. This is the date of Tacitus' <u>Annales</u>, which state that the Christians were the scapegoats of Nero. The date of composition is therefore between 95 and 115 AD. Given that some years passed after Josephus' writings were fully absorbed and the fact that the Gospels were well circulated at the time of Tacitus, I would place the date of composition of the Gospel of Mark at 105 AD and Matthew, Luke and Acts, a generation later. These were fully Gentile Christian documents, trying at every turn to denigrate the Fourth Philosophy and the familial ties of Jesus. In fact, since none of the authors knew Jesus or any of his original followers, the Jesus of the Gospels is nothing more than a composite of Paul and various other Jewish figures.

APPENDIX 5

NAME GAMES

The New Testament is filled with name games which are intended to befuddle the reader. We have already encountered the confusion which accompanies the names James, Simon and Judas. By combining many individuals into one person, the Gospels effectively eliminated certain main characters, such as Simon, the son of Judas the Galilean. This Simon was combined with Cephas to arrive at the composite, Peter. In the same way, James the brother of Jesus and James, the son of Judas/Jesus were combined into the fictitious James, the son of Zebedee. And Judas the Galilean was renamed Judas Iscariot, Barabbas and even Jesus, although Jesus was merely a title.

But besides these name games, there are other more subtle obfuscations. Letters in names have been switched to hide the real meaning in said names. A few such examples are listed below.

A. Matthias (Acts 1:23)
   Matthan (Matt. 1:15)
   Matthat (Luke 3:24)

As noted in Appendix 3, the Gospels have slightly altered the name Matthias to arrive at their own peculiar genealogies. In doing such, they have successfully hidden any tie between Jesus (Judas) with an older father figure, Matthias.

B. Judas the Galilean
   Judas Iscariot
   Jews

The most obvious and ingenious name game concerns the name Judas with the Jews. In the Greek, the names are nearly identical. Thus, the villification of Judas on an individual basis simply follows the same treatment of the entire religion. Judas Iscariot was the traitor and thief while the Jews were children of the devil.

C. Barabbas
   Barsabbas

As we discovered in our study, the name Barabbas was attached to Judas/Jesus in a most personal way. The reference, son of the father, referred either to Jesus' relationship to God or his relationship to his physical/spiritual father, Matthias. This being the case, the writer of Acts had to slightly alter the name of Judas/Jesus' sons, Joseph and Judas, to Barsabbas. The insertion of an S has confounded scholars for two thousand years.

D. Magdalene
   Magdala

Mary Magdalene should properly be called Mary of Magdala, a town in Galilee not far from Cana. This Mary was most likely the wife of Judas/Jesus and has been purposely distanced from him throughout the years. This was necessary to retain his virginity and to hide his familial relationships.

E. Iscariot
   Sicarios

A simple switching of the first two letters turns Judas Iscariot into Judas the Sicarios. This reference was to the latter stages of the Fourth Philosophy, when all hell broke loose. Just as Josephus described the Sicarii as being thieves (communists), the Gospel writers placed the money bag in Judas' hands. In the Gospel of John, Judas was said to have helped himself with the money. Thus, Judas Iscariot was a thief as well.

F. Zebedee
   Galilee
   Ezekias

Most scholars are at a loss in finding the meaning behind the name Zebedee. As we noted earlier, Zebedee was used as a code name for the family of Jesus. The sons of Zebedee, James and John, were really the brothers of Jesus. Thus, we must look into Judas/Jesus' background to arrive at the proper solution. In the Greek, the number of letters of Zebedee and Galilee agree with the final three being identical. The first part of Zebedee is simply a massaging of the name Ezekias, the father of Judas per Josephus. (Ezekias is the Greek form of Hezekiah). The Gospel writers simply switched the first two letters, E and Z, consistent with their handling of Iscariot and Sicarios. The l's in Galileans were also changed to b and d. Thus, the name Zebedee related directly to Judas the Galilean.

G. Alphaeus (Luke 6:15)
   Cephas (John 1:42)
   Cleopas (Luke 24:18)
   Clopas (John 19:25)

It is my belief that the family of Cephas has been disguised under the various designations above. Like the family of Judas the Galilean, the family of Cephas would have been major players in the early Jewish Christian movement.

H. Nazareth
   Nazirite

To further distance Jesus from Judas the Galilean, the Gospel writers named him Jesus of Nazareth. This geographical designation may simply be a twisting of the word Nazirite, or one consecrated to God. In addition, the town Nazareth was never mentioned in the Old Testament or in the writings of Josephus. In fact, Judas the Galilean was said to have gone to Sepphoris after the Golden Eagle Temple Cleansing. Sepphoris was only a few miles from the site of the second century AD city of Nazareth.

I. The Fourth Philosophy was modeled after the movement led by Judas Maccabee. It is interesting and revealing to compare the names of the Maccabee clan to the names of early Christianity as detailed in the New Testament and to the Fourth Philosophy as described by Josephus.

According to 1 Maccabees 2:1-6, Mattathias had five sons named John, Simon, Judas, Eleazar and Jonathan. These names run throughout the Gospels and Josephus. First, the New Testament's Twelve Apostle scheme has two Simons, two Judases, a Matthew and a Matthias, and a John. In addition, there was John the Baptist and the brothers of Jesus included a Judas and a Simon. (James will be discussed in the next section.) It should not be missed that the above mentioned characters were the main players in the early church. The other apostles were merely fillers. For example, what is known about Andrew, Philip, Bartholomew and Nathanael? Other apostle names such as Thomas (twin) and Thaddaeus are merely nicknames for Judas.

In Josephus' history of the Fourth Philosophy, the leaders were named Matthias and Judas. A Simon was instrumental in barring Herodians from the Temple. The two sons of Judas the Galilean, named Simon and James (see J), and a Theudas (corruption of Judas and Thomas) were all slain in the mid to late forties. The Jew from Galilee who converted King Izates to true Judaism (full circumcision) was named Eleazar. Also, the grandson of Judas the Galilean was named Eleazar. This Eleazar headed the group of Sicarii who defended Masada against the Romans in 73 AD. In short, the names of the Maccabee movement were popular in both the New Testament and Josephus' versions of history.

J. One other name needs to be addressed, because it was central to both the New Testament and to Josephus. James was the brother of the Lord (Jesus), and James was the son of Judas the Galilean. In fact, the New Testament mentioned three James in its history. The first James, the son of Zebedee, was a mythical character. The second James was the brother of Jesus. The third James was nicknamed the Younger or the Less. Josephus named only two James: the son of Judas the Galilean and the brother of the Messiah.

James is the English form of the Hebrew Jacob. The meaning of this name is supplanter or he that follows after.(1) Is it just coincidence that James replaced Judas/Jesus as leader of the Fourth Philosophy? The name itself may have been a nickname just as Cephas (rock) was a nickname for Simon. This is pure conjecture, but a link between the name Jonathan and James may be present. In <u>Ant</u>. 12.266, Jonathan was called Apphus. In the Gospels, James the Less was the son of Alphaeus. The Gospels may be preserving an earlier version of events, albeit twisted. It may be that Judas the Galilean named his son after his brother Jonathan. When this Jonathan was nicknamed Jacob or James, the son of Judas was also renamed as James the Less or James the Younger. The reference to an Alphaeus may be to his given name and not to his father.

APPENDIX 6

PAUL—I DO NOT LIE

The subject of Paul the Apostle is a complex one, but even our study of Judas the Galilean and the Fourth Philosophy is impacted by his life and beliefs. For Paul was opposed to the basic tenets held by Judas and his followers. That is why there is so much confusion concerning the New Testament. In its pages, we see a primitive Jesus and a Jesus following in Paul's footsteps. This Jesus is no doubt a composite character. It is up to us to sort out the real from the counterfeit. So it is necessary to better understand Paul in order to separate his beliefs from those of Judas/Jesus.

I. Paul and Herod

The Fourth Philosophy was a reactionary movement patterned upon the Maccabees, with Herod the Great as the chief antagonist. Herod introduced foreign practices amongst the Jews just as Antiochus Epiphanes did some one-hundred and fifty years earlier. That Judas the Galilean simply opposed Herod is an understatement. The disciples of Judas were willing to give their very lives in order to stop the hellenizing tendencies of Herod. This fervor continued from the time of Matthias, through the death of John the Baptist to the murder of James, the brother of Jesus. Thus, if we can tie Paul to Herod, his credibility is severely damaged. In fact, if Paul were a Herodian then our picture of Jesus is grossly distorted, because much of the New Testament Jesus comes from the life and teachings of Paul.

First, we will look to Paul's own writings for insights. In Romans 16:11, Paul said, "Greet Herodian the kinsman of me." The Greek word for kinsman is different than the word for brother. It is most likely that this kinsman would be a flesh and blood relative while brother could very well denote a spiritual relationship. This Herodian may be related by blood ties, but this by itself would still leave doubt. So Paul goes on and says, "Lucius and Jason and Sosipater the kinsmen of me." (Rom. 16:21). It is very possible that Paul had ties in Rome to several of his relatives who were Herodians. In all the other Epistles, Paul does not specifically mention any other relatives. So the case against Paul based upon his own writings is meager to be sure, but a possible tie to Herod is clearly present.

The Book of Acts, although historically flawed, may shed more light upon Paul's background. Saul, or Paul, was first mentioned in Acts 8:1 where he gave approval to the death of Stephen and to the general persecution of Christians. "But Saul began to destroy the church. Going from house to house, he dragged off men and women and put them in prison." (Acts 8:3) Saul intended to widen his search beyond Jerusalem so "he went to the high priest and asked him for letters to the synagogues in Damascus, so that if he found any there who belonged to the Way, he might take them as prisoners to Jerusalem." (Acts 9:2) Our focus should be upon Saul's influence at such a young age. Even though he was employed as a lowly thug by the chief priest, he did seem to have a certain pull with this particular priest. This does not prove that Saul was of Herodian descent, but the authority given him was extraordinary if he was from Tarsus and unrelated to those in power.

In Damascus, Paul escaped the governor of King Aretas by being lowered by a basket from a window in the wall. (2 Cor. 11:32,33) This scene was obviously altered in Acts 9:23-25, where Paul was lowered from the wall to escape the Jews. Certainly, the letter of Paul should be trusted more than the sanitizing Acts. And if this is so, the enemy of Paul was King Aretas, the same king who opposed Antipas (Herod the Tetrarch) over the murder of John the Baptist. (Ant. 18.109-119) This apparent hatred of Saul (Paul) may have had more to do with his Herodian background than with his preaching.

In the church at Antioch, there was one Manaen, a member of the court of Herod the Tetrarch (Antipas). (Acts 13:1) Saul was mentioned right after him and a few others as leaders of this particular church. Again, Saul is placed right next to a Herodian. Yet this association, though close, does not necessarily make Saul a member of the court as well.

Being a member of Herod's family had considerable advantages. For instance, they were given Roman citizenship at birth. Now in Acts 17:3, it is claimed that Paul and Silas were both Roman citizens. If Paul were a Pharisee, a Hebrew of Hebrews and a member of the tribe of Benjamin, it is doubtful that he would also have had Roman citizenship. Paul compared himself to the Jerusalem Apostles: "I was advancing in Judaism beyond many Jews of my own age and was extremely zealous for the traditions of my fathers." (Gal. 1:14) Here Paul used the term "zealous" for the law placing himself at an equal or superior position vis-a-vis Cephas and James. If this were true, then Roman citizenship is unbelievable.

After being threatened by the Jewish Christians (Fourth Philosophy), Paul was arrested by the Roman guard, thus saving his life. (Acts 21:27-36) It is interesting that Paul's nephew was there to protect Paul after the arrest, supplying information to the Romans. This information undoubtedly came from a mole, for no self-respecting Jewish Christian would knowingly help Paul. The nephew may have been keeping a close watch upon the activities of Paul and his knowledge of the Fourth Philosophy might have come from the High Priest, an employee of the Herodians.

After escaping Jerusalem, Paul was sent to Caesarea (58 AD) to answer charges in front of the Roman Procurator, Felix (52-60 AD). From the narrative in Acts 24:22-26, we learn that Felix was married to Drusilla, the daughter of Agrippa I and sister of Agrippa II. Felix often spoke with Paul, listening to Paul's Gospel. The reason for this frequent discourse was the hope for a bribe, for Felix believed Paul to have a large sum of money. That the friendly conversations occurred should not be doubted for Drusilla was a member of the Herodian family. This may indirectly indict Paul. And it is interesting to note that the bribe issue may relate to the sum of money sent by Paul's churches to the church in Jerusalem. (1 Cor. 16:1-4) Per this passage from Corinthians, Paul stated that he might accompany the money to Jerusalem. Obviously, the money never changed hands between Paul and Cephas.

In 60 AD, Felix was replaced by Porcius Festus. Felix never received his bribe for he left Paul in prison as a favor to the Jews. Festus convened a court, and it was decided that Paul should be sent to Rome to stand trial there. A few days later, King Agrippa II and his sister Bernice arrived in Caesarea to talk with Festus. (It should be noted that this Bernice later became the mistress of Titus, the Roman who destroyed Jerusalem. It was also rumored that she was having incestuous relations with her brother, Agrippa. (Ant. 20.145)) Festus informed Agrippa of Paul's case, and Paul was granted an audience. Paul made the most of his opportunity, praising the King with flattery upon flattery (Acts 26:2-3; 26:26-28). This action of Paul was opposite that of Jesus (based upon Simon and Agrippa I—Ant. 19.332-334) who was silent before Pilate. And consider Paul's attitude towards these Herodians—that of cordiality. The Fourth Philosophy, especially John the Baptist, would have vomited over this friendship.

The ties between Paul and the Herodians appear fairly secure, but Paul's teachings make it a certainty. In Romans 13:1-7, Paul wrote that the believers should pay their taxes to Rome and should also follow Caesar without reservation. From our analysis of Judas the Galilean, we know that his followers would rather die than be slaves to Rome. And it should be noted that Jesus was accused of teaching against the payment of taxes. However, since the Herodians were

Rome's tax collectors, it is easy to see why Paul sided with the power of Rome. This may also explain the passage attributed to Jesus where he was a friend of tax collectors and sinners. This was Paul and not Jesus!

Knowing all this about Paul, the passages in Josephus become more provocative. Most scholars have minimized the importance of a Saulus in the writings of Josephus because they have also overlooked Judas the Galilean and the Fourth Philosophy. But we know that Josephus centered much of his account of the times on the Fourth Philosophy (Jewish Christians). As such, the mention of a Saulus who is opposed to the Fourth Philosophy should send off warning signals. In his letters, Paul was very critical of the circumcision group's teachings, from the dietary laws to circumcision. His hatred of this movement probably hit a zenith when the Jewish Christians turned their backs upon him and his gospel (Galatians). With this in mind, let us look at Josephus' accounts of Saulus.

Costobarus, also, and Saulus did themselves get together a multitude of wicked wretches, and this because they were of the royal family; and so they obtained favour among them, because of their kindred to Agrippa: but still they used violence with the people, and were very ready to plunder those that were weaker than themselves. (Ant. 20.214)

This Saulus was a member of the royal family just as Paul claimed for himself in Romans. And as we know from Acts 8, Paul was able to obtain papers from the High Priest in order to arrest the members of the Way. This power, invested in the Herodian family, was also available to Costobarus and Saulus in the above passage. Saulus and Costobarus went about their business with a vengeance, attacking those who were weaker than themselves (Jewish Christians). In Jerusalem, Paul no longer needed to play his double game of identity. To the Jews, Paul was a Liar who taught against their Law and their way of life. Paul knew his position amongst the Jews and therefore used brute force in his persecution. It had worked once before (Acts 8; Gal. 1:13), and it would work again.

A second passage from Josephus comes from the Jewish War, where Saulus was a member of the Peace Party.

So seeing that the insurrection was now beyond their control and that the vengeance of Rome would fall upon them first, the most influential citizens determined to establish their own innocence and sent delegations to Florus and Agrippa, the former led by Simon, son of Ananias, the other distinguished by the inclusion of Saul, Antipas, and

Costobar, kinsmen of the king. They begged both to come to the City with large forces and suppress the insurrection before it got beyond control. (War 2.418-419)

Once again Saul is teamed up with Costobar and this time Antipas as well. Because of their Herodian background, they were sent to petition Agrippa. From our study of Acts 25:23—26:32, we know that Paul had a good relationship with Agrippa. And Paul's knowledge of the Way (Jewish Christians) would be invaluable in trying to defeat the insurgents. There is no doubt that Paul would have used his inside information to his own advantage.

The last mention of Saul also reminds us of his travels in the book of Acts.

After the disastrous defeat of Cestius many prominent Jews fled from the City like swimmers from a sinking ship. Costobar with his brother Saul and Philip, son of Jacimus, the commander of King Agrippa's army, slipped out of the City and went over to Cestius. But their companion in the seige of the Palace, Antipas, declined to flee and was put to death by the insurgents, as I shall describe later. Cestius sent Saul and his friends at their own wish to Nero in Greece, to acquaint him with their own plight and to lay the blame for the war on Florus; Nero's anger against Florus would, he hoped, lessen the danger to himself. (War 2.556-558)

Like Acts 21, Saul is fleeing the murderous Jews, finding comfort and support amongst the Romans. And like the account in Acts, Saul is sent to Nero to plead his case. In fact, it seems as though the account of Paul in Acts parallels the account of Saul in Josephus.

In Acts, Paul is attacked at the Temple and is rescued by the Roman guard. He is then taken to Caesarea where he is interviewed by Felix, Festus and Agrippa. After the interview with Agrippa, Paul is sent to Rome to meet with Nero.

In the account by Josephus, Saul is sent to Agrippa to plead the case for the leading citizens (wealthy and Herodians). He later returned to Jerusalem with his delegation and had to flee to the Upper Palace to escape the Sicarii (Fourth Philosophy splinter group). (War 2.425-429). Saul escaped from the city and went to the Roman commander, Cestius. Cestius then sent Saul, by his own wish, to Nero, where he petitioned Caesar for Cestius' and his own behalf.

The accounts are very similar. Knowing how Josephus was used in the building of Jesus, we must not think that the account in Acts is necessarily genuine. Note also that the first account by Josephus has Saul brutally attacking those weaker than himself. This may have been the model for Acts chapter 8. It is also interesting that Josephus mentioned two other individuals who may be in the book of Acts. In War 2.520, Josephus counted amongst the rebels "the

Peraean Niger and Silas the Babylonian; the latter had deserted to the Jews from King Agrippa, in whose army he had served." Acts mentions a Niger in chapter 13:1 and Silas was the traveling companion of Paul after the Jewish Christians had turned their backs upon him. (Acts 15:40; Gal. 2:11-13) Note that this Silas was also a member of the Herodian army. He would have been the perfect partner for Paul. But like Barnabas, it seems that this Silas also abandoned Saul and the Herodians to serve with the Fourth Philosophy.

The shift in Paul's later career to 58-62 AD (Acts) from 62-66 AD (Josephus) has tremendous implications. If Paul attacked the Jewish Christians after his so-called conversion, then all good attributed to him must be seriously questioned. In Josephus, Saul attacked those weaker than himself shortly after the stoning of James. This corresponds perfectly with Acts 7 and 8 concerning the stoning of Stephen. The Acts' version combines the later actions of Saul (62-64 AD) with a passage from Galatians.

For you have heard of my previous way of life in Judaism, how intensely I persecuted the Church of God and tried to destroy it. I was advancing in Judaism beyond many Jews of my own age and was extremely zealous for the traditions of my fathers. (Gal. 1:13-14)

According to Paul, he was a zealous Jew who tried to destroy the Jesus movement even though he was a young man. Now, if the Acts' version of Paul's early persecutions is not accurate, then is it possible to recreate the early persecutions described by Paul?

Concerning the year 19 AD, Josephus gave his reason why the Jews were expelled from Rome.

There was a man who was a Jew, but had been driven away from his own country by an accusation laid against him for transgressing their laws, and by the fear he was under of punishment for the same; but in all respects a wicked man:—he then living at Rome, professed to instruct men in the wisdom of the laws of Moses. He procured also three other men, entirely of the same character with himself, to be his partners. These men persuaded Fulvia, a woman of great dignity, and one that had embraced the Jewish religion, to send purple and gold to the temple at Jerusalem; and, when they had gotten them, they employed them for their own uses, and spent the money themselves. (Ant. 18.81-84)

When Tiberius heard of the swindle, he banished the Jews from Rome.

This passage has never been attributed to Paul because he has been viewed as a player of the late 30's and beyond. However, in Appendix 7, we have proved that the crucifixion of Judas/Jesus was shortly before this event in Rome. By moving the beginnings of the post-Jesus movement back in time by eleven to fourteen years (from 30-33 to 19 AD), the start of Paul's career could also be much earlier than previously thought.

It is interesting that Josephus did not name the Jew in the above story. He generally was quite adept at identifying individuals. It is possible that the name was deleted in the pious editing of Josephus as detailed in Appendix 7. Without the name Saul, we are left with similar behavior patterns, but we cannot place this action upon Paul with total certainty.

This Jew was driven from Judea because he had transgressed their laws. His flight from Judea was necessitated by the fear of punishment. This type of individual would never be able to openly mingle with the fanatical Jews again. After Paul's conversion, he traveled to Jerusalem twice by his own account (Gal. 1:18 and 2:1-2), but each time he only conversed privately with the leaders. Obviously, Paul knew of the dangers lurking in Jerusalem.

The unnamed Jew went to Jerusalem to make a living. Even though he had been forced to leave Judea for transgressing the law, he professed to "instruct men in the wisdom of the laws of Moses." This seems quite unusual. If a man knows the Law in Rome, he should know the same Law in Jerusalem. However, this pattern fits perfectly with Paul. Paul was always criticized by the circumcision (those from James, the brother of Jesus), but he claimed to have a superior knowledge of the Law to his own followers. These followers were generally Jewish converts, and later, simply Gentiles. These converts would know no better. They generally took Paul at his word, even though the circumcision called him a liar. In the Josephus passage, the unnamed Jew had convinced Fulvia, a rich Jewish convert, of his qualifications.

With the help of three other men, the unnamed Jew convinced Fulvia to contribute a vast sum to the Temple in Jerusalem. First, the unnamed Jew worked his scam with others. In the three passages about Saul in Josephus, this Saul was always accompanied by others, namely Costobarus, Antipas and hired hands. Note that Josephus called the followers of Saul "wicked wretches" (Ant. 20.214) just as he called the unnamed Jew a "wicked man" and his friends "of the same character as himself."

The scam concerned the contribution of purple and gold to the Temple in Jerusalem. This wealth never left the unnamed Jew's possession. Compare these actions to those of Paul.

Now about the collection for God's people: do what I told the Galatian churches to do. On the first day of the week, each one of you should set aside a sum of money in keeping with his income, saving it up, so that when I come no collections will have to be made. Then, when I arrive, I will give letters of introduction to the men you approve and send them with your gift to Jerusalem. If it seems advisable for me to go also, they will accompany me. (1 Cor. 16:1-4)

The instructions were for the Galatians and Corinthians. However, it seems as though Paul's credibility was being challenged by the Jews. 1 and 2 Corinthians as well as Galatians are merely documents which defend Paul's honesty and hard work. With the faith of a television evangelist, Paul stated:

Remember this: whoever sows sparingly will also reap sparingly, and whoever sows generously will also reap generously. Each man should give what he has decided in his heart to give, not reluctantly or under compulsion, for God loves a cheerful giver....This service that you perform is not only supplying the needs of God's people [Jews in Jerusalem] but is also overflowing in many expressions of thanks to God. (2 Cor. 9:6-12)

After calling the Jewish Apostles "deceitful workmen, masquerading as apostles of Christ" (2 Cor. 11:13), Paul repeated his claims of personal sacrifice and suffering (2 Cor. 11:16-33). He then topped his sales pitch with a boast that he was called up to heaven (2 Cor. 12:1-10). This all leads to the passage: "Now I am ready to visit you for the third time, and I will not be a burden to you, because what I want is not your possessions but you." (2 Cor. 12:14) However, I am sure that Paul accepted the possessions with open arms. These possessions never made it to the Jewish Christians in Jerusalem.

Although the above explanation about the unnamed Jew is conjecture, it should be noted that Saul met with Nero at his own wish in 66 AD. (War 2.556-558) This was the same Nero who tortured the Jewish Christians in Rome after the Great Fire of 64 AD. The Jewish Christians were crucified, set ablaze and torn apart by wild animals, all to satisfy the cruelty of Nero. I cannot imagine that Judas/Jesus would have freely consented to such a meeting. Only the most cynical, self-centered man would have met with Nero under these circumstances. Considering what we now know about Paul, such a meeting should not surprise us; he hated the Jewish Christians with a passion.

If this new history of Paul is correct, then the traditional time frame of his life must be wrong. In orthodoxy, Paul converted a few years after the crucifixion of Jesus, approximately 35 AD. By his own account of time in Galatians, Paul's participation in the Jewish Christian movement lasted from his conversion to his excommunication in Antioch, or about twenty years. This would have placed the year at 55 AD. He later went to Jerusalem, where he was captured and imprisoned. The year for this act would have been 58 AD, the dating for the Egyptian.

Of the above, the only verifiable dating is the twenty years in which Paul was a member of the Jewish Christian movement. If Judas/Jesus died in 19 AD, and Saul was a player in Rome at that time, his conversion may have been in the early 20's AD. Thus, his participation as a Jewish Christian may have been from 20-40 AD or a few years later. This may help explain a passage from the Pseudoclementine Recognitions 1.70, where the Enemy (Paul) attacked James and almost killed him. The dating for this attack was in the 40's, per Eisenman.(1) This could not have happened per the traditional dating, for Paul would have been a member of the Way during the 40's. However, if Paul had been excommunicated in the early 40's, then the motive for the attack on James would be evident.

A comparison of visits to Jerusalem between Acts and Paul's own account in Galatians should help solve the whole affair. Paul mentioned two visits to Jerusalem: one three years after his conversion and the second, fourteen years later. The Book of Acts detailed four visits: the first, at Paul's conversion; the second, at the famine (44 AD); the third, at the Council of Jerusalem (53 AD); the fourth, at Paul's arrest and imprisonment. Obviously, Galatians would have been written before the fourth visit. But what about the second visit at the time of the famine? Is it possible that Paul did not write about this visit because it had not yet happened? Remember that Paul was collecting money for the poor in Jerusalem. This is the same activity that Josephus described in his account of Queen Helena and King Izates. (<u>Ant</u>. 20.49-53) They also were sending money and food to Jerusalem during the famine. If Paul's collection activity were tied to the famine, then this solves the mystery of why Paul does not relate this 44 AD visit in the letter to the Galatians. In Galatians, Corinthians and Romans, Paul did everything possible to convince his followers that he was trustworthy. This was done so that the collection could go on.

In connection with the famine collection, Josephus also wrote about clashes between Pauline Christians and Jewish Christians; those who insisted upon circumcision and those who taught against it. (<u>Ant</u>. 20.34-48) This was no different than the excommunication of Paul in Galatians. If the Josephus account were in the early 40's, then it follows that the Antioch disagreement between Paul and Cephas would have been in the 40's as well. This earlier dating of Paul explains the unexplainable. The attack on James in the 40's and the visit to Jerusalem at the famine now fit into the time frame of Paul.

So what happened to the money that Paul had collected from those dear souls in Corinth and Galatia? Surely, the Jewish Christians did not receive any assistance from Paul. Most likely, Paul used the money to further his own goals and those goals of his Herodian friends and family. In the 60's, Saul had the resources to hire men to attack the Church. It is possible that he used the money in the 40's to stir up trouble for James and Cephas. In the 40's, the Fourth Philosophy came under attack; Theudas was beheaded and the sons of Judas the Galilean were crucified. Could Paul have had a hand in this persecution? The answer will never be known. However, we do know that Paul persecuted the Church in the 20's and the 60's. It is not too much of a stretch to assign him credit for one more persecution!

In all likelihood, the glowing account of Paul in the book of Acts is a total sham. To the very early church, Paul would have been an embarrassment, for his life was so unlike Judas/Jesus. The Gospels and Acts were designed to place the beliefs of the Gentile church onto Jesus and to make Paul the hero in the post-Jesus world. This post-Jesus world was not Jewish, but rather, Roman. Thus, Paul's harsh words and condemnations of Cephas and James were smoothed over, and it was the evil circumcision group who hounded the godly Paul. The reality was much different. In the next section, we will examine Paul's own letters against the book of Acts to solidify the above claims.

II. Paul and Acts

It is traditionally assumed that the writings of Paul and the Acts of the Apostles go hand-in-hand. In fact, the Acts of the Apostles is primarily the acts of Paul, with only slight mention of the other apostles. In this section, we will compare Paul's letters to what was written about him to see where there are agreements and where there are conflicts.

A. Acts 8:1-3 and Gal. 1:13—Persecution of the Church.

There is definitely agreement between Acts and Galatians concerning Paul's early years regarding the persecution of the Jewish Christian Church. Acts states that:

Saul began to destroy the church. Going from house to house, he dragged off men and women and put them in prison....He went to the high priest and asked him for letters to the synogogues in Damascus, so that if he found any there who belonged to the Way, whether men or women, he might take them as prisoners to Jerusalem. (Acts 8:3; 9:1,2)

Paul's hatred for the Way is not hidden. In fact, Acts makes him into a super-policeman. Note also that Paul was employed by the high priest who was appointed by the Herodians. The author of Acts may have unitentionally connected Paul to the ruling authorities. As we have seen above, this was probably the case.

Now Paul's version differs only slightly, but each discrepancy will loom large in our study.

For you have heard of my previous way of life in Judaism, how intensely I persecuted the church of God and tried to destroy it. I was advancing in Judaism beyond many Jews of my own age and was extremely zealous for the traditions of my fathers. (Gal. 1:13,14)

In this, Paul agrees with Acts: he did violently persecute the church. However, he gives no details of his methods. As discussed in the earlier section (Paul and Herod), the account in Acts mirrors a later persection by Saul. (Ant. 20.214) But it is possible that Paul persecuted the Jewish Church in the beginning of his career and also at the end. Or more likely, the author of Acts used the account in Josephus to add flavor to the story of Saul, the persecutor.

The main difference in the stories deals with Saul's friends. In Acts, the high priest was behind the stoning of Stephen, and Saul consorted with this high priest to obtain letters to arrest members of the Way. In Galatians, Paul blamed the whole episode to his zealotry for the law and the traditions of the fathers. Nothing could be father from the truth. Paul may have been zealous, but it was not the same fervor exhibited by the Fourth Philosophy (Jewish Christians or the Way). The reason for this sleight-of-hand is obvious: Paul wanted his Gentile audience to consider him an equal or superior to the Jewish Apostles. Thus, even though Paul rejected the law now, he once followed it closer than any of his peers. This deception becomes obvious when one reads the whole of Galatians.

B. Acts 9:1-30 and Gal. 1:15-17—Damascus

The story of Saul's conversion on his way to Damascus is familiar to most Bible students. The Lord appeared to him in a vision, and from that point on, Saul followed Jesus. He was led into the city of Damascus by the hand as the confrontation with the Risen Jesus had momentarily blinded him. There he met disciples of the Way, and the Holy Spirit entered him. At that moment, Saul transformed into Paul, champion of the Christian movement.

However, Paul's account of the conversion is considerably different.

But when God, who set me apart from birth and called me by his grace, was pleased to reveal his Son in me so that I might preach him among the Gentiles, I did not consult any man, nor did I go up to Jerusalem to see those who were apostles before I was, but I went immediately into Arabia and later returned to Damascus. (Gal. 1:15-17)

According to Paul, he did not consult any man, for his vision of Jesus had made him the apostle to the Gentiles. Once again, Paul was probably twisting the truth in order to impress his Gentile audience. There was no need to get the approval of Cephas and James, for he had been called by God's grace. His sojourn into Arabia was never mentioned in Acts, but there may be some truth here. Saul may have been sorting out his vision of Jesus into a coherent Gospel. After this was finished, Saul headed to Damascus. Never does he mention the helping hands of Ananias or Judas. To Paul, the conversion was between him and Jesus. The author of Acts tried to soften Paul's account by having members of the Way assisting him in the early days of his faith. The truth may lie somewhere between the two versions.

C. Acts 9:19-25 and 2 Cor. 11:32,33—Escape from Damascus

The story of Paul's escape from Damascus through a window in the wall demonstrates the working method of Acts.

After many days had gone by, the Jews conspired to kill him [Paul], but Saul learned of their plan. Day and night they kept close watch on the city gates in order to kill him. But his followers took him by night and lowered him in a basket through an opening in the wall. (Acts 9:23-25)

The object of hate was Paul and those desiring to kill him were the Jews who Paul had defeated in argument. Acts said these Jews were baffled by Paul's arguments about Jesus. Consistent with the Gospel presentation of Jesus, the Jews also hated Paul. And just as they killed Jesus, so too would they attempt to murder Paul.

Unfortunately for the author of Acts, his credibility is placed in question by Paul's own account of the situation.

In Damascus the governor under King Aretas had the city of the Damascenes guarded in order to arrest me. But I was lowered in a basket from a window in the wall and slipped through his hands. (2 Cor. 11:32,33)

The antagonist in Paul's story was King Aretas, not the Jews. Paul's purpose in relaying this story was to set forth the many trials and tribulations that he had endured for the Gospel. For Paul was in competition with Cephas and James for control of his churches. He hated those apostles by this time. If anyone would have blamed the Jews it would have been Paul. But he matter-of-factly placed the blame squarely on King Aretas. How was he to know that the later account in Acts would misrepresent the facts.

Now King Aretas had an ongoing feud with the Herodians. Josephus relates how the people believed that the destruction of Herod's (Antipas) army to Aretas was a sign from God. And this because Herod had John the Baptist killed. (Ant. 18.116-119) Thus, at the time of Paul's escape, the wounds inflicted on the Baptist and on Aretas would have been fresh. That Aretas was trying to capture a well-known Herodian should not surprise us. So in this instance, the story of Paul rings true while the account in Acts is twisted in order to villify the Jews.

D. Acts 15:40 and 2 Cor. 1:19; 1 Thes. 1:1; 2 Thes. 1:1
   Silas or Silvanus?

This next difference may seem petty but there is a possibility that the Silas mentioned by Paul was not the same Silas cited in Acts. Paul referred to his companion as Silvanus while Acts called him Silas. It is possible that the author of Acts used Silas the Babylonian as his character model. This Silas the Babylonian was mentioned by Josephus near his references to Saul. (War 2:520) Since the author of Acts shaped his history upon the writings of Josephus, why not Silas as well?

E. Acts 15:1-21 and Gal. 2:1-10—The Council at Jerusalem

Most Christians believe that the Council at Jerusalem, described in Acts, was the official reconciliation between the Jews and the Gentiles. The following list will detail the major points in this agreement:

1. Acts 15:1-3—Some men from the circumcision group had traveled from Judea to Antioch. These men were telling Paul's disciples that "Unless you are circumcised, according to the custom taught by Moses, you cannot be saved." So the church in Antioch sent Paul, Barnabas and a few others to Jerusalem to see the "apostles and elders about this question."

Paul's version is somewhat different. According to Paul, he went to Jerusalem with Barnabas and Titus in response to a revelation, where he was to tell the Jewish Apostles about his Gospel to the Gentiles. And he met in <u>private</u> with those who "seemed to be leaders." First, he went because of a revelation from Jesus. This is much different than the story in Acts where he was sent to settle an argument. Secondly, Paul said he met with only the leaders. This is not the sense we are given by the author of Acts who has all parties represented in the discussion. Thirdly, Paul denigrated the Jewish leaders by referencing them as those who "seemed to be leaders". He did the same thing in Gal. 2:9 where he named Cephas, James and John, those seeming to be the pillars. Obviously, Paul was trying to paint a picture where he was in the right and the Jewish leaders were somewhat illegitimate, for they had not been appointed by the Risen Jesus as he had been.

2. Acts 15:4—When Paul and his party arrived in Jerusalem, "they were welcomed by the church and the apostles and elders, to whom they reported everything God had done through them." Now this is totally different than Paul's version where he met privately with the leaders. The author of Acts was trying to bring this whole issue out in the open so that his readers would think that Paul had public support for his position. By Paul's own words, he met privately with the leaders to tell them of his gospel. However, even this may be somewhat misleading. Paul's modus operandi was: "to the Jews I became like a Jew, to win the Jews." (1 Cor. 9:20) So the private meeting between Paul, Cephas and James may have lacked much of the pertinent information. For example, Paul did not tell Cephas and James that the law was dead. This type of belief was only communicated to the Gentiles, for again, "to those not having the law I became like one not having the law...so as to win those not having the law." (1 Cor 9:21) In reality, the famed Jerusalem meeting was an attempt by Paul to buy time. Obviously, the Fourth Philosophy would never accept Paul's gospel, which was diametrically opposed to the teachings of Judas/Jesus. When the Jewish Christians finally understood Paul's game, they abandoned him in Antioch. (Gal. 2:11-13)

3. Acts 15:5-21—This part of Acts is mostly fantasy. The speech by Peter was based upon his meeting with Cornelius, per Acts 10. We have already described the real events as related by Josephus. So the writer of Acts was trying to bridge the gap between Paul and James with the vision of Peter. This vision gave the Pauline doctrine an equal or superior standing next to the antiquated Jewish system.

In addition, those opposed to Paul were represented by the Pharisees who wanted the Gentiles to be circumcised. Now we know that the Fourth Philosophy was comprised of Pharisees and Essenes and all freedom loving people. Their basic beliefs were following God's law and attempting to gain their liberty from Rome and the Herodian leadership. It is likely that James would have stressed the Law, telling Paul to teach Moses. In the event that the Gentiles would not completely convert, then they would be covered under the covenant with Noah. (Acts 15:20,21) Thus, the message would be: convert them to Judaism if possible; if not possible then through the covenant with Noah they could be God fearers, not full Jews.

Obviously, Paul did not understand this message for he stated, "They agreed that we should go to the Gentiles, and they to the Jews. All they asked was that we should continue to remember the poor, the very thing I was eager to do." (Gal. 2:9,10) It is likely that the pillars (John, Cephas and James) did tell Paul to go to the Gentiles. This is because the Gentiles did not figure heavily in their goals, that is to await the return of Jesus for the redemption of Israel. Note that the one thing they asked of Paul was that he remember the poor. By this they were asking Paul to collect money for those in Jerusalem. And this is the activity that was going on in Paul's churches in regards to the collection. The money was to be sent to Jerusalem. (1 Cor. 16:1-4) After the Jewish Apostles abandoned Paul (Gal. 2:11-13), that money probably stayed with Paul instead of going to the Jerusalem church.

In fact, Paul's claim that the Jewish Apostles asked only one thing of him (to remember the poor) does not ring entirely true. The Jesus movement was founded on dual precepts: love God and love thy neighbor. To love God meant that one followed God's Laws. To love thy neighbor included the sharing of wealth. The Jewish Apostles instructed Paul to do both. Paul only included the one command because he never intended to follow God's Law, and the command to help the poor was a wonderful fund-raising instrument. In the earlier section on Paul and Josephus, we encountered an unnamed Jew who swindled money from innocent naive Jewish converts. The same process may have been ongoing in the Galatian and Corinthian churches. To help in this later collection, Paul used the Jewish Apostles insistence on equality in his attempt to raise money.

4. Acts 15:22-31—One last piece of misinformation concerns the letter that was sent to Antioch. According to Acts, this letter confirmed Paul's teachings, telling the Gentiles that they did not have to be circumcised. The only possible letter to Antioch came from followers of James. (Gal. 2:12) And this letter told Cephas and the other Jews to withhold fellowship from Paul and his followers. So the two accounts are once again completely different.

F. Acts 15:36-41—According to the author of Acts, Barnabas and Paul parted company over a disagreement concerning John Mark. Barnabas wanted to take him along while Paul opposed such a move. "They had such a sharp disagreement that they parted company." (Acts 15:39) This is the sanitized version. According to Paul, when the Jews in Antioch heard the message from James, they all separated themselves from Paul and his disciples. "The other Jews joined him [Cephas] in his hypocrisy, so that by their hypocrisy even Barnabas was led astray." (Gal. 2:13) So the split between Paul and Barnabas was not over John Mark but rather due to Paul's interpretation of Jesus. To James and Cephas, the law was alive and well. Gentiles were to be taught the law and encouraged to follow it, including circumcision. Paul's teachings were obviously contrary to the pillar apostles and this caused all the Jews to abandon Paul. His double game was over. He would never trick the Jews again.

G. Acts 24:12-16—In the trial before Felix, the author of Acts has Paul say that he had never done anything against the law or the prophets. In addition, per Acts 21:24-25, Paul joined in a purification rite so that "everyone will know there is no truth in these reports about you, but that you yourself are living in obedience to the law." These two passages stretch our imaginations to the maximum. We already know that James and the Jewish Christians understood Paul's game, and that they rejected him and his gospel in Antioch. There is no way that James would have had Paul go through a purification rite knowing that Paul taught against the law. And Paul did preach against the law.

The following passages touch upon Paul's feelings about the Law:

1. Romans 14:1-6; 1 Cor. 8—Paul taught his disciples that all foods were clean and that only the weak were concerned about the dietary issues. "For the kingdom of God is not food and drink but righteousness and peace and joy in the Holy Spirit." (Rom. 14:17)

2. 1 Cor. 7:19—Paul downplayed the role of circumcision in his letters to the Gentiles. "Circumcision is nothing, and uncircumcision is nothing; but obeying the commandments of God is everything." This seem logical until one realizes that one of the most important commandment of God was circumcision. In fact, circumcision was the sign of God's covenant with the Jews.

3. 1 Cor. 13:3—This is perhaps the most famous passage from Paul, the importance of love. "If I give away all my possessions, and if I hand over my body (to be burned) so that I may boast, but do not have love, I gain nothing." It is interesting that the Fourth Philosophy believed in pure

communism and were willing to die for the law. In fact, Matthias and many of his followers were burnt alive by Herod the Great for their part in the Golden Eagle Temple Cleansing. So it is clear that this passage on "love" was nothing more than a slap in the face to James and Cephas.

4. 2 Cor. 3:7-18—Here Paul talked about the fading covenant with Moses and the Jews. In fact, Paul also stated that the Jewish branch was removed by God and the Gentile branch grafted in. How do you think the Jewish Christians would have responded to this?

5. Gal. 1:6-10—The most damning evidence against Paul concerned his feelings about the Jewish covenant with God, preached by James and Cephas.

I am astonished that you are so quickly deserting the one who called you by the grace of Christ and are turning to a different gospel—which is really no gospel at all. Evidently some people are throwing you into confusion and are trying to pervert the gospel of Christ. But even if we or an angel from heaven should preach a gospel other than the one we preached to you, let him be eternally condemned.

This same hatred of the Jews and their everlasting covenant was echoed in 2 Cor. 11:3-15, where Paul compared himself to the super-apostles (James and Cephas) and called these Jewish heroes, apostles of Satan.

From these first two sections, we must start questioning the whole book of Acts. The passages concerning the election of Matthias (Acts 1), the speech by Gamaliel (Acts 5), the death of Stephen (Acts 7), the persecution of Saul (Acts 8), the conversion of Saul (Acts 9,22 and 26), the story of Peter and Cornelius (Acts 10), the story of James' death and Peter's escape (Acts 12), the Council at Jerusalem (Acts 15) and the reason for Barnabas' separation from Paul (Acts 15) are all a twisting of facts and times. It is very possible (and I think very likely) that the last few chapters of Acts are also fiction. The passages from Josephus concerning Saul occurred between 62-66 AD, some four to eight years after the account in Acts. And the story in Josephus seems more probable considering the background of Paul. When Paul arrived in Jerusalem, he arrived as an Herodian, not as a member of the Fourth Philosophy. The thought of James having him go to the Temple is laughable. Most likely, Paul did what Josephus said he did: he aligned himself with Herodian henchmen and represented Herodian interests before Agrippa II and Nero. The timing of Paul's arrest in Jerusalem (58 AD) coincides with the uprising led by the Egyptian (War 2.261-263), and the passage where Felix desired a bribe from

Paul may be taken from War 2.273, where a few sentences after the mention of Felix, Josephus wrote this about Albinus: "he allowed those imprisoned for banditry...to be bought out by their relatives, and only the man who failed to pay was left in jail to serve his sentence." This became part of the picture painted of Paul in the last pages of Acts. The author of Acts could not tell the true story; that Paul once again opposed the Way (Jewish Christians). So Acts had him imprisoned where he talked to Agrippa and then set sail for Rome. It may be a happy ending but it is not consistent with any of the facts.

The twisting of Paul's life in the book of Acts is on par with what the Gospel writers did to Judas/Jesus. At every turn, the true story was either slightly tweaked or downright misrepresented. The final acts of Paul with his entrance into Jerusalem in 58 AD may be the last and most ingenious trick played on us by the author of Acts. By placing Paul in Jerusalem in 58 AD, in jail from 58-62 AD and in Rome thereafter, our attention has been diverted from the actual activities of Saul in Jerusalem, up to 66 AD. Note that this Saul was persecuting the church not long after the murder of James (62-64 AD). And it would not be a stretch that this Saul had some part in the plot against James. Robert Eisenman argues throughout his book, James, the Brother of Jesus, that the stoning of Stephen actually had many things in common with the stoning of James. In fact, in Eisenman's opinion, Stephen was a stand-in for James. Now, it just so happens that Josephus' mention of Saul comes only a few verses after the stoning of James. (Ant. 20.200 and 20.214) Considering their stormy past, it is conceivable that Saul approved of James' death just as Saul approved of Stephen's death in Acts 8:1. Thus, taking Paul out of the picture in 58 AD stops all such inquiries. It has worked for two thousand years, but no more.

III. Paul versus the Law

Much of Paul's emphasis throughout his letters focused on circumcision and the Law. To fully understand Paul, however, we must first identify the audience to whom Paul was writing. His churches were primarily composed of Gentiles and a few fringe Jews. Thus, his gospel or good news was applicable to them while the Law only applied to Jews and Jewish converts. And this was the sticking point between Paul and James: James wanted the Gentiles to convert if at all possible while Paul discouraged any such action. This eventually placed Paul on the outside looking in. The Jewish Christians turned their backs upon him as soon as they realized his true teachings. In this section, we will compare and contrast Paul's teachings with those of James and Cephas.

A. Grace—The underlying basis of Paul's teachings is grace, that gift of forgiveness that only comes through <u>faith</u> in Jesus Christ. And to have faith in Jesus, one can be circumcised or uncircumcised. (1 Cor. 7:19) Thus, circumcision and the law was not necessary for a follower of Christ. However, this contradicted the very teachings of Jesus, Cephas and James. They emphasized doing the law with a spirit of love. To them, one could not possibly love God if one purposely disobeyed his commandments. Thus, if God commanded the Jews to be circumcised, how could a good Jew disagree? And if a Jew were preaching to Gentiles, how could he withhold God's teachings on the law and circumcision?

This all comes into clearer focus when we examine a few passages from Genesis.

Then the word of the Lord came to him: "This man [Ishmael] will not be your heir, but a son coming from your own body will be your heir." He took him outside and said, "Look up at the heavens and count the stars—if indeed you can count them." Then he said to him, "So shall your offspring be." Abram believed the Lord and he credited it to him as righteousness. (Gen. 15:4-6)

This is the cornerstone of Christian belief from the time of Paul to today. In Romans chapter 4, Paul used this passage to prove that Abraham was justified through faith and not by works, which includes circumcision. As Paul stated, "Abraham believed God, and it was credited to him as righteousness." (Rom. 4:3) To Paul, the only thing necessary for righteousness was faith, with that faith centered upon the sacrifice of Jesus Christ.

But there was another view of this passage related in the New Testament. James, the opponent of Paul, will be quoted below:

You foolish man, do you want evidence that faith without deeds is useless? Was not our ancestor Abraham considered righteous for what he did when he offered his son Isaac on the altar? You see that his faith and his actions were working together, and his faith was made complete by what he did. And the scripture was fulfilled that says, "Abraham believed God, and it was credited to him as righteousness," and he was called God's friend. You see that a person is justified by what he does and not by faith alone....As the body without the spirit is dead, so faith without deeds is dead. (James 2:20-26)

Both Paul and James used the same passage from Genesis with completely different interpretations. Paul simply took the passage out of context. For the whole story of Abraham centers upon his obedience to God. God did establish an everlasting covenant between Himself and Abraham's descendants, but there was a catch.

Then God said to Abraham, "As for you, you must keep my covenant, you and your descendants after you for the generations to come. This is my covenant with you and your descendants after you, the covenant you are to keep: Every male among you shall be circumcised. You are to undergo circumcision, and it will be the sign of the covenant between me and you. For the generations to come every male among you who is eight days old must be circumcised, including those born in your household or bought with money from a foreigner—those who are not your offspring....Any uncircumcised male, who has not been circumcised in the flesh, will be cut off from his people; he has broken my covenant. (Gen. 17:9-14)

After reading this passage from Genesis, can you doubt the utter hatred of Paul emanating from the Jewish Christians? When Paul was playing his double game of deception, the Pillars (James, Cephas and John) were willing to allow him amongst the Gentiles, for they hoped that he would bring them into their fold. But when Paul's teachings were fully understood, the Jewish Christians could not tolerate such disobedience to God. Paul had purposely broken God's covenant and was teaching others to do the same.

But did not Paul teach a much superior philosophy based upon the circumcision of the heart? To Paul, the circumcision of the flesh was meaningless. But to the observant Jewish Christian, one could not have a circumcision of the heart if one refused to obey the commands of God. Therefore, circumcision in the flesh was a necessary component of the covenant. The Jewish Christians also believed in the circumcision of the heart. In fact, Jews had believed in this concept since the writings of Deuteronomy (Deut. 10:16). So there was nothing new in this concept of circumcision of the heart.

B. There were major problems in Paul's churches due to his interpretation of the law. First, Paul was hounded by those of the circumcision, those who insisted upon the Jewish law. Paul spent much of his time bashing these individuals in his letters. Re-read Romans, 1 and 2 Corinthians and Galatians. These letters are filled with references to the circumcision.

1. 2 Cor. 3:1,2—Many of Paul's disciples were questioning his authority because he had no letters of recommendation from the Pillar apostles in Jerusalem. To this, Paul insisted that his followers in Christ were his letters of recommendation. But this charge followed Paul wherever he went.

2. Gal. 1:11,12—To draw criticism away from his lack of authority from the Jerusalem Pillars, Paul boldly stated (to the Gentiles) that his gospel did not come from any man but was delivered to him by revelation from the Risen Christ. Thus, his credentials were superior to the apostles who only knew Jesus in the flesh.

So the problems with the circumcision were two-fold: the belief systems were different—different gospels; and there was an ongoing questioning of Paul's qualifications. This is why so much effort was expended in defending his positions with his own disciples.

Another difficulty relating to the law was the doctrine of Grace and its application in real life. Theologically, grace is a wonderful thing: all believers are forgiven with no effort on their own part, just pure simple faith. In reality, such a doctrine leads to all sorts of depraved behavior. Paul discovered that his disciples, who had no law, were living worse lives than the pagans. (1 Cor. 5) Paul had to respond to those who believed that grace would cover all sin. So the reasoning went as this: if I sin then the glory of God is revealed through grace. Therefore, to sin is good. Even today, the doctrine of grace is used as an excuse for impure living. What does it matter? God will forgive the believer whatever the circumstances. So you see, the doctrine of grace (or absence of law) was an embarrassment to Paul and an abomination to most Jews.

IV. Paul and his wild Revelations

Paul was not shy when revealing his source of information, for he had a direct line to the Risen Christ.

I want you to know, brothers, that the gospel I preached is not something that man made up. I did not receive it from any man, nor was I taught it; rather, I received it by revelation from Jesus Christ. (Gal. 1:11-13)

He also stated that any other gospel was false and those teaching these false gospels would be eternally condemned. (Gal. 1:6-9) By this he meant Cephas, James and John and all the other Jewish apostles, for they taught the law and circumcision. This is a shocking revelation! Could it be that our churches today teach the visions of a dreamer while the original teachings from Jesus have been long since forgotten? The answer is yes.

Paul's dreams or revelations were kept from Cephas and James as long as possible. But when they found out his game, Paul was shunned by the Jews. So how is it possible that we hold to Paul's teachings today and consider them the authentic utterings of Jesus? The credit for this grand deception can be laid at the feet of the early second-century Gospel writers. They molded the teachings of Paul with a pseudo-history based upon the framework of Josephus. In this section, we will look at Paul's revelations and how they were integrated into the life of Jesus.

A. The Lord's Supper and the Last Supper can be attributed to Paul, although most believe it was Jesus who instituted this church sacrament.

For I received from the Lord what I also passed on to you: The Lord Jesus, on the night he was betrayed, took bread, and when he had given thanks, he broke it and said, "This is my body, which is for you; do this in remembrance of me." In the same way, after supper he took the cup, saying, "This cup is the new covenant in my blood; do this, whenever you drink it, in remembrance of me." For whenever you eat this bread and drink this cup, you proclaim the Lord's death until he comes. (1 Cor. 11:23-26)

First, note who transmitted this information to Paul. He received it from no man but from Jesus himself. This also implies that the Jewish Christian movement, instituted by Jesus himself and maintained by Cephas and James, never practiced this particular rite. Secondly, Paul's audience was Gentile, and his use of mystery religion imagery merged quite well with their religious notions. Thirdly, Paul had Jesus rejecting the everlasting covenant with God, calling his own blood the new covenant. From what we know of the Fourth Philosophy, this is beyond credibility. Judas/Jesus supported the Law just as his earthly followers did, led by Cephas and James. As such, the sacrament of communion has absolutely nothing to do with Jesus and everything to do with the dreams of Paul. The Gospel versions have simply been taken from Paul's revelation.

B. The next passage from Paul certainly would have earned him a spot in a mental ward today.

I must go on boasting. Although there is nothing to be gained, I will go on to visions and revelations from the Lord. I know a man in Christ who fourteen years ago was caught up to the third heaven. Whether it was in the body or out of the body I do not know—God knows. And I know that this man—whether in the body or apart from the body I do not know, but God knows—was caught up to Paradise. He heard inexpressible things, things that man is not permitted to tell....To keep me from becoming conceited because of these surpassingly great revelations, there was given me a thorn in my flesh, a messenger of Satan to torment me. Three times I pleaded with the Lord to take it away from me. But he said to me, "My grace is sufficient for you, for my power is made perfect in weakness." (2 Cor. 12:1-9)

Here Paul is certainly boasting of his company, a name dropper for sure. But this was done out of competition, for the circumcision group was making inroads with his disciples. So Paul related this fantastic out-of-body experience with his followers to gain their respect and trust. After all, a large collection of money was underway and Paul had promised to escort it to Jerusalem. (1 Cor. 16:1-4) So, either Paul was a lunatic or a very sinister charlatan. If one reads only the New Testament, then the sincerity of Paul is beyond doubt. Therefore, he was just a dreamer. However, if the passages from Josephus concerning Saul are taken into account, then the purity of this "saint" comes into question. His opposition to the Way (Fourth Philosophy) in Jerusalem in 62-66 AD verged upon police terror tactics. We will never know for sure. But one thing we do know: the vision was a means to impress his listeners.

One other point must be observed. Paul asked the Lord three times to take away a thorn in his side. This reminds me of the speech put into Jesus' mouth in the Garden of Gethsemane. Three times Jesus petitioned the Lord, hoping to avoid the inevitable. And Jesus, like Paul, learned to accept God's answer.

C. I do not Lie! This is the refrain that Paul repeated over and over again against the accusations put forth by the circumcision group. The following passages contain this protestation:

1. Romans 9:1—"I speak the truth in Christ—I am not lying, my conscience confirms it in the Holy Spirit."
2. 2 Cor. 6:8—"We are treated as impostors, and yet are true."
3. 2 Cor. 11:31—"The God and Father of the Lord Jesus, who is to be praised forever, knows that I am not lying."
4. Gal. 1:20—"I assure you before God that what I am writing you is no lie."

Obviously, the charge of lying to the Gentiles was put forth more than once. Note that the denial was to the Romans, Corinthians and to those in Galatia. In fact, the charge of lying followed Paul wherever he went. This may be one reason why Paul developed such an overwhelming hatred for the Fourth Philosophy and was active against them as the Jewish war drew near (66 AD).

In Chapter Seven, it was noted that Robert Eisenman equated the Liar of the Dead Sea Scrolls with Paul. This was a most likely scenario, although Paul may have been just one in a long list of Wicked Priests and Liars. His association with the Herodians and his teachings against the Law made Paul the perfect Liar to those of the Fourth Philosophy.

V. Paul and Jesus

When one reads the letters of Paul, one cannot escape the numerous times he refers to Jesus. But his use of Jesus in not in the form of a regular name but rather a title. Thus, Paul uses the following interchangeably: Jesus Christ, Christ Jesus, Jesus, Christ, and Jesus Christ our Lord. If my hypothesis of Judas the Galilean is true, then Judas/Jesus would have been dead for nearly twenty-five years when Paul wrote his letters. This may be why any reference to Jesus comes as a Savior title and not as a real human being. Paul was so far removed from the real Jesus that he could not connect with his humanity. That may also be why he could not understand Cephas and James, contemporaries of Judas/Jesus. And since he was so far removed, his use of titles such as Jesus Christ and Christ Jesus hid the real figure, Judas the Galilean. The Gospel writers were imbibed with this terminology and also used the titles with no thought as to the real flesh and blood Judas/Jesus.

Through his writings, Paul demonstrated that he knew nothing of the flesh and blood Judas/Jesus. All of his contact with Jesus came from miraculous visions and revelations. That may be another reason why the Jewish Apostles called him the Liar. He was not only a Liar but a dreamer as well.

But truth is not always remembered. Paul's "lies" had more staying power throughout the ages than the dry truth of Judas the Galilean. And it was Paul's Jesus who survived. But this Jesus was a curious mix, a composite of Paul's own teachings as well as the outline of Judas the Galilean's life. Thus, the birth narratives follow the time line of Judas' life from the works of Josephus. And the crucifixion of Jesus mirrored the treatment of Judas and his two sons. However, some of the Gospel Jesus' teachings were straight from Paul. How else can one explain why Jesus ate with tax collectors and sinners when the whole Fourth Philosophy movement condemned such individuals. John the Baptist was murdered by those who Jesus supposedly befriended. In fact, this friendship with the world belonged to Paul and not Jesus. Also, Jesus would have never overthrown the dietary laws as the Gospels claim. Even by the late fifties, James and Cephas were still following such laws. So it is hard to imagine that this was truly a teaching of Jesus. But we know it was a central teaching of Paul.

As a general rule, when things appear too similar between the Gospels and Paul's writings, then something is amiss. Would Jesus have discarded the everlasting covenant between God and the Jewish nation? Would he have replaced this covenant with a new covenant in his own blood? Would Jesus have conversed freely with Nero, knowing full well that Nero had just massacred the Jewish Christian population in Rome? The answer to all questions is a resounding no. Such teachings and actions were from Paul, that dreamer who insisted he had a pipeline to God.

Thus, the true Jesus has never been exposed until now. Judas the Galilean was the flesh and blood Jesus. And Judas' movement was the same as Jesus' Jewish Christians. But to understand this, we must peal away two thousand years of Pauline bias. For the Jesus of the Gospels is merely a dim reflection of Paul.

THE PROBLEM OF PAUL

Acts (1)

```
                    Stephen              Council    Paul        Paul
                    Stoned               of         arrested    sails
                     (3)                 Jerusalem  in          to
                    Saul                 (1)        Jerusalem   Rome
                    converted    Paul               (6)   Paul  (6)
                    (2)  Paul's  and                Paul        and
                         first visit   Famine       and    L    Agrippa
                         to Jerusalem  (Acts 11)    Cephas E    (6)
                         (1)           (5)          disagree T
                         ---3yrs-------14 years----  (2)    TERS (5)
|---------|---------|---------|--------|--------|--------|--------|--------|--------|------|
19        25        30        35       40       45       50       55       58       62     66
AD
Jew      --3 yrs--  First    ---14 years---  Simon   Paul              James      Paul
swindles            visit                    and     and               is         and
Roman               to                       Agrippa Cephas            stoned     Agrippa
Jewess              Jerusalem                (4)     (2)               (3,6)      (6)
(7)                 (1)                      Izates  Paul                         Paul
                                             converted attacks                    and
                                             (4)      James(3)                    Nero
                                             ---FAMINE---                         (6)
                                             (5)
```

Josephus and Pseudoclementine Recognitions (1)

1. Both the New Testament and Josephus timelines incorporate the two meetings in Jerusalem as detailed by Paul in Galatians: 3 years after his conversion and then 14 years later. Note that Paul never mentioned a visit to Jerusalem during the famine. This is due to the fact that the letters to the Corinthians, Galatians and Romans preceeded his eventual trip to Jerusalem for the famine relief.

2. Since the actual crucifixion of Jesus occurred 14 years earlier than traditionally thought (19 AD vs. 33 AD), the beginning story of the Church would have also been 14 years earlier. Thus, it is possible that Paul persecuted the Church in 19 AD and converted to the faith in 20-24 AD. If this scenario is true, then Paul would have been excommunicated by Cephas and James around 40-44 AD.

3. The Book of Acts claims that Saul persecuted the early Church and approved of Stephen's stoning around 35 AD. In Josephus, Saul persecuted those weaker than himself after the stoning of James, around 62-64 AD. This description of Saul was used by Luke to invent his own version of history. Also, the Pseudoclementine Recognitions claims that Paul attacked James in Jerusalem in the 40's. This could not have occurred based upon the chronology of Acts, but it does fit with the earlier positioning of Paul within the movement.

4. The two passages from Josephus concerning Simon and Agrippa as well as King Izates, Ananias and Eleazar, show that a struggle was underway for the hearts and minds of Jewish converts. In the early 40's, Jewish Christians were being sent out from Galilee to ensure converts were accepting full conversion, which included circumcision. This is the exact argument described by Paul in Galatians. This helps prove that Paul's career with the Fourth Philosophy (Jewish Christians) was nearing an end by 40-45 AD.

5. Scholars date 1 and 2 Corinthians, Galatians and Romans at 57 AD, based upon the chronology of Acts (which is absolutely useless in dating events). According to the early placement of Paul within the movement, these letters were written shortly after Paul's excommunication (early 40's). Note that Paul was collecting monies for those in Jerusalem. This effort probably related to the famine which Josephus placed between 44-48 AD. If Paul travelled to Jerusalem at the time of the famine, he may have come in contact with James, and a struggle may have ensued (Ps. Rec.). In any event, the monies probably went into the Herodian coffers and not to the Fourth Philosophy (Jewish Christians).

6. The story of Paul's later career in Jerusalem is dated a few years earlier in Acts than in Josephus. This earlier dating of Acts (58-62 AD) helps to distance Paul from the following: the stoning of James in 62 AD; Saul's petition for an army from Agrippa in 66 AD; and Saul's appeal to Nero in 66 AD, two years after Nero massacred Jewish Christians in Rome. In short, Acts sent Paul to Rome before the Saul of Josephus could do his dirty deeds in Jerusalem and beyond. This being the case, the entire ending chronology of Paul's life is bogus. It is therefore possible to shift Paul's career with the Fourth Philosophy to an earlier time.

7. In full circle, the beginnings of Paul's career may be traced back to an unnamed Jew who extorted money from a wealthy Jewess in 19 AD Rome. This unnamed Jew worked with others, professed to be knowledgeable in the Law and convinced converted Jews to send monies to Jerusalem. All this fits in nicely with Paul's methods as described by himself in Galatians, Corinthians and Romans. Paul's anti-Law attitude may have actually preceeded his "conversion" to Jewish Christianity. The "conversion" for Paul was the synthesis of anti-Law teachings

with the death and resurrection of Jesus. It was through this "grace" that Paul could soothe his own conscience.

APPENDIX 7

PILATE'S REIGN

The traditional dating for Pilate's governorship is 26-37 AD. This is arrived at by adding up years contained in certain passages in Josephus. Per the existing documentation, Josephus stated that Gratus was appointed procurator shortly after the succession of Tiberius (14-37 AD). If Gratus arrived in 15 AD and served eleven years (Ant. 18.35), then his successor, Pilate, must have arrived in Judea in 26 AD. So the story goes.

This traditional dating of Pilate is crucial to support the Gospel story of Jesus. In Matthew, Jesus was born right before the death of Herod the Great, appoximately 6-4 BC. Luke mistakenly placed the birth at the census of Cyrenius, or 6 AD. Also, Luke stated that the ministry of Jesus began in his thirtieth year. Assuming his ministry lasted three years, Jesus would have been thirty-three at his death. From the birth in 6-4 BC, the death would have occurred thirty-three years later, from 28-30 AD. This fits in quite nicely with the traditional dating for Pilate. (Note that Luke's dating would have placed the crucifixion at 39 AD, two years after Pilate.)

However, I believe there is overwhelming evidence within the writings of Josephus and Tacitus to question the later dating of Pilate. From an analysis of their histories, we will place the reign of Pilate in Judea from 18-37 AD. This early date will be shown to approximate the crucifixion of Judas/Jesus. If this is the case, then the Gospel Jesus would have been in his early twenties by Matthew's reckonings and twelve by Luke's. Surely, the early date for Pilate would spell trouble for the orthodox story of Jesus.

JOSEPHUS ON PILATE

In analyzing the dating for Pilate, the passage concerning Pilate's rise to power will be quoted in context in order to ascertain the proper year in which he arrived in Judea.

He [Tiberius] was now the third emperor [14 AD]; and he sent Valerius Gratus to be procurator of Judea, and to succeed Annius Rufus. This man [Gratus] deprived Ananus of the high priesthood, and appointed Ismael, the son of Phabi, to be high priest. He also deprived him in a little time, and ordained Eleazar, the son of Ananus, who had been high priest before, to be high priest: which office, when he had held for a year, Gratus deprived him of it, and gave the high priesthood to Simon, the son of Camithus; and when he had possessed that dignity no longer than a year, Joseph Caiaphas was made his successor. When Gratus had done those things, he went back to Rome, after he had tarried in Judea eleven years, when Pontius Pilate came as his successor. (Ant. 18.33-35)

From the above passage, Gratus became procurator in 15 AD, right after the death of Augustus and the corresponding rise of Tiberius. Josephus stated that he appointed Ismael to be high priest in 15 AD and quickly replaced him with Eleazar. This Eleazar held the office of high priest for one year, from late 15 to late 16 AD. He was then replaced by Simon who also held office for no longer than a year (16-17 AD). In his final act, Gratus replaced Simon with Joseph Caiaphas (18-37 AD). After these appointments, Gratus returned to Rome. Per the years listed by Josephus, his governorship lasted only three years, from 15-18 AD. Note that this passage curiously listed his tenure at eleven years. After this, Pilate was introduced by Josephus to his readers.

Interestingly, the Gospel of John may provide valuable information concerning the above high priests. At the arrest on the Mount of Olives, Jesus was bound and sent to Annas, where he was interrogated. After questioning, Jesus was then sent to the reigning high priest, Caiaphas. (John 18:12-24) Per the account in Josephus, Annas was originally appointed high priest by Cyrenius and Coponius in 7 AD, replacing Joazar. (Ant. 18.26) It is at this time that Judas the Galilean began his tax revolt. (Ant. 18.1-6) The arrest of Judas/Jesus would have concerned no one more than Annas.

Annas was deprived of the high priesthood by Gratus in 15 AD. Of the other high priests appointed by Gratus, Eleazar was the son (15-16 AD) and Caiaphas the son-in-law (18-37 AD) of Annas. The Gospel of John may have inadvertently given us a clue as to the year in which the crucifixion occurred. If Jesus were taken first to Annas, then it would appear that this Annas was still held in high esteem by other officials. In fact, Annas may have been the one calling the shots. This would have been true in 18 AD, but not so likely in 30-33 AD. In the later time frame, Annas may have been long since dead and or Caiaphas would have been more firmly entrenched after being high priest for twelve to fifteen years. In addition, the charge of tax revolt against Jesus rings true with the interrogations by Annas, the high priest of Cyrenius and Coponius.

The author of the Gospel of John may have given us one last clue. Concerning the high priest, Caiaphas, he wrote: "They bound him [Jesus] and brought him first to Annas, who was the father-in-law of Caiaphas, the high priest that year." (John 18:13) From Josephus' account of the high priests, Annas was high priest from 7-15 AD. However, during the governorship of Gratus, the high priests served only one year. After Gratus, during the tenure of Pilate, Caiaphas may have served from 18-37 AD. So when John described Caiaphas as being high priest that year, he may have unwittingly pointed to the year 18-19 AD.

If the tenure of Gratus actually spanned eleven years, and if Pilate became procurator beginning in 26 AD, then one would expect the following history related by Josephus to be post 26 AD. But that is not the case. Right after the introduction of Pilate, Josephus described how Herod the tetrarch had built the city of Tiberius. This city, under construction for nine years, was dedicated in 18 AD. (Ant. 18.36-38) After this, Josephus spent time discussing obscure Parthian history, leading into his mention of the death of Germanicus, the Roman general who was assassinated in 19 AD. (Ant. 18.39-54)

After this 19 AD reference, Josephus wrote about Pilate again. The first story concerned the introduction of standards into the city. The Jews vehemently opposed this action and forced Pilate to withdraw the standards. Next, Pilate used the Temple treasury for the purpose of constructing an aqueduct. The Jews were outraged, and many were slaughtered in their opposition.

After these two events, the spurious passage about Jesus follows. In traditional calculations, the passages about Pilate were early in his career, around 26-27 AD. The passage about Jesus would therefore be shortly thereafter, anywhere from 28-30 AD. This passage about Jesus is not authentic, but it may have replaced the original story of Judas the Galilean's death at the hands of Pilate.

This assertion is bolstered by the two episodes related by Josephus after the spurious Jesus passage. If Jesus was crucified in 30 AD, then the following sections of Josephus would logically be post 30 AD. But once again, that is not the case. The story of the Roman woman, Paulina, who was tricked into prostituting herself in the Temple of Isis coincides with a similar tale told by Tacitus. However, Tacitus firmly placed the dating to 19 AD.(1) Secondly, Josephus explained why the Jews were expelled from Rome. (Ant. 18.65-84) Compare these two mentions by Josephus to this 19 AD reference by Tacitus.

There was a debate too about expelling the Egyptian and Jewish worship, and a resolution of the Senate was passed that four thousand of the freedman class who were infected with those superstitions and were of military age should be transported to the island of Sardinia, to quell the brigandage of the place, a cheap sacrifice should they die from the pestilential climate. The rest were to quit Italy, unless before a certain day they repudiated their impious rites. (Tacitus, Annals, II.85)

This same event was recorded by Suetonius, except that he stated that the "Jews of military age were removed to unhealthy regions, on the pretext of drafting them into the army."(2) The motives are slightly different but the events are the same. And this is the same event described by Josephus.

So once again, the narrative of Josephus returned to 19 AD. The explanation for this is simple. Pontius Pilate became procurator in 18 AD and the death of Judas/Jesus was shortly thereafter, in 19 AD. With this explanation, the text of Josephus makes perfect sense. The traditional Gospel story put Jesus at the hands of Pilate a decade later. So why did the Gospel writers need to tamper with history?

First of all, the story of Judas/Jesus being crucified under the governorship of Pilate was very early indeed. This element of the Jesus story could not be altered. The Gospel of Mark, therefore, used this original outline where Pilate was procurator. Mark did introduce other elements into his story, such as the 4 BC Barabbas incident, but his Roman procurator could not be changed. However, since Mark did not have a birth narrative, the actual dating of Pilate was not necessary. This purposeful imprecision of dating Pilate became outdated with the birth narratives of Matthew and Luke. According to these Gospels, Jesus could not have died before 28 AD. When these were set in stone, all other documents had to be adjusted.

The pious editors simply went to work on Josephus, the only source of evidence concerning the early movement. The term of Gratus was extended from three years to eleven even though the text can be calculated to three years. By doing this, Christians throughout the ages have discounted the problems noted above, that the Pilate and Jesus texts fall within the discussion of Judea in 19 AD. The death of Judas the Galilean was expunged and replaced with the obvious counterfeit passage of Jesus. This explains why the life of Judas was detailed by Josephus but his death was not covered. And this also explains why only the death of Jesus was included in the writings of Josephus.

The greatest editing actually occurred after the 19 AD narratives. From 19-37 AD, all information was erased from Josephus. This corresponds to the early church as found in Acts chapters 1-9. What Josephus had to say about this activity is anybody's guess. But we can be sure it would have differed wildly from the book of Acts. Throughout this book, I have noted the inaccuracies and plain misrepresentations given by the author of Acts. This was achieved by utilizing a different time frame, that of Judas the Galilean. Without this shift in perspective, it would have been impossible to ascertain the truth. And that is why the section covering the years 19-37 AD was deleted from Josephus. Without his valuable information, the detective work would be insurmountable for those trying to find the flesh and blood Jesus. Luckily, tracking Judas the Galilean exposed these clever tricks.

BIBLIOGRAPHY

Baigent, Michael and Leigh, Richard. The Dead Sea Scrolls Deception. New York: Summit Books, 1991.

Barclay, William. The Daily Study Bible. Philadelphia: The Westminster Press, 1978.

Bettenson, Henry. Documents of the Christian Church. New York: Oxford University Press, 1979.

Eisenman, Robert. James the Brother of Jesus. New York: Penguin Books, 1997.

Ellegard, Alvar. Jesus One Hundred Years Before Christ. New York: The Overlook Press, 1999.

Grant, Michael. The History of Ancient Israel. New York: Charles Scribner's Sons, 1984.

Johnson, Paul. Civilizations of the Holy Land. Atheneum, New York: 1979.

Maccoby, Hyam. Revolution in Judaea. New York: Taplinger Publishing Company, 1980.

Maccoby, Hyam. The Mythmaker. New York: Harper and Row Publishers, 1986.

Robertson, J.M.. Pagan Christs. New York: Dorset Press, 1987.

Suetonius. The Twelve Caesars. London: Penguin Books, 1979. Translated by Robert Graves; Revised by Michael Grant.

Tacitus. The Annals and The Histories. Chicago: Encyclopedia Britannica, Inc., 1952. Translated by Alfred John Church and William Jackson Brodribb.

Vermes, Geza. The Complete Dead Sea Scrolls in English. New York: Allen Lane, The Penguin Press, 1997.

Whiston, William. The Works of Josephus. Mass.: Hendrickson Publishers, 1984.

Williamson, G.A.. Josephus The Jewish War. New York: Penguin Books, 1981.

NOTES

CHAPTER ONE
1. Paul Johnson, <u>Civilizations of the Holy Land</u>, pg. 130.
2. Tacitus, <u>The Annals</u>, ii.85.
3. Suetonius, <u>The Twelve Caesars</u>, Claudius 25.
4. Robert Eisenman, <u>James, the Brother of Jesus</u>, pg. 66.
5. <u>Ibid</u>., pg. 23; See also, Seutonius, <u>The Twelve Caesars</u>, Vespasian 4 & 5.
6. William Barclay, <u>The Daily Study Bible</u>, The letters to Timothy, Titus and Philemon, pps. 1-13.
7. In the first century, the Docetists believed Jesus to be only of spirit, not of the flesh. To this, the Gospel of John replied, "The Word became Flesh…"
8. J.M. Robertson, <u>Pagan Christs</u>, pps. 5-6.

CHAPTER TWO
1. Tacitus, <u>The Histories</u>, v.8.
2. Suetonius, <u>The Twelve Caesars</u>, Domitian 12.
3. <u>Ibid</u>., Augustus 94.
4. Israel Finkelstein and Neil Asher Silberman, <u>The Bible Unearthed</u>, Chapters 2 and 3.
5. N.K. Sandars, <u>The Epic of Gilgamesh</u>, pps. 108-113.
6. Robert Eisenman, <u>James, the Brother of Jesus</u>, pps. 243 and 303.
7. J.M. Robertson, <u>Pagan Christs</u>, pg. 122.

CHAPTER THREE
1. Henry Bettenson, <u>Documents of the Christian Church</u>, pg. 2; Tacitus, <u>Annales</u> xv.44.

CHAPTER FOUR
1. Robert Eisenman, James, the Brother of Jesus, pg. 864.

CHAPTER FIVE
1. Tacitus, The Annals, ii.42.
2. Hyam Maccoby, Revolution in Judaea, pg. 136.

CHAPTER SIX
1. Robert Eisenman, James, the Brother of Jesus, pg. 320. The quote of James' age comes from the writings of Epiphanius.
2. Eisenman correctly deduces that the replacement was for the slain Jesus, not the mythical Judas Iscariot. He also makes it clear that the Twelve apostle scheme was never confirmed by Paul and may have been an invention of the Gospel writers.
3. Robert Eisenman, James, the Brother of Jesus, pg. 178.
4. Ibid., pg 178.
5. Ibid., pg. 320.
6. Hyam Maccoby, Revolution in Judaea, chapter 15.
7. Robert Eisenman, James, the Brother of Jesus, pps. 271-3.
8. Ibid., pg. 389.
9. Ibid., pg. 615.

CHAPTER SEVEN
1. Baigent and Leigh, The Dead Sea Scrolls Deception, pg. 196.
2. Geza Vermes, The Complete Dead Sea Scrolls in English, pg. 478
3. Baigent and Leigh, The Dead Sea Scrolls Deception, pg. 157.
4. Geza Vermes, The Complete Dead Sea Scrolls in English, pg. 127.
5. Ibid., pg. xvii.
6. Paul Johnson, Civilizations of the Holy Land, pg. 102.
7. Robert Eisenman, James, the Brother of Jesus, pg. 167.
8. Hyam Maccoby, Revolution in Judaea. To Maccoby, James was like a prince ruling the land until the rightful king returned.
9. Geza Vermes, The Complete Dead Sea Scrolls in English, pg. 482.

10. Ibid., pps. 97-98.
11. Michael Grant, The History of Ancient Israel, pg. 210.
12. Ibid., pg. 216.
13. Ibid., pg. 216.
14. Ibid., pg. 218.

CHAPTER EIGHT
1. C. Randolph Benson, Thomas Jefferson as Social Scientist, pg. 201.
2. Ibid., pg. 206.
3. Ibid., pg. 203.
4. Hyam Maccoby, Revolution in Judaea, pps. 127,128.
5. J.M. Robertson, Pagan Christs, pg. 20.
6. Ibid., pps. 40,41.
7. Ibid., pg. 112.
8. Ibid., pg. 118.
9. Ibid., pg. 110.
10. Hyam Maccoby, Revolution in Judaea, pps. 143,144.
11. Ibid., pps. 147-149.
12. J.M. Robertson, Pagan Christs, pg. 110.
13. Ibid., pg. 110.
14. Robert Eisenman, James, the Brother of Jesus, pg. 581.

CHAPTER NINE
1. Karl Marx and Friedrich Engles with intriduction by AJP Taylor, The Communist Manifesto, pps, 37,38.
2. In Ant. 14.159-177, Josephus mentioned Hezekias, a captain of robbers who was hunted down and executed by Herod. Mothers of those slain went to the Temple and mourned, and charges were brought against Herod because he by-passed the sanhedrin. Instead of standing trial, Herod fled to Damascus. This occurred around 48 BC. A decade later (40-37 BC), Herod hunted down the robbers who lived in caves in Galilee. Some of the robbers "underwent death [suicide] rather than slavery [to Herod]." (Ant. 14.415-430) And finally (approx. 24 BC), when Herod

introduced foreign practices to Judea (athletic games and theatre productions), the Jews were outraged and even tried to assassinate him. (Ant. 15. 267-289)
3. Paul Johnson, Civilizations of the Holy Land, pg. 123.
4. William Whiston, The Works of Josephus, pg. 815.
5. Ibid., pg. 815.
6. Antiquities was not finished until 93 AD. Since the Book of Acts is heavily dependent on this, the composition of acts must be later than 93 AD.
7. Tacitus, The Histories, v.9.
8. Robert Eisenman, James the Brother of Jesus, pg. 870.
9. Suetonius, The Twelve Caesars, Claudius 28.
10. Tacitus, The Histories, v.9.
11. Suetonius, The Twelve Caesars, Claudius 25.
12. Henry Bettenson, Documents of the Christian Church, pg. 2.
13. Alvar Ellegard, Jesus One Hundred Years Before Christ, pg. 85.
14. William Whiston, The Works of Josephus, pg. 815.
15. Tacitus, The Annals, xv.38.
16. Ibid., xv.44.
17. Suetonius, The Twelve Caesars, Nero 16.
18. Henry Bettenson, Documents of the Christian Church, pg. 37.

CHAPTER TEN
1. Henry Bettenson, Documents of the Christian Church, pg. 3; Letter of Pliny to Trajan.

CHAPTER ELEVEN
1. Robert Eisenman, James, the Brother of Jesus, pg. 21.
2. Falwell stated this inflammatory charge on *Hardball* with Chris Matthews and on *60 Minutes*, during the week ending October 6, 2002.

APPENDIX 5
1. Flora Haines Loughead, Dictionary of Given Names.

APPENDIX 6
1. Robert Eisenman, <u>James, the Brother of Jesus</u>, pg. 452.

APPENDIX 7
1. Tacitus, <u>The Annals</u>, ii.85.
2. Suetonius, <u>The Twelve Caesars</u>, Tiberius 36.

0-595-32197-6

Made in the USA
Lexington, KY
23 October 2015